Text and Presentation

TEXT AND PRESENTATION

The University of Florida
Department of Classics
Comparative Drama Conference Papers
Volume VIII

Edited by Karelisa Hartigan

UNIVERSITY
PRESS OF
AMERICA

Lanham • New York • London

Co-published by arrangement with the
Comparative Drama Conference, University of Florida,
Department of Classics

Library of Congress Cataloging-in-Publication Data

University of Florida Department of Classics Comparative Drama
Conference (1987)
Text and presentation / edited by Karelisa Hartigan.
p. cm.—(The University of Florida Department of Classics
Comparative Drama Conference papers ; v. 8)
Includes bibliographies.
1. Drama—History and criticism—Congresses. I. Hartigan,
Karelisa. II. Title. III. Series: University of Florida Department
of Classics Comparative Drama Conference. University of Florida
Department of Classics Comparative Drama Conference papers ; v. 8.
PN1621.U55   1987   88–3536 CIP
ISBN 0–8191–6907–2 (alk. paper)

PREFACE

TEXT AND PRESENTATION

The University of Florida Department of Classics
Comparative Drama Conference, March, 1987

The University of Florida Department of Classics Comparative Drama Conferences began in 1977 with the intent of emphasizing the humanities endeavors at the University. The aim of the conference has been to bring together persons from many areas of academia and theatre to share their mutual interests. The conference is unique both in its multi-disciplinary nature and its insistence that drama be both discussed and performed. Thus each program includes scholarly papers, addresses by leading figures in literature and theatre, and dramatic performances. The number of participants has been kept to a discreet size so that ample opportunity exists for individuals to meet and exchange ideas. During the years since its inception the conference has attracted scholars in the areas of Classics, Germanic and Romance Languages, English, Anthropology, Philosophy, and all areas of Theatre from more than eighty colleges and universities around the United States, Canada, and Europe.

The papers presented at the conference were of such consistently high quality that the publication of selected papers was undertaken. Each text is submitted to the examination of two to three referees before being accepted for inclusion in the volumes. This is the eighth volume in the series. It is expected that the wide range of topic offered here will be of interest to the many persons who study and enjoy comparative drama.

Karelisa V. Hartigan
Conference Director

v

For Volume VIII the assistance of the following guest
referees is acknowledged with gratitude:

Irving Deer
Kenneth Johnson

William Mould

TABLE OF CONTENTS

Conference Address

Incoherence as Meaning: From the Real to the Expressive

William R. Elwood
University of Wisconsin

We are approaching the end of the twentieth century; and we note profoundly the passing of 100 years. 1887 was a long time ago, yet the study of the transition to 1987 is important for us.

Many will say that we are headed for disaster as this century draws to a close. If we look, though, at the pessimist in the latter part of the nineteenth century we find similar predictions. David Rosen in Madness in Society quotes a medical officer in 1857:

> I doubt if ever the history of the world, or
> the experience of past ages, could show a
> larger amount of insanity than that of the
> present day. It seems, indeed, as if the
> world was moving at an advanced rate of
> speed proportionate to its approaching end.[1]

And closer to my time frame of 100 years in (1873) another source speaks of wear and tear and high pressure, the increase of casinos and gin-palaces and betting rings.[2]

Or we can paraphrase Schopenhauer who, rather than exalt history speaks of the assertion of value-lessness and the meaninglessness of existence. He said reality is malignant. I quote more specifically:

> Unless suffering is the direct and immediate
> object of life, our existence must fail of
> its aim.   It is absurd to look upon the
> enormous amount of pain that abounds
> everywhere in the world, and originates in
> needs and necessities inseparable from life

---

[1] Rosen (1968, 187).

[2] Rosen (189).

1

itself, as serving no purpose at all and the result of mere chance. Each separate misfortune, as it comes, seems no doubt, to be something exceptional; but misfortune in general is the rule.[3]

In fact Nietzsche said as much in 1872. He affirms for us the classical view of gloom and doom. In his The Birth of Tragedy, he quotes Silenus: "O wretched ephemeral race, children of chance and misery. Why do you compel me to tell you what it were beyond your reach forever: Not to be born, not to be, to be nothing. But the second best for you quickly to die."[4] I don't share the opinion of those who voice gloom and doom; that we are headed for disaster. I mean what my title implies: we are really progressing not into disorder but from one kind of order to another. I think we need to understand the shift of 100 years.

There is indeed something special about the turn of a century even acknowledging that developments in our history don't fit into neat decades. Seen from our perspective, clearly there was a major shift in the perception of reality from 1880 to approximately 1907. This perception of reality signalled a major emphasis on the material world, its rejection and its inevitable return in altered form. There are two goals I have set in this paper, one considerably easier to reach than the other:

1) I propose to articulate for you the meaning of the shift in the perception of reality from the latter quarter of the 19th century to the first quarter of the twentieth century.

2) I propose to make some projections regarding the latter quarter of the 20th century and into some perhaps not clearly defined period of time in the 21st century. Hopefully if what I have to say is meaningful some scholar in the year 2087 will tie it all in for the 22nd century.

---

[3] Schopenhauer (1962, 85).

[4] Nietzsche (1927, 962).

Not long after <u>Hernani</u> signalled the triumph of romanticism, over neo-classicism in the February 25th and 27th 1830 premiere at the Comedie Francaise, the world began to move fast and a number of changes forced a shift away from the perception of reality articulated by romanticism with its reliance on emotion and feelings as indicators of truth. The Industrial Revolution brought in its wake demographic changes, technological innovation and a major change in the <u>Weltanschauung</u> of Europe. Cities became places of potential for great opportunity and wealth and of course poverty and misery. Overcrowded conditions, free-wheeling capitalism and the birth of industry changed the way we looked at things. Responsibility for life choices shifted from the individual to the collective. Social divisions, classes and groups created new problems and shouldered the burden of the common good.

In the theatre playwrights chose a new framework: empirical verification and cause and effect became dramatic devices. The philosophy of materialism emerged as the informing mind-set for roughly the latter half of the century. In Zola's essay "The Experimental novel," he sounded the call for the socio-psycho mechanism on stage. I quote:

> In fact the whole operation [of naturalism] consists in taking facts in nature, then in studying the mechanism of these facts, acting upon them, by the modification of circumstances and surroundings, without deviating from the laws of nature. Finally, you possess knowledge of the man, scientific knowledge of him, in both his individual and social relations.[5]

Identifying the playwright as experimenter and observor Zola attempted to bring life unadorned to the stage. He exhorted actors "to be" and not to act. For the first time in the history of the theatre playwrights contended that the avant-garde was not contrivance. We would see <u>tranche de vie</u> on stage, real life. The obvious <u>beneficiary</u> of such an aesthetic would fall to those desiring social change.

---

[5] Stone (1959, 53).

For example Hauptmann wanted us to see the plight of the weavers. Indeed if social change were to be affected we would have to see the line, form and color of Käthe Kollwitz (1867 - 1945) on stage, not that of Maxfield Parrish. (1870-1966)

In the script we saw character, language, plot incident and theme as real taken from life as we know it, or knew it to be, casually articulated and empirically verifiable. Did attitudes of male chauvinism and the repression of the individual we saw in A Doll House really exist? Was the Silesian weaver's revolt truthfully depicted on stage? Indeed the great figures of late nineteenth century play-writing focused on what they deemed to be "real" phenomena, either physical or psychological. The "Big Four" of the turn of century playwriting, in different modes, wrote plays informed by materialism, con-structed to the laws of causality and verified empirically. Ibsen's realism was ideational; Strind-berg's was psychological; Hauptmann's was environ-mental and Chekhov's was a combination of sociology, psychology and environment, a pastel environmental "psychism" if you will.

On stage, the scene designer had to construct physical environment down to the last detail. Real earth was hauled on stage for Hauptmann's Rose Bernd (1903) real carcasses of beef hung for The Butchers (1888) by Fernand Icres and the box set came fully into its own where interiors were required. Lighting was made to resemble real sources, actors dressed according to socio-economic status, time period (usually contemporary) and sound effect were real or appeared to be so.

A new aesthetic had arrived, and plays, produc-tions, and acting style reflected the materialistic perception of reality. We solved problems within the framework of realism; more importantly we decided that the search for the truth was a search for understand-ing matter in all its varied and multiple physical, psychological and ideational forms. It is no accident that in the latter half of the 19th century, science emerged as the primary discipline and mode for this search for the truth. Even Freud and Jung communicated psychology in a scientific rather than literary or occult framework. We believed that truth could be empirically verified and once we arrived at its tangible core, we would be possessed of meaning for our lives.

4

Of course it would not be long before empirical verification would be challenged. Neo-romanticism and symbolism asserted that while a core of meaning existed it lay in a different direction. They contended that the symbol was the primary means of communication and that empirical verification only occluded our view. In Maeterlincks's L'Intruse (1890) or in von Hofmannsthal's Der Tor und der Tod (1893), death is painted not as it is in Strindberg's Dodsdansen (1901) -- his stage directions indicate a "realistic" death. Rather, there is a conversion to symbol; and abstraction in von Hofmannsthal and an absence/presence in Maeterlinck's work. Death, particularly its impact on survivors is palpable and a heavy emotional response, but difficult to verify empirically. Maeterlinck says it is better reproduced as he does in The Intruder.

While realism was still dominant and gaining a momentum that still informs if not dominates theatrical, cinematic and television production today, a more specifically oriented challenge captured the theatre's attention. Taking impetus from the field of painting, expressionism primarily in Germany proposed that the way to the truth lay in the ich or soul of man. That is the internal perception of reality was the proper view of defining truth. The playwrights and theatre artists utilized the symbol previously described but only as means of communication from a specific locus of consciousness: the ich. I define German expressionism as the attempt to articulate the essence rather than the appearance of reality through the use of non-realistic symbols and the juxtaposition or ordinarily non-related symbols.

In expressionism for example instead of an external articulation of anger, to cite an elementary example, the lighting artist might tinge the set with red. I would like to read the stage directions indicating anger in Rice's The Adding Machine (1923). Mr. Zero's anger is portrayed as follows:

(His voice is drowned by the music. The platform is revolving rapidly now. Zero and the Boss face each other. They are entirely motionless save for the Boss's jaws, which open and close incessantly. But the words are inaudible. The music swells. To it is added every off-stage effect of the theatre: the wind, waves, the galloping horses, the locomotive whistle, the sleigh bells, the

5

automobile siren, the glass-crash. . .
Suddenly it culminates in a terrific peal of
thunder. For an instant there is a flash of
red and then everything is plunged into
blackness.) (Scene 2)[6]

Compare those with stage directions in Rose Bernd:

Rose (clenching her fists, stares at him in
a surge of rage, hate and fear; finally
feeling that she is powerless, she drops her
hands and, almost whimpering, blurts out)
I'll see that justice is done. (Act I)[7]

Or, examine the monologue is Kaiser's Von Morgens bis
Mitternachts (1916) in which the cashier attempts a
definition of self:

Cashier: (looking around him) Grandmother
at the window. Daughters--at the table
embroidering. . . playing Wagner. Wife busy
in the kitchen. Four walls. . . family
life. Cozy. . . all of us together.
Mother--son. . . child under one roof. The
magic of familiar things. It spins a web.
Room with a table. Piano. Kitchen. . .
daily bread. Coffee in the morning . . .
chops at noon. Bedroom. . . bed. . . in. . .
out. More magic. In the end flat on your
back. . . white and stiff. Table pushed
against the wall. . . in the center a pine
coffin. . . screw lid. . . . silver mount-
ings. . . but detachable . . . a bit of
crepe on the lamp. . . piano unopened for a
year. (Scene 4)[8]

In Hasenclever's Humanity (1918), the restaurant
reflects attitudes regarding a sensational murder:

---

[6] Rice (1965, 14).

[7] Hauptmann (1961, 289).

[8] Block and Shedd (1962, 497).

Scene II

A Hall.

Night. The table is set. In the back

ground, a curtain, right and left, a niche.
The hall become bright. The old waiter a
guest.

The old waiter. (Reads the newspaper)
Murderer!

The guest. (lustfully) The legs?

The old waiter. The head is missing.

The guest. A beer!

Alexander. (enters through the curtain with
the sack)

The guest. Sex crime?

The old waiter. Reward.

The guest. Check please.

The old waiter. A roast beef.

The guest. A man?

The old waiter. $3.90.

The guest. (exits)

Alexander. Mankind.

The old waiter. Alexander!

Alexander. Who am I?

The older waiter. Disappeared.[9]

---

[9] Sokel (1963, 174).

Finally, in Toller's <u>Masse Mensch</u> Sonia's despair is articulated as follows:

The Man: I warned you against the masses.

Root up the masses and you root up hell.

The Woman: Hell? Who made that hell?

Who built the torture of your golden ills

That grind and grind out profit day by day?

Who put up prisons...who cried "holy war"

Who sacrificed a million human lives.

Upon the altars of some desperate game?

Who threw the masses into festering holes

In which, each day, is piled the filth of yesterday?

Who robbed these brothers of their human features,

Who drove them into factories,

Debased them into parts of a machine?

The state!...You!...

The Man: My life is duty.

The Woman: Oh yes...duty...duty to the State.

You're so respectable...

Didn't I say I saw you all too clearly?

You've been so well brought up.

You-tell all your right-thinking people

They never have been right...

They are the guilty ones...

We are all guilty...

Yes, I am guilty... guilty to myself,

Guilty to all mankind.[10]

In expressionism we are accorded an internal view of how one feels. There were two sub-units of the genre--mystical and political -- but all were written as if we are on the inside of an individual or a collective of individuals. Slanting walls, telegraphic speech, distorted human form and action were the devices of the expressionist playwright.

H.F. Garten added that they were foreshadowing the sinister and horrendous events to occur in 1933.[11] That could be true though difficult to verify. I prefer to classify the genre as a readjustment of balance vis à vis realism. It is clear that too heavy a reliance on the material of this world can impede our also important need for transcendance. The expressionists were proposing an alternate perception of reality.

Expressionism is usually dated from 1907-1925. For many the expressionist perception of reality was too remote and too abstract. Neue Sachlichkeit emerged in the German theatre in the twenties; indeed even the expressionist playwrights turned to neo-realism. It appears that the vicissitudes of everyday life demanded a more realistic aesthetic. Hasenclever's Ein Besserer Herr (1926), represents a clear and strong shift from his Humanity.

Without question, of course, Brecht represents the most important rejection of expressionism as the appropriate mode for communicating the truth. Decrying the "O Mankind!" school of expressionism Brecht created a new form of theatre, not realistic, strictly speaking, but anchored in a empirical verification. His Weltanschauung was a heightened realism of social idea. He transcended realism with

---

[10] Dukore and Gerould (1975, 100-101).

[11] H.F. Garten (1959).

his Verfremdungseffekt and bade us to perceive of the "true" reality in the context of social (chiefly economic) systems.

Still, though there were interesting protests and deviations from the norm, realism held sway until the sixties in America where the Living Theatre and other forms challenged once again the basic perception of reality that through matter, (science, psychology, economics, etc.) the core of meaning of our existence could be ascertained.

While Richard Schechner sought in Dionysus in 69 to return the theatre to what he considered its true ritual form, the social and political system engaged in its own upheaval, but more in line with Brecht than the Becks; more in line with Schiller than Schechner. That is to say the moral institutions of society were challenged and revised in the context of an ordered perhaps re-ordered materialistic perception or reality. The Viet Nam war was made concrete on television and on my campus, for example, the protests were quite empirically verifiable: a young man died in the bombing of the math research center in August of 1972.

Yet despite the theatre of Ridiculous, despite Bread and Puppet and the Manhattan Theatre project-- just as was the case in Europe in the 20s and 30s-- there was a return to the empirical verification, to the many variant forms of realism in theatre in America. After the war society returned to la vida cotidiana. Careers in dental technology increased and careers in theatre history and Shakespeare decreased. Funding in the sciences took vast leaps; the well ran almost dry in the arts and humanities.

As we progressed through the last half of our century theatre forms remained essentially realistic. The excitement came in the conventional treatment of heretofore "untouched" themes and ideas. Since I am tracing ideas, I take the liberty of branching into television and cinema, although my focus will remain chiefly on theatre. What then, has changed in the last part of this century? I will delineate themes and examples of plays manifesting those themes a little later on. Let me say at this point that there are clearly two schools of thought where late twen- tieth century theatre and society are concerned. One school sees an awesome deterioration and destruction of the values we hold dear. Indeed there is plenty to support such a contention. Nuclear threats, AIDS, dishonesty in government, the jeopardy of the middle class, violence, etc. I subscribe to the other school, however. That is to say, I believe that all this confusion is simultaneously house cleaning and reconstruction.

Let us now consider a few themes which had been basically untouched prior to the sixties. Most of them concern sex, for that was one important revolution in our country. Hair (1967) offered us the cafeteria of taboos to be rejected. Agnes of God 1980 a nun has had a child and we never know if she knows what happened. It is true that the play is about faith but the theme fits in the category of late 20th century shifts of thought. In Night Mother (1983) we see suicide treated as it is occurring on stage. Norman retains the 3 neo-classical unities interestingly, and allows us to see the actual mechanism of suicide.

An important spin-off in society and in theatre is the treatment of teenage suicide, treated before in Romeo and Juliet to be sure but not in this particular context. The idea of suicide epidemics, of serial suicides is new or at least this particular focus of it is new. We were reminded again with the 1986 so-called "pact suicides" in New Jersey and Illinois.

Homosexuality has made the grade if treatment and scrutiny are signs of arrival. Consider how far we have come from The Children's Hour (1934) and Tea and Sympathy (1953). In the sixties Boys in the Band (1968), in 1970 Find Your Way Home treated male homosexuality with considerable frankness. Hopkins'play is about a closeted homosexual who finally leaves his wife and returns to his lover Julian. A "friend" in sleazy fashion attempts to drive a wedge between the two men. It is not a good play, but unlike Tea and Sympathy there is no question about the sexuality being treated. I will mention contemporary plays that deal with the subject in a minute.

Where female love is concerned we begin, as I said with The Children's Hour and progress through the Killing of Sister George (1965) and plays by Cixous such as The Portrait of Dora (1979), where Freud's patient attempts to articulate a bonding to another woman, to Benmussa's adaptation of the short story "Albert Nobbs," The Singular Life of Albert Nobbs (1977), adapted by the French director Simone

11

Benmussa, a woman is forced to assume the persona of a man in order to survive in the world. It is a charming play which examines the question of what it means to be an man or a woman. It also implies parallels between the nineteenth century and ours and poses questions about a marriage between two women. Eve Merriam's The Club (1977) is similar in that it challenges our conceptions of sexuality.

In Jane Chambers A Late Snow (1974) the treatment of female love achieves a level of quasi-respectability. The women experience problems all of us experience: love, commitment, its fading and the existential crisis of what to do about a relationship that doesn't work in the face of new possibilities. One's sexuality for many segments of society is no longer a hush-hush topic; it is a fact of life and gradually has been integrated into the social aesthetic fabric of society. Plays like As Is (1985) and Normal Heart (1985) have already gone beyond the question of sexuality to a new yet old theme: cruelty in the multiple forms of ignorance in the context of a specific sexuality. As Is is a play about the devastation of a relationship by a hideous disease. It is true that the relationship is a same-sex relationship but the illness and its effect is what we see, not why, nor, should, the two men love each other.

The Normal Heart is without question a play about ignorance and the evil it perpetrates on us. Though it is labeled an AIDS play, it is about ignorance. The disease has been likened, in terms of social attitudes, to leprosy in literature. In the medieval period there were treatments of the disease leprosy, and the ignorance of society vis à vis the disease.

Indeed leprosy was called "The dreadful manifestation of an inner diseases, a disease of the soul."[12] In Der Arme Heinrich, (ca. 1195) Hartmann von Aue describes how Heinrich was struck with leprosy for not thinking correctly on the hereafter. There are other works of literature: Frauendienst (1215) by Ulrich von Lichtenstein, Tristram und Isalde (ca. 1170-1180) by Eilhart Henryson The Testament of Cresseid (1470?) all associate leprosy with spiritual

---

[12] Brody (1974, 148).

defilement [so]...pervasive in the literature of the Middle Ages.[13]

More specifically, Brody says, leprosy was perceived to be due to lust. In a 19th century Norwegian poem entitled "A Lament", the Young Man says:

For other illnesses found here
Wise doctors on the scene appear,
Who understand disease.
To hospital those sick are brought,
And for their plight a cure is sought.
Thus their ills are relieved,
And all their wound are dressed.

We lepers can no doctors get:
Here must we stay and wait and fret,
Until our time is up.
Peter from prison did escape
Because on God's grace he did wait.
O God, break now the chains
Which bind our limbs with pains.

Sometimes I softly walk about
The silent house of evening time:

Sorrowful sounds I hear.
One bitterly cries "woe is me"
Another sighs and groans that he
must creep away to bed.
Tell me O God-how long?[14]

Does that sound at all like the problems of AIDS patients today?

The theme of homosexuality can now be perceived as merely a sexuality not a dark perversion. In the novel and its movie version, <u>The Kiss of the Spider Woman</u>, (1979) the relationship between the two prisoners, though enforced by an unnatural confinement, develops quite naturally. The conditions were there for an expression of sharing and caring.

---

[13] Brody (189).

[14] Richards (1977, 159).

Consider wife and child abuse as late 20th century themes. The Burning Bed, a made-for-television movie, gives us a grim but important view of repression. Sam Shepherd's A Lie of the Mind published in 1986, produced in 1985, at the Promenade Theatre, is a story of a man who beat his wife so severely that she suffers brain damage. Neatly positing two families with the same number and sex of children, Shepherd engages in a grim analysis of how such things come about. The brother of the beaten woman seeks revenge on the man who beat his sister and when he has the chance to extract a humiliating apology, his father remains unconcerned in rather typical Shepherd fashion. He busies himself with the proper way of folding the American flag. The brother enraged but impotent to do anything about it says: "Doesn't anybody recognize that we've been betrayed? From the inside out. He married into this family and he deceived us all. He deceived her! He told her he loved her!" (III,3).[15]

Shepherd is telling us that wife abuse is nothing more than an extension of unfeeling and uncaring family environment.

Madeline Puccioni's Two O'Clock Feeding (1978) is a work depicting causes for child abuse, in this case, infant abuse. A mother of a new born infant with a busy and ambitious pediatrician husband resorts to abuse. The play begins too abruptly without sufficient articulation of the mother's deterioration and the reconciliation is too pat. Still, the fact that the play was written and produced attests to our demand for treatment of the issue. What makes the play interesting is the process of deterioration which makes a young parent perceive that physical abuse is a viable option.

Certainly we must include the tremendous and extensive coverage of women's right as the century draws to a close. Women can now participate in the heart attack track where striving for the good life is concerned. From wife abuse to freedom we are now able to recognize that there is a need to be equal partners.

---

[15] Sheperd (1987, 125).

The obvious side benefit for men has accrued as well. We can cry, feel and even let women take the lead without fear of loss of masculinity. Though hardly a trend, there are significant examples of role reversal in the positive framework. Most recently there is the television program <u>Dads</u> where the male consciousness functions as a single parent.

What does all this mean and what parallels can we draw from 1887 - 1987? let me attempt a wrap-up of our century first. I think we got blown out of the water in the sixties. Schechner, the Becks, Ronnie Davis and El Teatro Campesino among others did that for us. We were right, arrogant and powerful, preaching freedom while drilling for oil off the shores of Viet Nam. We were counseling our allies to stand up to the Soviet Union and at the same time dealing with them. Most recently we condemned terrorists, vowing never to negotiate with them and selling them arms to fight our allies <u>and</u> sending the money to Nicaragua. Thanks to a healthy chorus of critics we have the chance to see ourselves for what we are. If we disabuse ourselves regarding illusion of self, we are on the road to growth and recovery.

It is true that aesthetically we have remained in the framework of realism, but style is less important -- we have decided -- than idea. We have decided to shake convention and tradition, to the core, a kind of philosophical zero-based budgeting of ideas. We can use the functional components of existentialism to assess our core of being and take it from there. We simply don't accept any form of theatre of social form <u>argumentum ad veridunciam</u>.

In Munich last summer I saw some productions which without question support my contention. Walter Jens' <u>Die Troerinnen des Euripides</u> (1982) begins with the women tied to chairs and we hear an ominous, loud and metallic sound increasing in volume. It is the machinery of war. After a few moments, an enormous load of approximately one-inch square pieces of black and gray paper is dumped on the actresses. the paper clings to them throughout the act. The Trojan Horse was about twenty feet high, a skeleton of wire, and the trees were stark, gnarled winter, yet war-torn, trees. In a Kroetz play <u>Bauern sterben</u> (1985) a man wants to cut off his "lover's" hair, wrap her excrement in it and take it home. In another production of <u>Der Nusser</u> (1986) (adapted by Kroetz from Toller's <u>Hinkemann</u>) a disabled WWI veteran works in a research center biting off the heads of rats. The prop man made the rats in such a way that we saw brains, intestines, etc. The concern with fecal matter and gore is hardly the province of the German theatre. There are sufficient examples on the American stage and screen.

Leaving that particular topic for the moment, in Boston Robert Wilson's _Alcestis_, (Boston, 1985) apparently we must free ourselves of the addiction to the narrative frame by being bored interminably. The laser beam splitting of the rock was impressive, but boredom is boredom. Even the brilliantly performed comic moments lacked cohesion. Indeed the play has little to do with Euripides' play.

Still it must be said, we need to reevaluate the narrative frame as an inviolate truth. There is no question that the conventions we hold dear are no longer functional if they ever were. One only needs look at an interesting book the Garreau's _The Nine Nations of North America_ (1981) to recognize that we are functioning more in terms of larger regions. I quote one rather humorous reference to demonstrate my point:

> "...each nation has a distinct prism through which it views the world. The foundry, the declining industrial nation of the northeast for example, still tends to see the other eight nation as subservient, was the real center of paying colonies they once were. It views itself as the real center of power in the continent, shrugging off the inexorable slide of population and ambitions to other place as temporary abberations susceptible to some quick fix, to some new 'program'...Yet the northern Pacific Rim nation of Ecotopia views the Foundry in yet another way -- as irrelevant... Its natural markets and its lessons about living are in Asia."[16]

I think it is not correct or fair to say that we are coming apart--even in light of the Contra Arms Deal. What it is fair to say is that we are emerging from a period of crisis and transition. Perhaps

---

[16] Garreau (1981, 2).

analogously we are no longer adolescents but young rich adults facing up to the fact that with money, power, and prestige, there is work to do, and responsibilities to assume, yet we are uncertain of the form. For example in an article in the NY Times two or three summers ago we made the top of the list as the most violent nation in the world. Do I need to provide you with examples of violence on the stage? It has been said that if we look at our Theatre we will know the kind of nation we have. All the scrambling, all the sex, violence and taboo-busting on stage and in society don't mean that we're coming apart; it means we are realigning ourselves and attempting a reconstruction of values.

At the end of the 19th century they may have been realigning as well, but I prefer to identify that shift as a progression from one order to another. After all, it was possible to overrun Europe as the worst that could be done. It was not possible to destroy the planet. That achievement belongs to our century.

What was occurring was the turning away from emotion and transcendence as vehicles for arriving at the core of meaning in Romanticism to knowledge, scientific casuality and empirical verification. Truth was defined as only available through empirically verifiable matter whether in object, system or psychology. Realism and naturalism took definition from a tangibly articulated reality.

In the nineteenth century, definitions of reality shifted from A to B. In the twentieth century we have challenged a finite definition of reality. We were iconoclasts where A or B or indeed the alphabet was concerned. I can't resist reminding you that while we are clearly a materialist nation, our form of government was born in the period between die Aufklärung and die Romantik, between the age of enlightment and romanticism. If what I have articulated is true, what will happen between 1987 - 2010? There must be in that period a termination of iconoclasm and a restructuring of a different value system. One cannot destroy icons forever; eventually someone will pick up pieces and build something new. I don't think we are finished destroying or challenging old values. The injustices to the American Indian must be redressed finally. The economic inequities will continue to plague us until they are at least restructured. I notice for example the disappearance

17

of the middle class in New York City. I see a play
about bands of poor raiding Trump tower. Today the
rich in Jamaica, for example, live in armed fortres-
ses. What makes us think it can't happen here?

There is a serious problem where the role of the
poet and artist are concerned. There is a connection
between our rating as most violent nation and social
attitudes toward the artist. Our soul is in trouble
and the one to help -- the artist -- is only barely
tolerated if not scorned. The teacher is another
source of salvation, less scorned but equally under-
valued.

I could go on but I am essentially an idealist
and I believe the 21st century will effect a cohesion
of values more appropriate to life which will include
colonization in space, greater advance in diagnosing
physical and mental illnesses and yes greater dangers.
There will be interplanetary wars by the 22nd century.
But let me come back here though.

Dietrich Schwanitz in an interesting work
entitled Die Wirklichkeit der Inszenierung und die
Inszenierung der Wirklichkeit (The Reality of Production and the Production of Reality) (1977) articulates
some interesting principles of aesthetics where the
theatre is concerned. As his title indicates, the
perception of reality vis à vis the illusion created
on the stage [with, of course, its own reality] can be
described as a process of double distinction and the
renewal of one's sense of reality vis à vis that
double distinction. He says, "The fictionality of the
drama is confounded with the reality of the production."[17] There is a phenomenon of accepting reality,
the Coleridge's willing suspension of disbelief, of
allowing that acceptance to become a new reality.
Schwanitz says that the theatre can exist on the basis
of its double character: image and extension of
reality.

There are clear overtones of existentialism in
this aesthetic when he says that the individual
emancipates himself from his own sense of being object
and impulse and participates in the world of the
other. Man exists only in the divestiture of self in
terms of the reality in which he finds himself. We

---

[17] Schwanitz (1977, 297).

internalize the new reality of a theatre production but it is a specific reality with its specific purpose and we come away with a newly shaped definition of our own reality.

To be horrified at the lack of love in Shepherd's A Lie of the Mind is to miss the point of what is occurring at the end of this century. The old value system--being concerned about the proper folding of the flag-- and our adherence to it despite its obviously horrendous consequences are what need to be replaced with a different, hopefully better concept to love. It is not that the Catholic Church is inherently corrupt in Agnes of God. It is that faith has been improperly defined, faith, I would add, in the efficacy of empirical verification. The gay life style is viewed as evil by some and indeed perverted often by its own practitioners. The value system proposed in the play The Normal Heart however, is that love is sufficiently strong to transcend gender if those who would love care to understand its meaning.

Instead of seeing contemporary theatre in terms of representing the decline of a civilization, what can be happening is that creation of a new process. To paraphrase Schwanitz, the cycle of theatre reflecting life which reflects theatre is disrupted in modern drama and theatre practice since it confuses reality and reflection. It is in this disorientation of reality that contemporary theatre functions.

We are not declining because we are allowing negative ideas and activities on the stage; we are re-processing the concept of illusion and reality into a new problem [or perception of reality]--initially. What remains to be done is to identify the perception of reality we now have as more viable for our time.

I teach my students to assess theatre, drama and life with a theory which I call the theory of symbolic interconnection. That is we interpret action, artifact, and attitude as interconnected and possessed of meaning. All of this confusion is nothing more than a progression toward a more functional set of values. Regardless of one's status, one operates with a set of values, even if one insists on no set of values, a value system as clear as any.

What we will do is take the positive and core elements of confusion and rebuild. All of the themes in theatre I mentioned have peripheral and core value.

We as a civilization will go for the core. Wife and child abuse are bad and we have to stop it by knowing how it starts. What we will take from that theme is the exhortation to help both abused and abuser. The wife and child abusers have been bused. We will look in the theatre for ways of caring. Homosexuality per se is neither here nor there. Committed relationships are what enrich our lives, not differences in anatomy and sexual techniques. Women are on their way to equality. They don't want a new Amazon society. They want partnership and communication first. Equal pay and other rights are important but they only affirm communication; they are not at the core. Suicide is the feeling of no growth and no further options in life. In the 21st century we will work less on hot lines and more on what can be learned about self. The potential suicide should be glad to be alive, not for the good day, because there will be bad days, -- but for new information he/she has about self. We will not abandon technology, nor will it destroy us. We are that smart. We will refine it and, for example, create holographic theatre.

Let me conclude with where I think the theatre will be aesthetically. As I said we will continue to examine more taboos until a new value system presents itself. Then we will see the theatre as an extension of the mind, not tied to the narrative frame-- performance art has helped -- but anchored in a multi-layered perceptual and aesthetic framework which forces us to search for a personal value system consistent with a social one. If Proust is correct in saying that the quality of an experience can only be grasped in recollection, then the theatre will present us with recollected and reflected modes of perceiving reality. We will have greater control of our theatre by manipulating its components during performance to suit our needs, our quest for larger meaning. We are all in search of the truth and the 21st century theatre, a true theatre of the mind will enable us to project from our minds onto a stage which will consist of live actors trained differently, projections, movies, holographs and other technologies unknown to us at this time. We will come back upon ourselves in multiple time frames and on multiple levels of reality. Maybe we are looking in the way Schopenhauer looked. Maybe we are finally understanding the precariousness of reason and the futility of opposing the will with mere idea.

In my study of the history of theatre one finite truth remains: theatre never really dies; its forms change because the impulse to create is a biological drive.

While looking at the transition from the 19th-20th century from the perspective of this imminent transition is a little scary, it is finally more comforting than frightening. We are more on a razor's edge but the rewards seem greater. Imagine a theatre even more sophisticated than the holographic theatre in Bradbury's Fahrenheit 451. I don't know how far I will get into the 21th century (in this physical form) but I sure plan on being on the razor's edge. See you there.

References

Block and
Shedd, 1962:   Haskell Block and Robert
                      Shedd, Masters of Modern
                      Drama: (Random House).

Brody, 1974:   Saul Brody, The Disease of the
                      Soul (Ithaca: Cornell University
                      Press).

Cixous and
Benmussa, 1979:   Helene Cixous and Simone Benmussa,
                      Benmussa Directs: Portrait of
                      Dora and The Singular Life of
                      Albert Nobbs (Dallas and London:
                      John Calder Pub. LTD).

Copleston, 1946:   Frederick Copleston, S.J., Arthur
                      Schopenhauer-Philosopher of
                      Pessimism (Jesuit Fathers of
                      Heythrop College, Pub.).

Dukore and
Gerould, 1975:   Bernard F. Dukore and Daniel C.
                      Gerould, Avant-garde Drama: A
                      Casebook 1918-1939 (New York:
                      Thomas Crowell).

Garreau, 1981:   Joel Garreau, The Nine Nations of
                      North America (New York: Avon
                      Books).

Garten, H.F., 1962:   Modern German Drama (New York: Grove Press).

Grimm and Hermand   Reinhold Grimm and Jost Hermand, Deutsche Revolutions-dramen (Suhrkamp Verlag, Pub.).

Hauptmann, 1961   Gerhart Hauptmann, Five Plays (New York: Bantam Books).

Hoffman, 1979:   William M. Hoffman, Gay Plays-The First Collection (New York: Avon Books).

Hopkins, 1971:   John Hopkins, Find Your Way Home (Baltimore: Penguin Books).

Hughes, 1952:   Henry Stuart Hughes, Oswald Spengler - A Critical Estimate (New York: Charles Scribner).

Nietzsche, 1927:   Friedrich Nietzsche, The Modern Library), The Philosophy of Nietzsche (New York: Random House).

Proust, 1924:   Marcel Proust, Remembrance of Things Past (New York: Random House).

Rice, 1965:   Elmer Rice, 3 Plays (New York: Hill and Wang).

Richards, 1977:   Peter Richards, The Medieval Leper and His Northern Heirs (Cambridge: D.S. Brewer Ltd.).

Rosen, 1968:   George Rosen, Madness in Society (Chicago: University of Chicago Press).

Schopenhauer, 1962: Arthur Schopenhauer, The Essential Schopenhauer (London: Unwin Books).

Schwanitz, 1977:   Dietrich Schwanitz, Die Wirklich-keit der Inszenierung und die Inszenierung der Wirklichkeit (Meisenheim am Glan: Verlang Anton Hain).

Stone, 1959:   Edward Stone (ed.) <u>What was</u>
<u>Naturalism</u>? (New York: Appleton,
Century, Croft).

Teraoka, 1985: Arlene Akiko Teraoka, The Silence
of Entropy or Universal Discourse
- <u>The Postmodernist Poetics of</u>
<u>Heiner Müller</u> (New York: Peter
Lang Publications).

Valine, 1977:   Robert Valine, <u>West Coast Plays</u>
(Berkeley: West Coast Plays).

What! No Plot?
Rhetorical Inventio in French Court Ballet:
Les Incompatibles (1655)

Louis E. Auld
Central Connecticut State University

I

Ballet and mascarade constituted perhaps the most popular entertainments at the French court throughout most of 17th century. Although for four decades after the Ballet Comique de la Royne of 1581 important ballets frequently deserved to be qualified "comique," or as we would say, 'dramatic,' in their titles-that is, they developed a plot-production after that date, from 1621 to 1671, did so rarely. Even in the earlier works the putative plot was often of no more than peripheral value in the elaboration of the central idea. Unlike their English cousins, the court masques, these later production, know as ballet à entrées were not plays.[1] Not only did they contain no dialogue, but they depended on principles of organization foreign to dramatic theatre. This paper seeks to demonstrate that creation of such ballets called extensively upon the rhetorical inventio taught in the schools.

In modern scholarship it is normally taken as a given that French court ballets totally lacked conceptual rigor. A recent writer, J.-M. Apostolides, sums up accepted opinion, "the traditional ballet could accommodate all sorts of entrées, ... they were pasted in without the slightest concern for harmony."[2] In fact, it has become a sort of scholarly ritual to refer to it, in a deprecatory phrase that seems to have been the invention of the musicologist Lionel de

---

[1] H.C. Lancaster, "Relation between French Plays and Ballets from 1581-1650," Publications of the Modern Association 31 (1916), 379-394.

[2] Jean-Marie Apostolides, Le Roi-Machine. Spectacle et politique au temps de Louis XIV, Paris Minuit ("Arguments"), 1981, 61. Translations here, as elsewhere, are mine.

la Laurencie, as "cette scolastique minutieuse."[3] On
the evidence of the surviving livrets, one might well
conclude that those ballets were in fact vapid,
formless jumbles of unrelated ideas.[4]

How then, to account for the fact that time and
again those who wrote on the theory of ballet mentioned the coherence and intellectual rigor required
for a proper ballet design? One writer, known to us
only as St.-Hubert, maintained that the most difficult
part in the creation of a ballet was finding and
developing "un beau sujet." There are, he lamented,
"fort peu de gens qui sçach[ent] accommoder un beau
sujet, y observer l'ordre nécessaire" (La Manière de
composer et de faire réussir les ballets, Paris,
1641). Michel de Marolles (Mémoire, 2 vols., Paris,
1656-57) insisted that the ballets, parts "se rappor-
tent agréablement à un tout." Perhaps most clearly of
all, Michel de Pure called for a "judicieuse diversité," while at the same time insisting that all
entrées be drawn "sans effort et pour ainsi dire sans
feu, des entrailles du Sujet" (Idée des spectacles,
Paris, 1668, 243). As he explained it,

> The Subject is the Soul of the Ballet, which
> gives rise to the first Idea that the Poet
> may have conceived, which communicated the
> spirits to the diverse parts, and which
> gives them in conclusion their nourishment
> and their movement. ... It is a substantial
> and internal sap, which rises secretly and
> separately in each member of the body of the
> ballet, which communicates to all the heat
> and all the vigor necessary to live.

---

[3] Les Créateurs de l'Opéra français (Paris, 1911)
73. Cf. Marie-Françoise Christout, Le Ballet de cour
de Louis XIV, 1643-1672 (Paris, 1967), 147; M.
McGowan, L'Art du Ballet de Cour en France, 1581-1643,
(Paris: C.N.R.S., 1963).

[4] Les Contemporains de Molière, ed. Victor
Fournel, t.II, "Théâtre de Cour," (Paris, 1863-65;
facs repr., Genève: Slatkine, 1967); Ballets et
Mascarades..., ed. Paul Lacroix, 6 volumes (Genève,
1868-70; fasc. repr., Genève: Slatkine).

Thus, it dominates uniquely during the entire action, and the entire length of the entertainment, even though in the separate entrée the unity may appear to be interrupted.[5]

By closely following the textual indications of the livret and related material, one can often recover much of the conceptual unity the governed the diverse and seemingly unrelated entrées of a given ballet. To penetrate the ballet's inner logic is to come closer to understanding a fundamental aspect of theatrical experience in the seventeenth century.

The sections which follow indicate first some typical ballet subjects and the ways in which they were developed; then the Ballet des Incompatibles, in which Molière participated in 1655, provides a specific instance; the final section suggests how the elaborative techniques thus discovered related in to Renaissance rhetorical training.

II

French court ballet was, of course, primarily spectacle. There is no doubt that it offered the visceral, kinesthetic satisfaction that dance coupled with music always affords. Nor may we doubt that pageantry and the opportunities for striking, even outlandish, costumes played an important part in the genre's appeal.

Furthermore, ballet performances, had a variety of social functions. Ballet was a social ritual in which all the court participated. Nobles and courtiers danced principal roles, royalty and the great nobility became part of the spectacle-whether as sponsor or active participants or both-and received exaggerated compliments; and everyone took great pleasure in it. A strong propagandistic element

---

[5] "Le Sujet est l'Ame du Balet, qui formente la première Idée que Poète peut avoir conceüe, qui communique les esprits aux diverses parties, & qui leur donne enfin la nourriture & le mouvement... . C'est une sève matérielle & intéieure, secrètement & séparément répandue dans chacun membre du corps, qui luy communique toute la chaleur en soit apparente & interrompue" (Idée des spectacles, p. 216).

explicitly connected the pageantry to the social hierarchy, and thus confirmed and consecrated the status quo.[6]

Subjects could be borrowed from mythology, legend, or literature; they could be derived from proverbs and sayings; they could reflect current events and passing sensations. The poets, as those who invented these entertainments were called, often sought out subject which naturally fell into several divisions. Marolles describes hypothetical ballets of the Planets, the Muses, the Elements, the four Parts of the World, the Seasons, the Nations, and the Beasts.[7] Many of these subjects were actually used: Les Saison de l'Année, in 1621; the Nations, closely related to the Four Corners of the World (Asian, African, European, and American) appeared both in the Douairière de Billebahaut (1926) and at the extended conclusion of the Bourgeois gentilhomme (1669). Marolles offered the plan of a "Ballet of the Night;" the sumptuous production under the name only a few years later (1653) remains one of the most famous in the genre. His project and the actual production may profitably be compared, as may his Ballet des Muses and the great festival of the name created by Molière, Lully and Benserade in 1667-68.

Some years later, the schoolman father LeJay would describe the detail how to set a "Ballet des Arts," with sections devoted to the liberal arts (the trivium and quadrivium) and the applied or practical arts (agriculture, navigation, architecture, printing, and so forth). But since the ballet was to be produced in the intervals of a five-act Latin play at the Collège Louis-le-Grand, a four-part division became imperative; therefore, the poet "envisaged the arts in their divers rôles within society:" "1) the necessary arts; 2) the useful arts; 3) the pleasure-giving arts;

---

[6] See McGowan and Christout, opp. cit.; L. E. Auld, "The Comedy-Ballet of Molière" (unpub. diss., University Microfilms, 1968); The Lyric Art of Pierre Perrin vol. I, The Birth of French Opera (Binningen/Ottawa/Henryville: Inst. of Mediaeval Music, 1986), 74-78.

[7] Marolles, Mémoires (Paris, 1656-57), t. II, 184.

and 4) those which serve for the glory and honor of humanity."[8]

Mythological subjects were fashionable in the early phase (1581 to 1621), and again after 1651; the topos 'Planets,' for instance, might yield the deities Mars, Venus, Jupiter, Saturn, and Apollo (the Sun). Allegorical figures abound throughout, and moral interpretation was never far from the surface. There was a steady fascination, too, with magic, transformations, enchantments. Many ballets had propagandistic intentions, whether inciting to national pride, as in Richelieu's Ballet de la Prospérité des Armes de France (1642), or simply extoling the virtues of the great who presided over their presentation.

In the Agronautes, a "ballet comique" danced in 1614, the subject on its most abstract level opposes Harmony and Discord-more specifically, Moral disorder and the stabilizing power of the monarch (and his mother, Marie de Medicis). What should we expect to see in a ballet of the Argonauts? In all likelihood, not what we get. The opening section is devoted to the entrancing Circé; the next, to the enchanter, Amphion, whose song moved stones to build the walls of Thebes; the next, Medea, yet another sorceress. In the finale Circé humbly yields before the greater power of their Majesties. The Argonauts, restored to their familiar forms (as elegant courtiers), dance a Grand Finale, preceded by twelve Pages still dressed as squirrels, and twelve musicians disguised as Sirens. Clearly, even in this supposedly dramatic ("comique") ballet, what plot there is operates only on the abstract, or moral, level.

The association of Jason, as representative of all the Argonauts, with Medea, whose charms and spells could not hold him, is reasonable enough. Indeed, some version of the legend tell of a brief visit to the island of Circé. But where is that talisman, the gold fleece, which most would consider central to the story of the Argonauts? There is no sign of it. The action portrays the evil power of Circé being overcome by the King's power for good and her charms bested by those of the Queen. A lively interplay between the

---

[8] From LeJay's De choreis dramaticis (Paris, 1725), in Ernest Boysse, Le Théâtre de Jésuites (Paris, 1880), 39-42.

legendary and the contemporary, between the moral sense and theatrical characterization notwithstanding, there is precious little story. The appearance of Amphion and Medea betrays a metonymic, or associative, method of development inimical to good dramatic plot construction.

We have noted briefly the allegorical, the mythological, the magical, and the propagandistic aspects of ballets, as well as the free shift of conceptual points of view. Several others deserve mention: The exotic, and inexhaustible source of subjects and material, was not unrelated to the magic and enchantment themes. Literary works, too could furnish subject. Ariosto and Tasso provided many a subject; in the later part of the century Marino's Adone offered a rich hunting ground.

The circumstantial nature of many ballet ideas could be closely related to the propagandistic, as when a production celebrated the birth of a dauphin or a military victory. But local events and absorbing topics of interest often took a much more earthy turn. There were ballets of Impatience (1661, when a promised operatic production was not ready in time to suit the King) and of the Resale of Costumes (La Revente des Habits, also 1661). Everyday life furnished the subject in ballets and mascarades of the Rues de Paris (ca. 1644), of Fashions, both in Clothing and in Dance (Modes, autant des habits que des danses, 1633), of Wine-Drinkers (Les Demandeurs de vin, 1646); there were the Grippés à la mode (The Latest Fashionable Flu. ca. 1640), and even a Ballet des Moyens de parvenir (How to Succeed at Court, ca. 1640).

In 1656 Lully and Benserade presented Le Ballet de Psyché, ou la Puissance de l'Amour, in the usual two parts, or "acts."[9] By this time, the last thing the reader should expect is that it enacted the story of Psyche and Eros. Sure enough, "in the first [act] are shown the beauties and delights of Love's Palace. In the second, Love Himself entertains the beautiful Psyché by representing some of the miracles he has accomplished." Nothing of the story of her fatal

---

[9] Livret, Ballet de Psyché (Paris, 1656); see Auld "The Commedy-Ballets of Molière," 38-9, n. 88).

curiosity is portrayed. She sits and observes, merely a framing-character.

A favorite mode of thought in ballets, as everywhere else, was opposition, paradox. One could cite the Ballet des Contraires, (ca. 1640), the Ballet des Renconires antipathiques (ca. 1644), les Impossibilitiés, (1627), or le Monde renversé (1625-a popular theme). A work in this mode, Le Ballet des Incompatibles, prepared and danced for the Prince and Princess de Conti, in 1655, affords a closer look at the ways individual entrées could related to the general subject.[10]

III

"Ballet des Incompatibles"-the title indicates the theme, or subject, and poses the challenge: the entire ballet depends on the single principles of "things incompatible," a category of polarity or binary opposition. The concept is worked out in a variety of ways: the dancer inappropriate to his role; types of characters inconsonant with each other; characters and moral qualities not to be discovered together, etc. Most of the dancers are nobles of the court, familiar to the audience. In the livrets the complex inter-relations among the dancers, their roles, and their social personae were further subjected to the wit of the court poets, who vied in exploring all the possible paradoxes involved, thus adding layers to the play of theatrical illusion.

"Things incompatible," such a subject or theme commits the poet to very little; this is the most common coin of the realm, the 'moon-June', the 'Boy-meets-Girl' of logical-rhetorical thought. Clearly, too, whatever intellectual excitement the ballet may engender must come from the ingenious or novel ways the poet, the costumer, and the dancers find to flesh

---

[10]Molière Oeuvres, ed. E. Despois, P. Mesnard, "Grands Ecrivains de France," (Paris, 1873-1893), t.I, 523-535; Oeuvres complètes, ed. G. Couton, Pléiade," (Paris, 1967), t. I, App. I, 987-995, notes, 1371-1373.

out their simple conceptual frame. The Incompatibles, then, took the following form:

Première Partie

Récit de la Nuit

Première Entrée:	La Discorde
Seconde Entrée:	Les Quatre Elements
Troisième Entrée:	La Fortune et la Vertu
Quatrième Entrée:	Un Vieillar et deux Jeunes Hommes
Cinquième Entrée:	Deux Philosophes et Trois Soldats
Sixième Entrée:	L'Argent. Un Peintre, un Poéte et un Alchimiste
Septième Entrée:	Un Chariatan et la Simplicité représentée Par un Vieux Paysan

Seconde Partie

Récit du Dieu du Sommeil

Première Entrée:	L'Ambition
Deuxième Entrée:	La Dissimulation et Deux Ivrognes
Troisième Entrée:	L'Eloquence et une Harengère
Quatrième Entrée:	La Sagesse et Deux Amoureux
Cinquième Entrée:	La Vérité et Quatre Courtisans
Sixième Entrée:	La Sobriété et Quatre Suisses
Septième Entrée:	Une Bacchante et Une Naiade
Huitième Entrée:	Le Dieu du Silence et Six Femmes

The opening récit, sung by the allegorical figure of Night, turns upon the inevitable binary: Day-Night. In this case that opposition does not, as it might have done, provide the structural principle for the two parts of the ballet. An apostrophe to the personified Day, calls upon him to make way for the prince's well-earned nocturnal pleasures.

> Dans le vaste sein de Neptune
> Laisse vite tomber ta lumière importune,
> O Jour trop envieux qui retarde mes pas.

> C'est aux voeux de ta soeur opposer trop
> d'obstacles:
> Un grand Prince aujourd 'hui m 'appelle à
> des spectacles
> Où l'on ne te veut pas.

Having banished Day in the first strophe, in the
second Night explicitly links the prince and his
exploits to the spectacle. Such propagandistic hype
occur frequently in the royal ballets. Thus, already
two different kinds of evocation have been planted in
the spectators' minds:

a) The world of military exploits subjected to a
process of idealization: "faits pleins de gloire;"
"une illustre vicroire; "Don't l'orgueil de l'Espagne
a poussé des soupirs.

b) A mythical world ("Dans le vaste sein de
Neptune") of elemental, opposed, and equal forces
which sets the stage, as it were, and begins to lift
the spectator out of the everyday world, into the
almost equality familiar one of a comfortable, ideal
illusionism-the escapist world of that time. clearly,
the poet drew upon a fund of familiar concepts.

Now begins the ballet proper, a series of
entrées, each figuring in one way or another the
concept of incompatibility. Often today the reader
needs to assemble clues from a variety of sources-
titles and headings, song texts and "vers pour les
personnages" in livret, as well as any surviving
musical scores or contemporary explanations and
analyses-in order to discover the point of a given
entrée.

In Les Incompatibles the allegorical figure of
Discord, dancing alone, opened the dance, and the
verses develop the paradox of the dancer too good to
play the part.

> En me vouyant si bien danser
> Et charmer par mes airs l'espirt le
> plus sauvage,
> On peut dire sans m 'offenser
> Que je fais mal mon personnage.

The Four Elements, Fire, Water, Air and Earth,
in Entrée Two, are in compatible in a quite different
sense. Although they must be combinable, they must
also by definition remain distinct, as irreducible

33

elements.   The verses explain each character's
relation to the theme.   The Marquis de Bellepont, as
Fire, burns for military, but not amorous, conquest.
The Vicomte de Larbourt, as Water,provides the pretext
for a parallel on inconstancy:

> Je suis de nature inconstante;
> Mon humeur est toujours flottante:
> Les autres éléments se déterminent mieux.
> Mon inquiétude est extrême,
> El loin d'être toujours bien d'accord avec
>   eux,
> Je ne suis pas toujours d'accord avec moi-
>   même.

The Marquis de Yillars, as Air, bathes in the light of
a great (royal) star; and M. de Fourques, as a nimble-
footed Earth, can claim:

> Je crois que personne ne pense
> Que je sois un lourd élément.

In the third entrée, Fortune and Virtue, in a
traditional moral opposition, provide and excellent
example of the interplay of social and stage roles.
The two stanzas of verse contrast the poverty of the
Marquis de Canaples with his allegorical portrayal of
Dame Fortune.

> J'ai beau même danser pour elle,
> Ce ne sont que pas perdus.

For Entrée Four, an Old Man and two Young Men--
the binary age/youth-the poet returns explicitly to
his theme of incompatibility, and verses for the Young
Men praise their amorous exploits.

It is worth nothing the shift from the allegorical to another level of portrayal, still relatively
abstract; the Old Man represents a class more than an
individual.   The individual dancer might have been
costumed to represent the class of Old Men metonymi-
cally, through elements of dress, a traditional mask;
and perhaps even attached attributes that could be
read as saying: Old Man.

Entrée Seven, A Charlatan and Simplicity,
represented by an Aged Peasant, will illustrate an
even more complex conceptual pattern, as allegory
takes on a greater degree of individualizing detail.
The audience sees an Aged Peasant, whom it is expected

to 'read' as the figure Simplicity. As a scene from everyday, rustic life it draws the spectator away from the court into low realism, almost certainly in a comic mode. Yet the moral implications of the scene are kept in view as well. The second set of verses is designated, in a departure from the norm: "For SIMPLICITY, speaking of [not to] the CHARLATAN." Not all that simple in truth, the rustic has misgiving: Happy though he is to see this personnage "whose divine secrets spare us from death!", he still does not fail to note that the Charlatan with his miraculous remedies seems to be subject to the same ills as the rest of us.

Unlike some ballets, this one introduces no new angle in the second part, but only continues to develop various polarities. It is worth pausing long enough to note only continues to develop various polarities. It is worth pausing long enough to note in Entrée Three the verse for Molière, who portrayed a fish wife. In a nicely turned compliment they praise the poet's incompatibility with all that is not eloquence.

A final Grand Bal lead the performers directly back into the social world of the spectators. Thus, a shifting play of theatrical illusion and allusion animated this typical ballet.

IV

In drawing their materials from allegory, myth, legend, popular wisdom and everyday life, the ballet's inventors ranged freely up and down the Porphyrian Tree, that long-established visual model for classifying types of being, from the most comprehensive or universal to the most individual.[11] Such lines of thought followed paths with which most of us have little acquaintance today, but which then constituted a main avenue for the development of ideas. The ballet designer, or "poet," proceeded from the central concept, or what he called the Subject, to the specific application, from the abstract to the concrete example.

---

[11] See Walter J. Ong, Ramus, Method and the Decay of Dialogue (Cambridge: Harvard u.p., 1983 [orig. 1958]), xv-xvi and 78.

In the instance just examined the ballet's creators set out to explore that area of logic which housed Incompatibilities, or what the logician and rhetorician called <u>repugnantes inter se</u>, things incompatible with each other. Now opposition and contrariety are basic logical categories. They would be among the first logical distinctions learned in school, since the Aristotelian <u>Organon</u>, and Prophyry's <u>Isagoge</u>, or introduction to the Categories, figured very early in the schoolboy's training.[12] But if these categories derived ultimately from Aristotelian logic, they had long since become a part of rhetoric as well. One of the sixteen topics in Ciceronian rhetoric, the <u>repugnantia</u> would be applied to the task of finding things to say or developing a given idea. "Emphasis on inventio is considered one of the hallmarks of Humanist logic;" often seen as a weakening of the Aristotelian tradition in logic, it reflects the "Ciceronian-rhetorizing" tendency, of which historians of logic speak.[13] Poets, like rhetoricians, had the habit of "searching the places" for materials. What did they find in those places? The very sorts of ideas that inform the ballet of the Incompatibles: the stories of antiquity, mythology, legend, the bible, history and hagiography, or the more recent tales of Ariosto, Rabelais, and Cervantes-any material from which a lesson could be drawn. Then, too, there was the real and present world: examples of tradesmen, and other walks of life; character types, age groups. And there were saying (<u>Chria</u>) <u>sententiae</u>, proverbs: <u>Omnia vincit amor</u>...

A ballet danced in 1627 went by the name <u>Les Français surmontent Tout</u>: it illustrated a motto or emblem. In order do develop such a subject, the poet

---

[12] C. de Rochemonteix, S.J., <u>Un Collège de Jésuites aux XVIIe et XVIIIe Siècles. Le Collège Henri IV De la Flèche</u>, (LeMan, 1881) t.III, 26-27. Cf. D. Mornet, <u>Histoire de la clarté française</u> (Paris, 1929), For Aristotle's treatment of contraries, see especially the <u>Categories</u>, 6.5.11, 11b15, and <u>De Interpretatione</u>, Ch. 6-7, 12-13, in Aristotle, <u>Organon</u>, tr. J.L. Ackrill (Oxford: Clarendon, 1963).

[13] Neal W. Bilbert, <u>Renaissance Concepts of Method</u>, (New York: Columbia U.P., 1960), 76.

would examine each aspect separately in this case the three ideas: Frenchmen, overcoming or conquest, and everything. Under each heading he would then run through all possible examples. Under Frenchmen, he might consider the three estates, nobles, merchants and peasants; he could certainly make a mental list of the various regions of France, with a view to contrasting Parisian and provincial, Norman and Picard, etc. He would look for exemplars, famous or legendary representatives in each category. He would then proceed similarly with the other two terms.

If, as I indicated at the outset, the ballet theorists insisted on the importance of strictly relating every entrée to the subject, they also specifically called for constant variety in material selected. The abbé de Pur, for instance, want a "judicieuse diversité: among the entrées should alternate, as Saint-Hubert indicated.

The metaphor of visiting the places and the spatial model of the Porphyrian tree suggest way of thinking of ballet logic in terms of what I sometimes call the "shot-group." Or since each of the topoi or places constitute a separate trove of potential material, since under each heading could be found a wealth of illustrations, one might also imagine the troves as a series of columnal lists, each ranked in ascending order of seriousness, with the most commanding items at the top and the most lowly, base or 'crotesque' at the bottom. The result is a grid or a sort of spreadsheet. Assuming that some ideas stand out as more appropriate than others to representation on stage, we derive a grid with a random pattern of entries. The ballet designer can choose among them. To maintain interest and pique the intellect, the less obivous the interrelations, the better. For the sake of variety the poet avoids choosing his materials either from the same column or from the same level twice in succession. Yet all entrées still relate the germinal idea. In this lies their harmony; far from being haphasard, they depend on a typically Baroque paradox of unity within diversity.

Thus, the method of elaborating a ballet can indeed be said to be "scholastic" in the sense that it derived to some extent from habits or though learned from Aristotle, and therefore basic to medieval philosophy. But more accurately, it was scholastic in another sense: in that it depended on ways of thinking taught in the schools--i.e. the rhetorical _inventio_.

The curious theatrical are of _ballet de cour_ would engender French opera, _tragédie lyrique_; interwoven between the act of the first Italian operas in France, ballets helped to keep the audience awake, and thus give _dramma per musica_ a foothold in that country; less than a decade alter, Molière, who was redefining dramatic comedy, would combine the two genres in his own proud invention, the comedy-ballet. When the court ceased to participate in ballet productions, the genre tood refuge in the Jesuit-run collèges. Yet its influences resonate throughout the eighteenth century-in the "opera-ballet" of Fameau, for instance-where it would again learn to tell a story.

The apparently haphazard and barren ballet plans grew out of, and returned the spectators to, structures of thought within their experience, structures by which they definded their relationship to society and the world. It is by understanding how such deeping ingrained intellectual habits worked to shape and give coherence to even the most circumstantial of courtly art forms that we can uncover the hidden springs of "cette scolastique minutieuse," seventeenth-century French court ballet.[14]

---

[14] Part of the work for this paper was completed during a Summer Seminar at Harvard University in 1986 sponsored and funded by the National Endowment for Humanities and direct by Professor Jules Brody.

The Power of the Evil Eye in the Blind:
Oedipus Tyrannus 1306 and Oedipus at Colonus 149-156

Eleftheria Bernidaki-Aldous
Creighton University

Focusing on the reaction of Sophoclean choruses before the blind, I examine the Greek belief in the evil eye: its definition and function. I also show how it relates to other beliefs such as transgression (hybris), envy (phthonos), pollution (miasma, agos) and that which maintains that suffering spoils the character. The blind are seen not only as having transgressed mortal boundaries and as a source of pollution, but also as capable of inflicting the evil eye.

The evil eye can be defined as that syndrome of interaction of psychic energies, according to which, some magic power exists in the eye, which, when motivated by envy, may be directed against the person of enviable good fortune. Blindness, as deprivation of the supreme good (eyesight), is a source of phthonos in the deprived person. Consequently, the blind are capable of inflicting harm through the power of the evil eye. If we accept the belief in the evil eye as real in ancient (as it is in modern) Greece[1], we will appreciate more fully the complexity of the scenes where the Choruses confront Oedipus. We will understand the consternation of the Theban citizens or of the Colonean elders, as they encounter, for the

---

[1] For a thorough account of the almost universal belief in the evil eye, see C. Maloney, ed. The Evil Eye (New York, 1976). What is there recounted of many contemporary cultures--modern Greek, Latin American and Navaho Indian--reasonably applies, I think, to ancient Greek society. The evil eye is a form of "institutionalized envy: whose purpose it is to function as a "method of social control" (p. 43). See pp. 42-61, on Greece and the evil eye. See pp. 223, 226, 240, for theories that link the evil eye with envy.

I have first hand knowledge of several practices still used in Greece to ward off the evil eye. The tradition of protecting oneself and one's family and animals from the evil eye continues, long after the belief in the power of the evil eye has subsided.

first time, the newly blinded king or the blind old beggar. We will gain insight to the ambivalent reaction of the choruses, which are torn between their awareness of mortality and the need for compassion, on the one hand, and their fear of pollution and the evil eye, on the other. I understand the attitudes of the Chorus to be representative of the average citizen and to reflect conventional wisdom, superstitions and practices. Such popular attitudes are very much part of the concerns of the intellectuals, but also distinct from them in many respects. Together, they constitute the Greek culture. There are, for example, significant distinctions between the "hero," the "sophron" and the "Chorus."[2] The Chorus, the people (laos, according to Aristotle), will be my focus.

---

[2] See E. Berndaki-Aldous, Blindness in a Culture of Light: Especially the Case of Oedipus of Colonus of Sophocles (Ph.D dissertation, The Johns Hopkins University), (Ann Arbor: University Microfilms International, 1985), 106-148. There, Sophoclean drama is viewed as a microcosm of Greek society. The three basic characters present in every Sophoclean drama--the hero, the sophron and the Chorus--include, although hero is the exceptional man, the transgressor; the sophron is the man aware of the rules imposed on him by his mortality, and the Chorus represent the citizens, influenced and directed by sophrones and heroes alike. These three categories illustrate the various responses to be expected from Greek society towards the blind.

See R. G. A. Buxton, "Blindness and limits: Sophocles and the logic of myth," JHS vol. c (1980), 22-37 (especially 22 and 26). Buxton recognizes "blindness as "one of the most important motifs in Sophocles," as characteristic of his "mood" in all the extant plays. Sophocles' treatment of the "blindness motif," i.e., the way in which the dramatist "explored the implications of blindness," is examined against the background of the mythical tradition and is compared with fifth century Greek thought. Buxton observes that "in using the blindness motif, Sophocles was drawing on a theme fundamental to a large number of mythical narratives from the time of Homer to that of Pausanias, and beyond" (p. 22). See p. 26 for a good presentation of the difficulties of placing "Sophocles' treatment of blindness within the wider context of Greek myth."

The Greeks viewed blindness as a fate which, potentially at least, cold befall anyone. They were always aware of the possibilities their mortality might hold in store for them. The Choruses in Sophocles, like the majority of Greek people, understood everything in terms of a "generic," "modal," or "archetypal" reality. What was true of Oedipus might be true of any man. It must be significant that in the fourth stasimon of the O.T., after Oedipus discovers the truth and rushes into the palace to blind himself, the Chorus sing of the "generations of mortals," not merely of Oedipus. It must be significant that they pity, not blame Oedipus, as he is found out to be an incestuous parricide and as they watch him falling from the peak of achievement and glory. Oedipus is the subject of their song, only as an intimate paradigm of human fate. They lament: "Oh, generations of mortals, ...keeping your own example in mind, your own fate, oh miserable Oedipus... (1186-1194)." The Chorus are aware of their own mortality, ass they confront the blinded king with pity and fear. Their fear is of the freshly discovered sinner and the fresh blinding.[3]

The decisive factor distinguishing the chorus from the sophron and the sophron from the hero is the degree and level of awareness. The same Chorus, who a few moments earlier had pitied Oedipus as a paradigm of the human condition, are now inspired to frenzy before the blind king: "what horror do you cause in me!" (1306). The Chorus of Colonean elders echo the same terror when they first confront the blind beggar (who has trespassed into the grove of the Eumenides). They exclaim: "Alas for your blind eyes!...You are indeed transgressing, you have overstepped the boundaries: (149-156). The Chorus (as common citizens) are not always able to change places with the sufferer. They are well-meaning and naturally sympathetic, but also frightened and judgmental. Their

---

[3] The question whether Oedipus' blindness is one more reason for his pollution and shame cannot be fully answered at this point. It is my belief that blindness, together with patricide and incest, was understood by the Greeks as a cause of shame and pollution. This claim will be substantiated when we consider more closely the case of Oedipus. For Oedipus' desire not to be seen by others in his condition of shame and pollution see O.T., 1410-12.

attitudes toward the sufferer are not always positive, not firmly established, and they are influenced according to the direction which protects against risky endeavors, established guidelines of behavior, but cannot always distinguish between form and substance, appearance and reality, falsehood and truth.

One such convention, which the Chorus are anxious to observe and which influences decisively religious and social law, is the belief in pollution.[4] It is fair to assume that blindness was viewed as pollution because it was felt to be a punishment for some transgression (intentional or unintentional). The blinded Oedipus, as a polluted object, arouses horror. Whatever blindness may be as a metaphor and a symbol, as a real experience it is overwhelming and capable of eliciting negative and contradictory reactions. Anyone marked with divine affliction (like Philoctetes, who literally entered the forbidden grove of Chryse and inflicted with a incurable wound by a sacred snake, or like Teiresias, who saw deity (Athena) at a time and a place which were tabooed, or like Oedipus, who found himself to have been where he

---

[4] Blindness is one of the many and most undesirable sources of pollution in Greek culture. See especially O.T. 1424-1431, where Creon gives orders that Oedipus the polluted (agos hieron) be hidden away from the sacred light of the sun. Oedipus is both ashamed and polluted, not only for his sins of patricide and incest, but also and more acutely because of his newly acquired blindness. See Sophocles: Oedipus the King, trans. S. Berg and D. Clay (New York, 1978). Especially p. 18: "at the end of his discoveries, Oedipus is the object of horrible curiosity. Creon calls him 'this cursed, naked, holy thing' ... He is an agos--both cursed and sacred...."

See also L.W. Lyde, Contexts in Pindar: with reference to the meaning of pheggos (Manchester, 1935), 12-14, especially p. 14, for an interesting translation of 1428. He says neither a "clouded sky," nor a "bright one" will accept Oedipus. He will be an offense in either case. Lyde also observes that in Greek tradition the sun, a source of light, can become a source of blinding as well. He claims, correctly I think, that Oedipus is aware of this binding effect of the sun when he bids farewell to the "phos" when he decides to enter the palace and blind himself.

should not with whom he should not) becomes a sacred curse (hieron agos): polluted. I suspect that blindness arouses the same fear of pollution as that associated with the dead. The blind share in the characteristic most typical of the world of the dead (Hades), namely, Darkness.[5]

However blindness is associated with pollution, Sophoclean Choruses fear the blind because they view them as a source of pollution. Hence the mixed responses of the Choruses in the O.T. and the O.C. Pity, compassion, willingness to help, on the one hand, and on the other, awe, fear, abhorrence. Their responses are predictable and informing: "What terror you cause in me!" (1306), and, "Alas for your blind eyes!...You are indeed transgressing" (149-156). Peras refers on one level to Oedipus' entry into the grove of the Eumenides. On another deeper level, these words recall Oedipus' ancient transgression (parricide, incest and his self-blinding). True, the Chorus do not yet know who the stranger is, but the association of Oedipus with transgression in the mind of the audience and of Oedipus is inevitable; the association of blindness and transgression must be in the mind of the Chorus as well. The Colonean Chorus make an indisputable case for the claim that blindness (regardless of the identity of the blind person and its cause) is feared as a source of pollution. What is more, the Chorus assigned to Oedipus the power "to attach curses" on them (153-154). At the outset, before the Chorus have any idea of the identity of the transgressor, it is because of his blindness that Oedipus is perceived as horrible and endowed with the power to curse. To avert the curses of the blind man, and because they are aware of their own mortality, they express their willingness to help him and they advise him how to leave the forbidden grove. Lest they be polluted, they keep their distance from the source of pollution, the blind beggar.

Pollution is one of many factors which contribute to the horror of the Choruses and is closely linked to the belief in the evil eye. The polluted are unfortunate, have reason to be envious and, as such,

---

[5] See H. Musurillo, The Light and the Darkness: Studies in the Dramatic Poetry of Sophocles (New York: Fordham University Press, 1967). _____, "Sunken Imagery in Sophocles' Oedipus," American Journal of Philology 78 (1957), 36-51.

capable of inflicting the evil eye. Consequently, the blind have every reason to translate their misery and envy to harm for others through the evil eye. The question may be asked, "how can the blind put the evil eye on someone when they cannot see?" At first sight, this might seem one more paradoxical aspect of the Greek beliefs about blindness. However, the paradox is easily explained, if we accept that the evil eye was possible not only by means of an admiring stare (which expressed desire for the missing thing), but also by means of words of thoughts. Belief in the evil eye, as it is found among modern Greek peasants, sheds light on similar beliefs in ancient Greece. The evil eye, a power of the eye activated by an admiring glance, a voiced compliment or thought, (motivated by envy caused by some deprivation of the admired thing), is bound to bring misfortune upon the person admired because of his good luck. The evil eye in modern Greece (vascania or matiasma) resembles ancient Greek beliefs. Such beliefs held that intentional or unintentional transgressions (hybris), or too much success (olbos), or the over-confidence resulting from such happiness (koros)--all are bond to cause envy (phthonos) and to result in punishment and misfortune (dysdaimonia). A human may not overstep mortal limits with impunity. A man who enjoys good fortune and happiness must take steps to ward off envy and the evil eye by refraining from boasting and bragging. Thus, the evil eye may be seen as a form of "institutionalized envy" whose purpose is to function as a method of social control, in ancient (as it is in modern) Greek society. In addition, some ritualistic gestures and procedures must have been in place, as antidotes to the magic power of the evil eye. I suspect that the Choruses accompanied their horrified exclamations with appropriate movements and gestures, which the audience must have recognized as meaning to ward off the evil eye.[6] In modern Greece, a compliment is accompanied by a balancing insulting gesture, such as spitting on the ground or opening the palm to give "five fingers." These gestures may be undertaken by the object of admiration (secretly, behind the back of the admirer) for protection, or by the admirer (openly) as an indication of good will an explicit denunciation of any intention to harm, through the

---

[6] See D. Seale, Vision and Stagecraft in Sophocles (Chicago: University of Chicago Press, 1982), who takes into account the blindness of Oedipus for the staging of the Sophoclean plays.

evil eye. The Colonean Chorus (a.) do not brag about their good fortune to be sighted, and (b.) try to avert the evil eye (the curses) of the blind. Their deep awareness of the change of fortune (their mortality) results in compassion. However, their very real fear of pollution and the harm which may result from the evil eye causes their panic.

The evil eye was only one of many ways in which an unfortunate person could harm others. Such a belief was related to the notion that it was natural, under great suffering for people to become evil. Extreme suffering--the kind that exceeded the threshold of human endurance--was expected to dehumanize the sufferer.[7] The belief that suffering spoils the character was moderated by the awareness that mortals, without exception, were meant to suffer. A state of absolute bliss was reserved only for the immortals. The question gain is one of degree: How _much_ suffering is enough to spoil the character and to render one harmful? The words of Achilles to Priam, at the moment of the hero's greatest humanity, are indispensable:

> To whomsoever he gives sufferings only, Him Zeus makes hateful, him evil madness Drives all over the surface of sacred earth, And he wanders honored neither by gods nor by mortals.[8]
>
> (_Il_. 24. 525-533).

Two points must be emphasized here: First, the distinction between mortality and immortality is firmly established in terms of the allotment of happiness. Second, human beings can deal with their

---

[7] See especially: _Iliad_ 24. 525-533; Euripides, _Medea_, and _Hecuba_ (W. Arrowsmith, translator, pp. 3-4, Introduction, in _Euripides III_, ed. Grene and Lattimore, Chicago, 1958).

See Simonides of Ceos, fragment 19. (Loeb Classical Library, 1924).

[8] I translate _boubrostis_ as "madness," since it brings to mind the gadfly. Translation of the same as "famine" undermines the vivid imagery which _bourbrostis_ brings to mind. See Murray's note on this line (_Iliad_, vol. 2 p. 602, Loeb, 1967).

mortality (can cope with misfortune and still maintain
their humanity) only so long as their suffering has
some relief. A resting place for the wanderer
(epaula) is necessary. Take away all hope, and
humanity is destroyed.[9] The concluding line of
Achilles' speech to Prima epitomizes the condition of
utter misfortune for the Greeks: to be dishonored
totally by god and man alike. In a shame culture
(where honor is the highest goods), utter dishonor is
the supreme misfortune. Blindness (associated with
death because of its darkness), at all times, vies
with dishonor to win the title of "the worst of
suffering." When the Chorus told Oedipus that he
would have been better off dead than blind, they
probably believed that he could not be blind and happy
at the same time. If so utterly unhappy, he must have
lost hope (which allowed for humanity). He must be
envious of their eyesight and capable of harming them
through the evil eye. The Colonean Chorus had also
good reason to react as they did, when they first saw
Oedipus. He was dishonored (apolis) and blind to
boot. It would take a wise man, the sophron Theseus,
to realize that suffering does not always create the
same dehumanized creatures, that some sufferers
(exceptional indeed) have very special ways of bearing
their misfortune.[10]

---

[9] The belief that extreme suffering may destroy
humanity finds its best spokesman in Euripides. He
draws the implications of what it feels like to
overstep human limits, to walk outside the boundaries
of humanity. This happens when one resembles the
gods in bliss (like Admetus), or the beasts in the
loss of humanity due to extreme suffering (like
Hecuba). A human cannot partake in either state
(divine or beastly) and still maintain the nature
proper to a mortal, i.e., humanity. Admetus has to
learn suffering and human subjection to ananke
(death). Hecuba turns into a bitch (soon after her
dehumanized condition, for which her unbearable
suffering was responsible).

[10] The way (tropos) in which suffering is endured
is very crucial for the Greeks, from Homer and Simonides, through the tragedians and Lysias, to Plato and
Aristotle. It makes the difference between pity and
compassion, or, contempt and blame towards the
sufferer. It also accounts for the difference between
a sufferer who is a terror and a curse (agos) and one
who can become a hero and a deity (like Oedipus).

Man in sophocles (as in Euripides and Homer) is tragic. Unbearable suffering brings the individual (the hero) to a state of utter despair and confusion which can best be described as madness. For this, I believe that the meaning of the word boubrostis (Il. 24. 533) is "madness." Boubrostis must be understood to mean something like that state of pain and madness to which a cow is driven when stung by a gadfly. The term not only brings to mind the component words (bous and oistros), but also the concrete situation on which the metaphor is based. The cow, stung by the gadfly, is forced to flee without stop for rest (like Oedipus and Io), and a danger to whomever might be in its path. If the sting of fate were too sharp, if the gadfly of misfortune allowed no respite, the afflicted character--mad with pain-- would remain in an animal-like condition (like Hecuba whose relentless misery turned her into a bitch). Such a person would be viewed not only as miserable, but terribly dangerous as well. The Chorus' reaction before the freshly wounded Oedipus is not surprising. The sting of fate was too sharp (the golden brooches of his wife-mother), the wound of blindness too deep and too visible. His fate, that of a self-blinded king and incestuous parricide, inspires the Chorus to frenzy. The man could very well be dangerous, as well as pitiable.

The Chorus could not anticipate that Sophocles would present them with an Oedipus who would become a hero and a deity, not a beast.[11] The essence of Greek attitudes is found in the existence of both options. The views on the affect of suffering on the character do not vary widely from Homer to Euripides (although differences in attitudes through time unquestionably exist). Attitudes vary from social group to social

---

[11] What determines the outcome, i.e., whether suffering would dehumanize one or make him a hero or a deity, is too vast a topic to be discussed here. We should note, however, that Oedipus (unlike Hecuba) had many reasons why he did not lose his humanity in suffering. E.g.: the love of his daughters, the humanity and friendship of Theseus and of the Colonean citizens, and a purpose (to die in Colonus and to avenge his enemies by blessing his friends and harming those who hurt him).

group to social group and from individual to individual, at all time. As a rule, attitudes differ
from common people (Chorus) to intellectuals and
nobility (Sophocles, Plato, Theseus). By the end of
the fifth century, when the O.C. was performed, the
Chorus express as much horror at the sight of the
blind old beggar as a contemporary of Homer or
Simonides might have, confronting a wretched man, who,
because of his suffering, was expected to be evil,
envious and harmful. The informing differences in
attitudes are found, not so much between the various
centuries of Greek literature,[12] but between, for
example, Theseus and Creon and the Chorus of the O.C.
Simonides of Ceos echoes the words of Achilles to
Prima, Hecuba (in Euripides) enacts them, and the
Chorus of Sophocles believe them.

The Colonean Chorus need Theseus' instruction and
further contact with Oedipus, in order to realize
that humanity may extend beyond this mechanism of
brutality. Sophocles presents the belief in the evil
eye as very real. But he also makes it very clear
that the best antidote against the magic of the evil
eye is compassion and humanity. Theseus (informing
contrast with the Chorus) is not afraid of Oedipus
because he is very much aware of his mortality: that
fortune changes and an uncertain future is common to
all. His words to Oedipus epitomize Sophoclean and
greek humanity. King Theseus comforts the blind
beggar, saying: "I know well, being a man (mortal)
that my share in the day to come is no more than
yours." (576-568). Theseus is protected from the
evil eye because he is not afraid of it.

---

[12] For a different view regarding the difference
of attitudes through time (especially from Simonides
to Plato), see C. Whitman, Sophocles, p. 202.

Spatial Metaphor in Schechner's
Environmental Theatre: Dionysus in '69 Makbeth

Paul C. Castagno
Ohio State University

Although a great deal of contemporary criticism is applied to textual and performance analysis, little scholarly thought has been directed toward significance of theatrical space. In the late nineteen-sixties, Richard Schechner and his designer Jerry Rojo, evolved the function and significance of space in theatrical production (McNamara, Rojo & Schechner 1975). Together with the Performance Group, Schechner and Rojo created environmental theatre, a form that was revolutionary in its assault upon the authority of assumptions in the traditional theatre. Schechner's use of <u>mise en scene</u>, however, had a certain sensationalism which led to prejudice against environmental theatre (Leiter 1986, 45-46). Such prejudicial attitudes against Schechner's practices obscured the logic behind his theory of environmental space. This paper will validate the spatial experiments of Schechner and Rojo during this period, and demonstrate how these findings contradicted assumptions regarding the traditional theatre of illusion (McNamara, Rojo & Schechner 1975, 14-21). I will conclude by positing the influence of Schechner and Rojo's findings upon contemporary performance practices.

Environmental theatre conceived space through three fundamental principles different from those of traditional or epic theatre. The first principle requires that the spectator and performer must share the same space. As Schechner defined it: "the environmental use of space is fundamentally collaborative" (Schechner 1973, 39). Conversely, the function of traditional theatre architecture has been to separate space into the liminoid areas of lobby, auditorium and stagehouse areas. This division of space establishes a system of differences that allocates specific areas for spectators, and separate areas for performers (Schechner 1973, 18). Shared space, on the other hand, diminishes the spatial separation of spectator from performer. It also eliminates fixed seating and the hierarchal nature of ticket pricing. Instead, the spectator is allowed to find his own place. Schechner elaborates:

There ought to be jumping off places where
spectators enter the performance; regular
places where spectators can arrange themselves more or less as they would in an
orthodox theatre; vantage points where
people can get out of the way of the main
action and look at it with detachment; there
ought to be pinnacles, dens and hutches.
(Schechner 1973, 30)

Rojo suggests that action derives its logic from
the space in which it functions. For this reason,
intimate scenes were usually played in private
spaces, where only a few spectators could hear or view
the action. Schechner defines these as scenes of
"local" focus. Occasionally, one scene of local focus
is played in consecutive locations, until it is heard
by most of the audience. An example of that is the
first scene from Dionysus in '69, between Tiresias
and Cadmus. It was played in five consecutive
locations throughout Rojo's environment (McNamara,
Rojo & Schechner 1975, 94-95). The spectators'
perception depends upon the physical proximity and
potential contact with performers. This closeness
permits the spectator to perceive the duality of the
performer and role, thereby offering the spectator a
dynamic alternative to the "willing suspension of
disbelief." Finally, it is this "immediacy" of shared
space that encourages spontaneity and participation in
performance.

The second environmental principle posits the
concept of transformed space. Transformed space
evolved from the nation of 'found' space. Found
space in 'Happenings' described any performance area
not originally conceived of as a theatre. The
theatre environmentalists transformed these found
sites in performance spaces. The role of the designer
was expanded to include the design of the total space.
This transformational process had clear implications.
It functionally re-defined the spatial dynamic
between the performer and spectator for each production. The new, flexible dynamic allowed for the
variable factor of participation, and the constant
factor of the audience as a scenic element. As a
result of those factors, spectator involvement played
a determinant role in shaping: a) the space itself,
and; b) the performance.

I will focus upon the Performing Garage on Wooster Street in lower Manhattan established by Schechner and The Performance Group in the late nineteen-sixties. At that time Schechner was interested in the possibilities of exploring the total space. To accomplish this, it was necessary to locate a space that combined substantial height with a sufficient floor area. Schechner solved the problem of height and sufficient floor area. Schechner had recognized the limitations of the low ceiling in his earliest environmental theatre work, Victims of Duty, which among other things, was plagued by poor sight lines (Telephone interview Rojo 1985). Schechner solved the problem of height and sufficient floor area when he leased an erstwhile auto garage on Wooster Street. The dimensions of that garage were 50' x 35' x 19'. Schechner had fond a space that allowed him to fully explore the, as yet untested, spatial style of environmental theatre. His designer, Jerry Rojo, designed multi-level environments that fully explored the vertical axes of three-dimensional space. By doing that, Rojo was revolutionary in integrally activating the "negative space;" that is, areas usually left open or undesigned. The first example of this are the towers from Dionysus in '69 which explore the high or vertical spaces of the Performance Garage (see plate 1). It should be pointed out that even critics who did not like or care for Dionysus in '69, such as Walter Kerr of the New York Times, were awed by the structural integrity of Rojo's environment (Kerr 1968, Section II, 11).

The third principle concerns the different
relationship of the theatrical sign in traditional
theatre and environmental space. Traditional theatrical design relies on the principles of imitation and
illusion. Illusion is created when the limitation
appears real or like the thing itself. The success of
failure of a design is measured by the quality of
imitation against the object in reality. In this case
the theatrical sign (signified) is a stand-in for the
objection reality (referent). For example, in the
traditional theatre of illusion a set may signify room
in New York. The signifier--room--is separated of
deferred from the referent--room in New York. Plate 2
demonstrates the different semiotic relationships
between referents and signifiers contrasting traditional design from environmental space.

[PLATE TWO HERE]
CAPTION: The Theatrical Sign

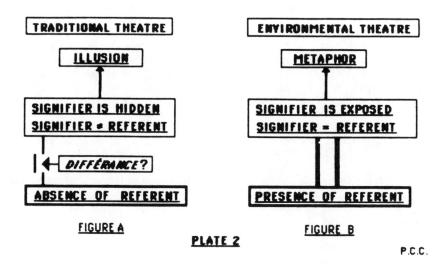

In Figure A the absent referent (object in reality) is always separate from the signifier (theatrical design). "According to this classical semiology, the substitution of the sign for the thing itself is both secondary and provisional: secondary due to an original and lost presence from which the sign thus derives; provisional as concerns this missing presence toward which the sign (theatrical design) is a movement of mediation" (Derrida 1985, 402). This ontological difference, in the Heidegegerian sense, illustrates the tenuous foundation in the traditional theatre of illusion (see broken line in Figure A), since it puts into question the authority of presence. In addition, Figure A points out that the signifier, for example, the construction material, is hidden. In Figure A, illusion derives its force from the craftsmanship of the signifier. To make this clearer, imagine a standard flat in a box

53

set. Its referent is a permanent wall. The signifier, made up of frame and muslin and coats of
paint, if seen from the necessary distance will create
the illusion of the wall in the spectator's mind (as a
signified). In environmental theatre space (see
Figure B), the signifier is the functional space
consisting of unpainted platforms, stairs, ladders and
wooden posts. These elements are exposed. There is
no ontological difference between the signifier and
referent. They are, in fact, synonymous. This is
because the referent does not exist outside the space
but rather has presence as the signifier. The unity
between signifier and referent is revealed as the
functional space. The spatial metaphor (signified)is
derived from the associative and attributive qualities
of the signifier or referent which are perceived or
conceived by the spectator.

In Plate 3, Figure A demonstrates that the
spatial metaphor (signified) is revealed through the
transaction of performers, spectators, and theatrical
text with the functional space (signifier/referent).
Figure B demonstrates that the performed text (signified) is revealed through the actor's "objective" or
"action" that he discovers in the subtext. In
traditional theatre the "actions" derived from the
subtext are revealed in the explicit presentation
(signified); whereas, in environmental theatre the
explicit "transactions" reveal the implicit spatial
metaphor (signified). Therefore, Figure A posits an
essential formal contradiction to Figure B. Figure C
demonstrates the "spine" or central principle that
governs performance. In traditional theatre the spine
is the play's "super-objective" found in the subtext.
In environmental theatre the spine exists as the
central image of the spatial metaphor (Rojo 1976).
Rojo has posited that there is one central spatial
metaphor in each one of his environments. This
spatial metaphor might be translated into kind of
super-objective (see Plate 3, Figure C).

PLATE THREE HERE]
[CAPTION: <u>Spatial Metaphor</u>]

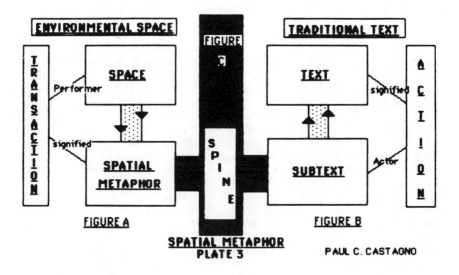

SPATIAL METAPHOR
PLATE 3

For instance, in <u>Dionysus in '69</u>, the central image was the two towers that dominated the corners of the space, a metaphor for the towers of ancient Thebes. The spectators sat or dangled over the edge of the levels and created the mass of the tower (see plate 1). During performance spectators were joined by performers, or they left the towers to participate in the celebratory rituals. When <u>Dionysus in '69</u> became a hit, Rojo constructed more of these towers to accommodate the increasing audience (Telephone interview Rojo 1987).[1] What had started as two monoliths now became integrated into an architectural scheme.

---

[1]Rojo had worked with Schechner on <u>Victims of Duty</u> while at Tulane University in 1967. The original designer for <u>Dionysus in '69</u>, Michael Kirby, did not work out.

According to Rojo, the floor of the space became a metaphor for the sensual and ecstatic nature of Dionysus in '69 (Telephone interview Rojo 1987). Layer upon layer of carpet matting contrasted the sensual dionysian nature of the floor, with the rigid apollonian plasticity of the towers. Much of the process in Dionysus in '69 explored physical body work evidence by the Total Caress, Ecstacy Dance, and the birth Ritual all of which became important floor scenes in the finished text. The spectators were encouraged to partake in the frenzied choric actions of the Performance Group or they might observe from the fixed, safe space of the towers. By their choices, spectators engaged in the conflict between the dionysian (floor/sensual), and apollonian (tower/rational) forces inherent in the spatial metaphor of Dionysus in '69. What Schechner's Performance Group had accomplished was the prophecy of Nietzsche's Birth of Tragedy: "that art owes its continuous development to the Apollonian-Dionysiac duality" (Nietzsche 1974, 820). Moreover, by introducing the dionysian choric element in frenzied, erotic rituals, Dionysus in '69 captured an aspect of the classic spirit that is too often ignored.[2]

If spectators to Dionysus in '69 were allowed freedom of participation and choice, in Makbeth they were subject to regimentation and manipulation. Whereas the towers and floor of Dionysus in '69 connotated bonding and ecstacy, the environment of Makbeth stated darker meanings. Makbeth was a piece about intrigue, revenge, spying and the distance between people and groups of people. The spatial metaphor for Makbeth was the catacombs of a medieval castle (Telephone interview Rojo 1985). This metaphor can be extended to include the divisions in the renaissance mind, between the rational and the magical--in other words, the Macchiavelian versus the irrational view of the world. In this sense the space evoked similar impressions to the imaginative carceri {prison} etching of Piranesi, which, for all their

---

[2] For instance, the plays of T.S. Eliot which attempted to resemble the classic spirit, became stiff an formal. Even Aristotle skirts by this issue in the Poetics, describing catharsis as the removal of an excess of pity and fear. I believe Nietzsche saw catharsis as the culmination of the dionysian element present in the Greek drama and spirit.

multi-tiered gloominess, also contained a sense of the capricci {fantastic} (Piranesi, 1754).

This "capricci" was first evidence as the spectator entered a lobby above the space, which had been transformed into a pre-show maze by Brook McNamara.[3] The purpose of the maze was to establish: a) an historical framework for the production, and b) a mental framework for the spectator. Represented in this liminoid maze were drawings and memorabilia from celebrated performances of Shakespeare's Macbeth. The memorabilia was grotesquely accented by groups of mirrors which gave the audience a sense of inclusion, while creating the bizarre effect of a carnival hall of mirrors (Telephone interview Rojo 1985).

The spectator proceeded down a tight spiral staircase to the environment's floor. The height of the space, and the descent into its tomblike levels became a metaphor for the transit from heaven to hell. Once there, the audience was divided into clusters, a reflection of the Renaissance notion of audience class-division. Choice was replaced with manipulation. Spectators were asked to crawl up and down ladders, and into tight spaces. The real danger of falling created fear within some spectators. A balcony surrounding the environment became a place for watching, and for private scenes of intrigue. Rojo has pointed out that the vertical wooden columns (rough cut 4'x4'), which supported the balcony, at certain moments created a natural sense of a forest and countryside. At lower levels, holes were cut into the platforms and heads would appear and disappear thereby accenting the action of spying (Telephone interview Rojo 1985).

Perhaps at this point it seems as though the spatial metaphor is defined by its changing nature. this is misleading because in Dionysus in '69 and Makbeth there was no changing scenery, only the changing transactions between performer, spectator and text within the functional space (Telephone interview Rojo 1987). These transactions created a chain of

---

[3] Schechner had originally promised the total design to Brooks McNamara, but after the success and recognition of Rojo's Dionysus, a compromise was worked out, with McNamara designing the pre-show, and Rojo designing the environment.

metaphors (signifies), that can be defined by the Derridean term, différance (Plate 2, Figure B) (Derrida 1985, 403).

In its simplest form, différance is the process of the changing signified in performance; its relation to past signs as trace, and to the potential procurement of other future signs (Levinas 1985, 345).[4] Différance defined the processual nature of the spatial metaphor (signified) in environmental theatre. As a result it created a far richer texture of signs than was possible in the traditional theatre.[5]

Makbeth, for a number of reasons, was unsuccessful. Within the complex range of this problem, however there was a spatial problem that was never overcome. The Performance Group created Makbeth during rehearsals in September 1969 at Baocic, Yugoslavia. Meanwhile, Rojo was building the environment for Makbeth at the Performance Garage. Although the scale model for the space had been approved by Schechner at the Group, when they returned they were overwhelmed by the completed structure. The process that had developed in the meadows of Yugoslavia, never translated to the confines and tight spaces of the Makbeth environment. The result was an unsuccessful and disappointing marriage of the absent spatial referent (the countryside and outdoors of Yugoslavia) with the signifier (the functional space). This spatial displacement of the referent (ontological

---

[4] Emmanuel Levinas posited the idea of trace. Here I use it to signify the indelibility of a previous signified upon the consciousness of the subject. Interestingly, Schechner uses the word 'associations' to describe the chain of subconscious images that are stimulated from certain psychophysical exercises. There exists a strong correlation between Derrida's meaning of the word différance, and Schechner's concept of associations. See Chapter on "Performance," in Environmental Theatre

[5] The traditional theatre is essentially a theatre of fixed sings, based in mimesis. In Schechner's theatre resemblances are based on the associational characteristics derived from the functional space during performance.

difference [as trace][6]) from the signifier created a
non-organic foundation for the performance. In
addition, the pre-show, liminoid maze of antecedent
Macbeth performances, while fascinating in its own
right, displaced the synchronic immediacy of the
performance with the diachronic scheme of an historical continuum. Ironically, these two spatial/temporal
practices contradicted Schechner's theories of
environmental space, and violated the principles that
had worked so well in Dionysus in '69.

To conclude. What is the significance and
influence of environmental space today in 1987?
Influence has been most noticeable in the areas of a)
theatrical architecture; b) scene design; and c)
staging practices. Certainly, the architectural
influence is seen in the proliferation of 'black-box'
flexible-space theatres that have been constructed
since the early seventies.[7] These flexible spaces
often supplement main stages or proscenium theatres,
and are usually utilized for new or experimental
works.

Scene designers have assimilated concepts like
the spatial metaphor into the mainstream of commercial
theatre with varying degrees of success. Sweeney Todd
re-created the working environment of a factory within
a traditional Broadway house. The structure extended
well into the audience. However, the movable as-
semblies connected to huge I-beams justified a scale
of production that overwhelmed the humble nature of
the story. Recently, Dreamgirls successfully used
movable light-trees as integral elements of the mise-
en-scene. Currently, John Napier's design for Lés
Misérables employs a multi-functional moving environment that transforms its image throughout the show.

---

[6] In a phenomenological sense it could be suggested that TPG had ensconced the Yugoslavian referent
during rehearsals and workshops of Makbeth. Therefore, upon, return to New York it would have been
impossible to separate the group consciousness from
the referent 'trace' of the Yugoslavian meadows.

[7] Many 'black-box theatres' have been converted
into fixed seat thrust stages--no longer used for
their intended purpose of providing spatial
flexibility.

These images are not based on object referents, but rather derive from a theatrical essence. Napier says that:

> "the most important thing about a set design is that it can never be naturalistic because you're in an unreal situation. But it has to be believable. You have to capture the audience's imagination and take them on a path where you're evoking things for them and not always being literal about it" (Kroll 1987)

Outside the United States, the designs of the Czech Josef Svoboda have been most successful in integrating advanced technology with the mise-en-scene. Svoboda often integrates film and other media with live actor. His settings consistently employ moveable levels and revolves, pre-programmed to create an ever-changing stage environment. Svoboda's designs best demonstrate the narrowing gap between the aesthetic and functional realm of stage design. Indeed, how his designs function are essential to their aesthetic effect. Through his daring approach to an integrated mise-en-scene, Svoboda has successfully merged the primarily functional mode of environmental theatre design, with the aesthetic pictorial mode of traditional scene design.

Environmental theatre practices have greatly influenced concepts of staging in the past fifteen years. Commercial theatres' use of the whole space for performer and spectator has met with varying degrees of success ranging from moderate, Candide, to the incredibly successful Cats. The widespread popularization of environmental staging has made it accessible and understandable to both professional and amateur director. Indeed, it is no longer a rare occurrence to see a community theatre production staged environmentally. Removed from its original 'radical' context, environmental staging has now become a convention or style that has been thoroughly assimilated into the theatrical mainstream.

Post-modern directors such as Robert Wilson and Peter Brook have extended the concept of environmental staging to the remote mountains of Iran, and the tribal hamlets of Africa. Performances extend for an indeterminate time period. Real-life actions mix with the aesthetic event. The divisions between performer and spectator are often blurred.

Recent examples of innovative environmental staging can be seen at the Squat Theatre in New York City. A large window facing the street allows the passer-by to look at the performance, while simultaneously allowing the spectators and performers to see actions on the sidewalk. Often dramatic actions are staged on this sidewalk but the spectator never really knows what is real-life and what is staged. These liminal modes of dramatic reality unleash the potential for spectator participation. ":Second-generation" performance groups like the Squat Theatre continue the interest in the staging experiments of the late sixties and early seventies.

Finally, it can be said that environmental theatre projects a greater role for space and time than the traditional theatre. The spatial/temporal aspects of performance become materials of the text, not mere by-products. Mood and atmosphere are of far less importance than immediacy and function. By basing his dramatic theory on revolutionary principles of space, Schechner demonstrated that space could play a metaphorical role concomitant to the text.

References

Derrida, 1985:   Jacques Derrida, "Différance, Deconstruction in Context, ed. Mark Taylor (Cambridge: Cambridge University Press).

Kerr, 1968:   Walter Kerr, NY Times, June 16.

Kroll, 1987:   Jack Kroll, Newsweek, March 30.

Leiter, 1986:   Samuel L. Leiter, Ten Seasons: New York Theatre in the Seventies (New York: Greenwood Press).

Levinas, 1985:   Emmanuel Levinas, "Trace of the Other" Deconstruction in Context, ed. Mark Taylor (Cambridge: Cambridge University Press).

McNamara, Rojo &
Schechner, 1975:   Brooks McNamara, Jerry Rojo,
                      Richard Schechner, Theatres,
                      Spaces and Environments (New York:
                      Drama Book Specialists).

Nietzsche, 1974:   Frederick Nietzsche, "Birth of
                      Tragedy," Dramatic Theory and
                      Criticism, ed. Bernard E. Dukore
                      (New York: Holt, Rinehart and
                      Winston).

Piranesi, 1754:   Piranesi, The Carceri Etchings
                      (microfilm reprints at Lawrence
                      and Lee Theatre Research
                      Institute) The Ohio State
                      University. Film no. 2507.

Rojo, 1976:   Jerry Rojo, Performing Arts
                      Journal, interview with editors,
                      Vol. 1; No. 1.

Schechner, 1973:   Richard Schechner, Environmental
                      Theatre (New York: Hamilton
                      Books).

Going A-Viking": Edward Gordon Craig's Production of Ibsen's "The Vikings"

James Fisher
Wabash College

On July 19, 1902 Henry Irving and Ellen Terry performed together for the last time in a revival of their mutual triumph, The Merchant of Venice. Irving's fortunes, and those of his Lyceum Theatre Company, were rapidly declining. The great actor-manager had failed to embrace, or even acknowledge, the new drama epitomized by the plays of Henrik Ibsen and George Bernard Shaw, and his repertory had stagnated with revivals of his earlier successes. Less than a year after this historical final performance Terry, who had a long-standing interest in the new drama, leased London's Imperial Theatre for a season of plays to be staged and designed by her son, the iconoclastic designer and director, Edward Gordon Craig (1872-1966). Craig had spent eight years as an actor in the lyceum company and had designed and staged four critically acclaimed, but commercially unsuccessful productions (Dido and Aeneas) (1900), The Masque of Love (1901), Acis and Galatea (1902), and Bethlehem (1902) on a shoe-string for the Purcell Opera Society. In each case, his controversial stage designs had dominated the productions, and Terry was eager to help her son bring his ideas into the English theatrical establishment. The Terry and Craig Imperial Theatre season opened during the spring of 1903 with the much-heralded first English production of Ibsen's mythical tragedy The Vikings at Helgeland.

It is interesting to note that among the dozen productions realized by Craig during his long and controversial career, The Vikings, Rosmersholm (1906), and The Pretenders (1926) were all by Ibsen, a significant exponent of the realistic drama. Craig maintained a serious interest in Ibsen's plays beginning with designs he made in 1900 for an unrealized production of Peer Gynt (which Craig longed to stage with himself as Peer) and ending in 1930 with a book of his designs for his 1926 production of The Pretenders in collaboration with Johannes and Adam Poulsen at the Royal Theatre in Copenhagen.

Craig's enthusiasm for Ibsen was largely restricted to the great playwright's least realistic plays. And when he later designed scenery for Eleonora Duse's production of <u>Rosmersholm</u> he created an abstract environment for a play that had traditionally been designed naturalistically. Craig was among the first and most outspoken critics of the theatre's dependence on realistic literary drama:

> "The modern Realistic Theatre, forgetful of all the Laws of Art, sets out to reflect the times. It reflects a small particle of the time, it drags back a curtain and exposes to our view an agitated caricature of Man and his Life, a figure gross in its attitude and hideous to look upon. This is true neither to life nor to art. It has never been the purpose of art to reflect and make uglier the ugliness of things, but to transform and make the already beautiful more beautiful,..." (Craig, 1913, 89)

Craig preferred the grand scope of Shakespeare's poetic tragedies, so it is not surprising that two of Craig's Ibsen productions were selected from among the playwright's early mythical plays, which superficially approximated the pageantry and emotional scope of Shakespeare's tragedies. <u>The Vikings</u>, a four-act romantic drama in blank verse drawn from the Icelandic family sagas and set on a Norwegian island in the tenth-century, focuses on the story of the tragic obsession of Hiordis, wife of Gunnar the Strong, with her brother-in-law Sigurd. Before 1900 the play proved to be one of Ibsen's most popular in his own country and, although it is rarely produced today, turn-of-the-century audiences were attracted to its stark setting and epic characters. These qualities undoubtedly also appealed to Craig who envisioned a mystically abstract setting with symbolic staging that stressed stylized movement set to music.

Perhaps due to the predominance of realism and naturalism, Craig saw little in the contemporary theatre that interested him. But Ibsen's mythical dramas presented Craig with unique challenges and he eagerly sought to produce these plays in England, hoping to make his mark as a designer and director. But English audiences were largely unfamiliar with Ibsen, and although George Bernard Shaw, William Archer and others had promoted Ibsen's plays, producing theses works even as late as 1903 was still very risky business, as Craig later wrote:

"At the time it was felt that if you did a play by Ibsen you had got your knife into poor old England, because, it was said, Ibsen dealt in things not often touched on in England, and dealt in them squalidly-- in a cold, damp way." (Craig, 1969, 146-147)

Beyond general resistance to Ibsen's plays, Craig faced many more difficulties, beginning with his own mother. Ellen Terry had maintained a long-standing interest in Ibsen's plays and had tried in vain to persuade Irving to produce John Gabriel Borkman. Irving was ill when the play was published in English in 1897 and Terry took advantage of his immobility to read him the first two acts of the play, while he read the third to her. But Irving was not impressed, as he sarcastically wrote in his notebook, "Threadworms and leeches are an interesting study; but they have no interest to me." (Irving, 1951, 601) But Terry, particularly acknowledged for her performances as light-hearted and witty characters, worried that an audience might not accept her in the leading role of Hiordis in The Vikings, "a fierce virago who kept chained bears in the house." (Shaw, 1929, 35) Terry recalled her fears about the role in her memoirs:

"Not in my most wildly optimistic moments did I think Hiordis, the chief female character - a primitive, fighting, free, open-air person - suited to me, but I saw a way of playing her more brilliantly and less weightily than the text suggested, and anyhow I was not thinking so much of the play for me as for my son." (Terry, 1982, 208-209)

Terry finally agreed to open her Imperial Theatre season with The Vikings, hoping her enormous popularity would counter any controversy generated by Ibsen's play and Craig's non-traditional staging and design. To further ensure success Terry engaged a cast of established British actors, led by Oscar Asche, Hubert Carter, Holman Clark, Hutin Britton, and Conway Tearle. Terry's daughter, Edith Craig, supervised construction of Craig's costume designs and Martin Fallas Shaw, Craig's conductor for his Purcell Opera Society productions, composed original music.

Craig threw himself into the design of the set, lights, and costumes for the play making, as he later recalled, "some fifty or so drawings and some hundred sketches, working, as the theatre-folk in those days had to work -- all day and nearly all night -- for months." (Craig, 1924, 36) Although he was disappointed in the stiff translation by William Archer that had been selected, Craig's imagination had full play in Ibsen's gloomy drama, as Martin Shaw remembered:

"Without being in the least realistic his setting was essentially Scandinavian in spirit. Some years later when we were both in Sweden for the first time, I remember pointing out to him a group of boulders which might have been the setting of the first Act of The Vikings. The banqueting scene in Act II was also a great triumph for him. That was the real beginning. My admiration for Craig's work increased with each new production."

Typically, Craig went so far as to rename the acts of the play (Act I - The Rocks, Act II - The Feast, Act III - Light, Act IV - The Storm), recreating the scenes as an allegorical battle of man versus nature, body versus soul, savagery versus civilization. He emphasized the elemental in his setting, eliminating extraneous detail and ultilizing carefully selected symbolic image, described by critics James Huneker as "a real unreality. For example, when the curtains are parted, a rocky slope, Nordish, rugged, forbidding, is viewed, the sea, an inky pool, misthemmed, washing at its base. From above falls a curious, sinister light which gives purplish tones to the stony surfaces and masks the faces of the players with mysterious shadows. The entire atmosphere is one of awe, of dread." (Heuneker, 1905, 32) The second act is set in the feast room at Gunnar's house for which Craig was able to create an extraordinary feeling of spaciousness in a "boxed-in: setting by using a circular platform "with a high seat at the back, and a long table with rough benches, railed in...A fire burns in a peculiar hearth in the centre, and there are raised places for the women." (Huneker, 1905, 32) Here again with startling lighting effects Craig was able to create an atmosphere of gloomy radiance with the light tempered by a painter's perception. The third act, which Craig had labeled "Light," was actually a simple hall with a large casement window and a dais "flooded by daylight. Here the quality of light was of the purest, withal hard, as befitted a northern latitude." (Huneker, 1905, 33)

To Huneker, and many others, the visual aspects of the
third act were the most impressive. Although some
critics felt that there was nothing extraordinary
about the fourth act design, Craig's use of a vast
black background with a starkly lit slope made an
impressive playing area for the suicide of Hiordis.
Craig gutted the backstage area of the Imperial and
abolished "foot and border lights, sending shafts of
luminosity from above...We see no 'flies', no shaky
unconvincing side scenes, no foolish flocculent
borders, no staring back-cloths" (Huneker, 1905, 32),
all of which were standard staging practices in that
era. The costumes for The Vikings were done in shades
of grays, greens and browns, with semi-circular cloaks
trimmed with golden ornaments and rope, and studded
shields of bold and simple design.

While Ibsen has attempted to humanize his legendary characters, Craig emphasized their larger-than-
life qualities with stylized movement heightened by
lighting effects. Craig saw that despite the colloquial language of the play, the characters existed
in an imaginary, dream-like world. All of this proved
unsettling to the actors who struggled to maintain a
more conventional approach. The colloquial language
of the play, coarsened by Archer's pedantic translation and the stilted acting of his cast, conflicted
with Craig's illusory design. Along with these
particular problems the actors resisted Craig's
staging ideas on every level, as Martin Shaw recalled:

> "...there was the mound across the stage
> which Asche and Holman Clark declared sloped
> too much for them to fight their duel on, as
> they used to fall down whenever they
> flourished their swords. However, they
> gradually acquired balance and brought off a
> most realistic combat. But all through
> rehearsals the actors made difficulties. The
> light was the chief cause of trouble. They
> complained bitterly that the audience could
> not see them. Of course a well-lit scene
> would have been quite out of place in the
> grim and fatalistic doom-play, and to-day no
> one would expect it; but in those far-off
> time actors were not educated up to such
> pitch of realism and self-sacrifice, and
> though that their facial expressions were
> the most important thing in the play."
> (Shaw 1929, 35)

The actors continually appealed to Terry with their complaints and she worked diplomatically to keep the peace, but all of this produced an atmosphere of extreme tension. Craig, feeling the pressure, became resistant to changes and the situation exploded when Terry's officious business manager outraged Craig by asking him to sign a contract with his own mother.

Ultimately, due to lack of sympathy with Craig's ideas and the melodramatic principles of nineteenth-century acting, most of the actors were unable to rise above stock poses and gestures. For the remainder of his career, Craig, although insistent on the centrality of the actor, and hoping for the return of the actor as artist in the manner of commedia dell'arte, disdainfully condemned most of the acting in his own day as the "swaggering artifice of the 'theatrical'". (Craig, 1960, 291n) The Vikings opened on April 15, 1903 to a large and enthusiastic audience who had come to see Ellen Terry in her first major role by a controversial contemporary dramatist. The Daily Chronicle reported the next day that "Miss Terry's reception on entering was enthusiastic, and after being summoned many times at the conclusion of each act, she was compelled at a quarter of an hour before midnight to lead forward Mr. Craig and to deliver a few words of thanks for the public recognition of efforts that she admitted had occasioned some anxiety." (The Daily Chronicle, 1903, 8) The critical reception was somewhat more guarded, particularly about the play itself, which was described as "a Scandinavian hodge-podge of sagas turned to dramatic uses" (The Times, 1903, 4) with a plot that is "mere blood and thunder, and the action indirect, heavy and uncertain" (Referee, 1903, 2) interesting only to "students of folklore." (The Times, 1903, 4) These criticism of the play extended to Archer's translation:

> "...I can only judge Ibsen by the translations of his plays, which, to do him justice, have a rigidity in English which they have not in the French, I have seen...I feel that such an expression as 'going a-viking', which is used more than once, may be a clumsy rendering of a perfectly acceptable Norwegian term". (Referee, 1903, 2)

Craig's set, costume, and lighting design created the expected controversy. Some critics found "an obvious discord between the story told on the stage, and the atmosphere of its mise-en-scene" (The Daily Telegraph, 1903, 7) and that although Craig "gives us a new sensation" (Referee, 1903, 2) and was to be praised for moving away from customary scenic practices, he "has not yet perfected the means of doing without them." (Referee, 1903, 2) Other critics acknowledged that Craig's "scene and costumes are good -- harmonious in colouring, broad and massive in design. He has his own system of stage lighting-- all illumination, if we are not mistaken, comes from above -- and the result is sometimes to leave the personages, where Dr. Johnson on a former occasion left the question of ghosts, in obscurity." (The Times, 1903, 4) But a few critics were completely enthusiastic. Max Beerbohm wrote that Craig:

> "...has had his chance, and has come off with flying colours. For the art of Ibsen and the art of Miss Terry our admiration has not been intensified; by the stage-manager-scene-painter-designer-of-all-costume-and-all-the-rest-of-it looms up illustriously with laurels on his brow...The Viking is excellently well suited to Mr. Craig's theory of stage-arrangement. I do not mean that he is incapable of varying his methods according to the kind of work he is illustrating. On the contrary, nothing could be less like the grim mystery of his Viking effects than was the sunny and childish gaiety of the effects wrought by him for The Triumph of Love [The Masque of Love]." (Beerbohm, 1903, 517-518)

The actors were generally praised, but Terry's anxiety was well-founded, for although the first audience gave "frequent and exuberant expression to their friendly feeling" (Referee, 1903, 2), subsequent performance were poorly attended and she was forced to close the play after three weeks. In hope of recouping her financial losses she hurried into production on May 23, 1903 with Much Ado About Nothing, playing Beatrice, one of her most acclaimed roles. Nearly thirty years later, Craig was able to explain the conditions he felt had cause the failure:

"...the London of 1903 which didn't want
Ibsen and loathed to see E.T. [Terry] in a
'wicked woman's part,' was a grievous
spectacle: and my way of producing a play or
an opera attracted very few people in
England at that time. Artists, and a few
hundred others were interested, and a few
thousand or so might have been quite willing
to pay for seats to see what I had to give
them - but in 1903 you couldn't run a full-
sized playhouse on the strength of a couple
of thousand eager enthusiasts..."(Craig,
1931, 138-139)

In her memoirs Terry generously took much of the
blame for the failure noting that she was, as Huneker
wrote, "woefully miscast. Once a creature capricious-
ly sweet, tender, arch, and delightfully arrogant,
Miss Terry is now long past her prime. To play
Hiordis was murdering Ibsen outright." (Huneker, 1905,
31) The Daily Telegraph was kinder, stating that
although she was not ideal in the role she acted "with
both charm and strength. If neither the charm nor the
strength were particularly Scandinavian, or endowed in
any sense with an epical quality, they were romantic
with all the unfailing romance and picturesqueness
which are Miss Terry's gracious privilege." (The
Daily Telegraph, 1903, 7)

William Butler Yeats, who would later accept a
set of Craig's patented scenic screens for use at the
Abbey Theatre, as well as some designs for a 1911
production of his own The Hour Glass, liked Terry's
performance but had mixed feelings about Craig's
design for The Vikings, writing to Lady Augusta
Gregory that Craig's "scenery is amazing but rather
distracts one's thoughts from the words." (Wade,
1955, 398)

Numerous other playwrights, directors and actors
were impressed with Craig's work. Sir John Martin-
Harvey recalled that:

"No one who saw it will forget the remarkable setting for Act II and in which the
long cloaks of the guests produced so fine
and barbaric an effect..." (Martin-Harvey,
1933, 137)

George Bernard Shaw, with whom Terry had maintained a long-time correspondence, also saw the

70

production and suggested that although Craig was "a young man of much talent" (Lawrence, 1972, 324), he was ultimately guilty of "matricide...In dealing with you his faculty for stage art totally deserted him." (Lawrence, 1972, 325) As well, Shaw accused Craig of "treachery to the author." (Lawrence, 1972, 324) He wrote:

> "If Master Teddy [Craig] wants to use plays as stalking horses for his clever effects, let him write them himself. To take an author of Ibsen's importance, and deliber- ately alter his play to suit the limelight man, is the folly of a child, not the act of a responsible man...If he did that to a play of mine, I would sacrifice him on the prompter's table before his mother's eyes." (Lawrence, 1972, 325)

Surprisingly, Shaw subsequently tried to inter- est Craig in designing some of his plays, particularly Caesar and Cleopatra for which Max Reinhardt commis- sioned Craig's designs in 1905. The production was never done and Shaw and Craig kept up an off-again-on- again feud that had begun with Shaw's scathing criticism of some of Craig's early acting perfor- mances in the 1890's and continued through a highly publicized dispute over the publication of the Shaw/Terry correspondence after her death. Craig himself recognized many of the problems with The Vikings and frankly shared his feelings about the

distance between his ideal visual concept and the reality of the staged performance in a letter to Martin Shaw:

> "...I feel convinced that no Vikings can be done unless each character will listen to the stage manager and hear what character he is to play. What the hell is the use of Act I -- what's all the bother about on the rocks, the ROCK and the Giants, the swords ten inches thick and blood flowing, wres- tling of limb and brain, if Hjordis is not the exact opposite of all this exterior might. What is the storm at the center of the play but the counterpart of the storm inside her heart, and what has exterior storminess to do with her -- absolutely NOTHING. 'to side with wild sisters' and all that is the cry of her soul not the

71

instinct of her physique. Soul is to her
what physique is to every other one in the
play. Sigurd is little short of God, Gunnar
absolute man...You did the <u>Vikings</u> -- and I
did the <u>Vikings</u> -- and the rest were doing
jokes -- and never got rid of their skins,
much less into any others. And only
because, as it goes today, that is an impos-
sibility -- The stage is upside down."
(Craig, 1968, 171-172)

Without a doubt very few actors, audience, and
critics in 1903 were ready for Craig's concepts, as he
himself was painfully aware: "I take it I was a
little before my time, a very careless thing to be;
after this [the Imperial Theatre season] I was out of
work for many months." (Craig, 1924, 36) But as a
result of <u>The Vikings</u> experience Craig impressed
several fellow artists, including Yeats, who would
later contribute articles to <u>The Mask</u>, Craig's journal
of the art of the theatre which he published from 1908
to 1929, as well as seriously experiment with Craig's
screens. Perhaps more importantly, Count Harry
Kessler who had seen Craig's Purcell Opera Society
production, was most impressed with <u>The Vikings</u> and
wanted to bring Craig to the German theatre. But
despite several attempts to arrange collaborations
with Max Reinhardt, Otto Brahm, and Hugo von Hofmannsthal, Craig was only to contribute a few designs for
a production of <u>Venice Preserved</u>, under the super-
vision of Brahm. However, Craig was to have an
enduring and profitable relationship with Kessler
that culminated in the 1928 publication of an extraordinary edition of <u>Hamlet</u> illustrated by Craig for
Kessler's distinguished Cranach Press.

Craig and Kessler met through artist William
Rothenstein who wrote a letter to <u>The Saturday Review</u>
scolding Max Beerbohm on his review of <u>The Vikings</u> for
failing to adequately recognize that "...so beautifully was the play staged, so nobly were the figures
grouped in scene after scene, that I felt that
something important had happened to the English
stage." (Rothenstein, 1932, 54) Rothenstein went on
to air his grievances at the English theatre of his
day:

"A feeling against the wanton extravagance
and low standard of taste which prevail in
the theatre in England has been slowly
gaining ground, but Mr. Craig is the first

72

to show us that the particular qualities which excite our enthusiasm for other arts may also be brought upon the stage, and that it is possible for a play to be produced which may be judged by the same standard and enjoyed to the same degree as poetry, painting and music. Mr. Craig's genius, his unique perception of all the qualities which to make an atmosphere of dignity and beauty of dramatic theatre in England. It were a pity, however, if that active encouragement without which theatrical achievement is almost impossible in existing circumstances were not forthcoming from all those who hold that beauty is one of the essential elements of life." (Rothenstein, 1903, 588)

The Vikings was most certainly a commercial failure, but Craig had the opportunity to demonstrate and experiment with his theories. Elements of his design ideas would later turn up in his productions of The Pretenders and MacBeth (1928). His attempts to integrate the characters into an abstract scene was undermined by his cast's inability and unwillingness to appreciate his concepts, unlike the cast of Craig's previous Purcell Opera Society productions who were willing amateurs he could mold into his visual scheme. When Craig later published his essay, "The Actor and the Ueber-marionette," theorizing that the modern actor should be replaced by a super-puppet, he was undoubtedly influenced by his unhappy experiences with the rigid nineteenth-century traditions of his cast in The Vikings.

The production had also contributed to growing interest in the works of Ibsen in England (although the only other major English production of The Vikings, in 1928, was unenthusiastically received). The earliest English productions of Ibsen's plays in the 1880's were vilified by critics, with the notable exceptions of Archer and Shaw, but after the ban on performances of Ghosts was lifted in 1914, Ibsen's plays were slowly accepted by English audiences. Craig's production, with the added public credibility of Terry's presence, helped, in a modest way, to elevate respect for Ibsen's works. But perhaps most importantly, less than two years later, and undoubtedly influenced by his experience with The Vikings,

Craig's controversial book The Are of the Theatre generated a furor among artists that would radically change ideas about performance and production in the twentieth-century theatre.

REFERENCES

Beerbohm, 1903

Max Beerbohm. "A Notice," The Saturday Review XCV (April 25, 1903).

Craig, 1913:

Edward Gordon Craig. Towards a New Theatre (London and Toronto: J.M. Dent & Sons, Ltd.).

Craig, 1924:

Edward Gordon Craig. Woodcuts and Some Words (New York: E.P. Dutton & Co., Inc.).

Craig, 1931:

Edward Gordon Craig. Ellen Terry and Her Secret Self (New York: E.P. Dutton & Co., Inc.).

Craig, 1957:

Edward Gordon Craig. Index to the Story of My Days (New York: The Viking Press).

Craig, 1960:

Edward Gordon Craig. On the Art of the Theatre New York: Theatre Arts Books).

Craig, 1968:

Edward Gordon Craig. Gordon Craig. The Story of His Life (New York: Alfred A. Knopf).

Craig, 1969:

Edward Gordon Craig. Henry Irving (New York: Blom).

Craig and St. John, 1932:

Edith Craig and Christopher St. John, eds. EllenTerry's Memoirs (New York: G.P. Putnam's Sons).

The Daily Chronicle, 1903:

Unsigned Notice. The Daily Chronicle (April 16, 1903).

The Daily
Telegraph, 1903:   Unsigned Notice. The Daily
                      Telegraph, (April 16,1903).

Huneker, 1905:   James Huneker. Iconoclasts
                      (London: Scribner's).

Irving, 1951:   Laurence Irving. HenryIrving
                      (London: Faber & Faber).

Lawrence, 1972:   Dan H. Lawrence. Collected
                      Letters 1898-1910 (NewYork:
                      Dodd, Mead & Co.)

Martin-Harvey, 1933: Sir John Martin-Harvey. The
                      Autobiography of Sir John
                      Martin-Harvey (London).

Referee, 1903:   Unsigned Notice. Referee
                      (April 19, 1903).

Rothenstein, 1903:   William Rothenstein. "A
                      Letter to the Editor," The
                      Saturday Review XCV May 9,
                      1903).

Rothenstein, 1932:   William Rothenstein. Men and
                      Memories 1900-1922 (London:
                      Faber & Faber Ltd.).

Shaw, 1929:   Martin Shaw. Up to Now
                      (London: Oxford University
                      Humphrey Milford Press).

Terry, 1982:   Ellen Terry. The Story of My
                      Life (New York: Schocken).

The Times, 1903:   Unsigned Notice. The Times
                      (April 16, 1903).

Wade, 1955:   Allen Wade, ed. The Letters
                      of W.B. Yeats (New York: The
                      MacMillan Co.).

Brecht's Gestic Vision for Opera: Why the Shock of Recognition is more Powerful in The Rise and Fall of the City of Mahagonny than in The Three Penny Opera

Rebecca Hilliker
North Dakota State University

Written by Bertolt Brecht and Kurt Weill, The Three Penny Opera and Rise and Fall of the City of Mahagonny were two of the first operas that attempted to turn Jazz and popular music into a legitimate idiom for serious composers. Thematically, both bitterly satirize postwar bourgeois society morally corrupted by money. Like the cry of Büchner and Berg's Wozzeck, Brecht's operas shout "With us poor people--its money money money. . . . People like us can't be holy in this world." Although initially described as indigestible, The Threepenny Opera ultimately became a classic and made Brecht and Weill famous. It is still considered one of the rare cases of a serious avant-gar-de work capable of simultaneously achieving lowbrow and highbrow popularity. Mahagonny on the other hand, which was written after Brecht had developed his opera theories more fully, never achieved such popular success, but is in some ways more powerful in achieving Brecht's gestic vision for opera.[1]

In both The Three Penny Opera and Rise and Fall of he City of Mahagonny Brecht and Weil offer a lurid vision of morality and capitalistic corruption. Weill's scores mingle the lyric beauty of the ballad with the acrid melodies of the cabaret for success and Brecht's texts thematically fight against the creation

---

[1] For a comprehensive analysis of Brecht's gestic vision for music see "On Gestic Music", pp. 104-105 and "On the Use of Music in an Epic Theatre", pp. 84-90 in Brecht on Theatre, translated by John Willet (New York: Hill and Wang, 1964). In this analysis Brecht provides a definition of what he means by a social "gest" and describes the political relationship to the musical score. See also "The Modern theatre is the Epic Theatre" (pp. 33-42 in the same text), Brecht's notes to the opera The Rise and Fall of the City of Mahagonny. In German consult Schriften zum Theater. **Seven volumes edited by Werner Hecht (Suhrkamp Verlag, 1963-4).**

of a false harmony and the smoothing over of contradictions. In both operas the "cheap" music is
never allowed to overpower the text. In the gestic
sense the music serves to punctuate or underline the
words. There are marked differences in the methods
of forcing the spectator to confront and study what
he sees, however. In the former the authors were
establishing a precedent for a new musical convention
and there is a clear division between songs and text.
In the latter they moved beyond the obvious attack on
outworn conventions and back toward a more orthodox
form (the music is almost continuous). Although the
forms are very different, both pay tribute to what
Brecht and Weill viewed as the "idiocy" of the
operative form and both create the desired shock of
recognition which produces the famed Verfremdungseffekt. However, in Mahagonny there is greater suspense
created in the process than in awaiting the outcome.
This helps to prevent the opera from becoming classic
and safe. There is less of an opportunity for
Mahagonny to develop its own outworn conventions.

At the beginning of Act I of Three Penny Opera,
Peachum lets us know that Brecht was aware of his
dilemma early on when he says:

"Between 'giving people a shock' and
'getting on their nerves' there's a difference my friends. Only an artist can give
people the right kind of shock!"[2]

A closer analysis of the methods of creation helps to
clarify why Mahagonny is potentially more successful
in meeting Brecht's long term criteria for gestic
opera than Three Penny, why the shock of recognition
for the latter was only temporary, and why Three
Penny was destined to become too popular and too easy
to take.

When Three Penny Opera premiered at the Theater
am Schiffbauerdamm in Berlin, Brecht and Weill's
attack on sacred musical conventions initially
produced a strident reaction. Those who attended the
first dress rehearsal in the late Summer of 1928 felt
that it had no hope for survival and Berlin producer

---

[2] Bertolt Brecht, The Threepenny Opera in The
Modern Theatre: Five Plays, edited by Eric Bentley
(New York: Doubleday Anchor Books, 1955), 140.

Ernst-Josef Aufricht wanted an alternate production prepared in case of failure. Lotta Leyna, 23 years later, described the farcical nature of the experience:

> "it [the rehearsal] lasted until five in the morning. Everybody was completely finished. We were all shouting and swearing at one another. Only Weill remained calm... We learned that Aufricht was already going around asking everybody if they did not know of a new play for him; he needed something new on the spot, otherwise he was lost.

> Well-known Berlin theatre prophets, as soon as they left the dress rehearsal, told all who cared to listen that Brecht and Weill intended to insult the audience with a wild mixture, neither opera nor operetta, neither cabaret nor drama, but a bit of each, with the whole thing bathed in an exotic jazz sauce: in other words it was indigestible. They suggested that the most sensible thing would be to cancel the play before the first night.[3]

The premiere, produced just the sort of "shock" that Brecht was looking for. Lotte Leyna described the legendary performance and its outcome:

> Upon to the second scene, which plays in a stable, the audience remained cool and non-committal. They gave the impression that they were convinced in advance that the play would be a flop. Then came the Cannon Song. An unbelievable storm of applause. The audience was beside itself. From this moment on nothing could go wrong. The audience was enthusiastically with us. We could not believe our eyes and ears. Until the next morning we could not really believe in our success. . . . Berlin was gripped by a Threepenny Opera fever. Everywhere, even in the streets, the tunes were whistled. A

---

[3] Brecht as They Knew Him, translated by John Peet, edited by Hubert Witt, (New York: International Publishers, 1974), 60-61.

> Threepenny Opera Bar was opened, where no
> other music was played. Immediately all
> sorts of scribblers imitated to death the
> "Brecht style" and the "Weill style," or
> what they understood by these words.[4]

Within five years of its premier, The Threepenny Opera
had transformed traditional music and had been
produced throughout Europe.[5]

Brecht was able to change the ordinary, well-
known world into a strikingly unexpected one, making
the self-evident incomprehensible in order to make it
all the more comprehensible. When it was first produced, Threepenny caused Brecht's desired "jerk" in
perception. Furthermore, not since the late nineteenth century Italian opera had a composer and writer
been capable of such a complex infusion of banal
popular forms with complex emotions, bridging that
cultural gap which exists between "highbrow" and
"lowbrow" society. it is partly for this reason that
it has been so aptly described as the weightiest
possible lowbrow opera for highbrows and the most
full-blooded highbrow musical for lowbrows.

Eventually, however, the traditionally "cheap"
taboo music forms (jazz, cabaret and popular) which
were meant to prevent the audience from irrational
culinary enjoyment became their own narcotic.
Audiences developed a more sophisticated understanding
of the language of jazz and cabaret music was further
legitimized and romanticized by the American film
version of the musical Cabaret which mesmerized its
audience and possessed a comfortable aura of decadence
lost in sentimentality. Brecht discussed the dehuman-

---

[4] Brecht as They Knew Him, 61-62.

[5] The success of the opera received a temporary
setback in 1933 when the Nazis party placed a ban on
the work and requested that all foreign organizations
return scores to Germany for destruction. Even some
of the staunchest supporters lost faith in the power
of the opera. Some twenty years later Threepenny
revealed itself as a timeless masterpiece with the
stunning success of the 1950s New York City revival at
the theatre de Lys. Thus the opera took its proper
place in musical history.

izing process of becoming too comfortable in a crucial paragraph (44) from the "Short Organum":   "We are always coming upon things which are too obvious for us to bother to understand them."[6]   To prevent this from happening Brecht depended upon amazing his public--by alienating the familiar.   But what happens when that amazement disappears over time?   Is a production destined to become to popular?

The very popularity of The Penny Opera ultimately made the music so common place that it became too obvious for the audience to bother to understand it. Cabaret music, which initially possessed a natural gestic character in its attack upon the outworn lyricism of the culinary opera, eventually became its own convention and is accepted in the same manner as other Brechtian tactics now taken for granted. The singers of the cabaret songs have lost their easy power to effectively comment upon the music while communicating its essential content.

Although the separation of the music and text helps to a degree, performers have to rely primarily on an effective gestic approach to acting in order to distance their audience and American actors are not well trained in the Brechtian style. The Three Penny Opera lives in the United States today primarily by its songs, not by its gestic effectiveness, reaching its ultimate romantic outlook in such vocal inter- pretations as Bobby Darren's Mack the Knife and textual interpretations as the G.W. Pabst film version which a right wing paper described as having "such a fairy-tale-like effect . . . told with such charm and humor that in the end one completely disregards the intended meaning and just enjoys the story."[7]   Without the moritat sharpness of a razor's edge, the teeth of the shark, in the United States at least, have lost their bite.

Such a romantic view of Threepenny Opera is not wholly the outcome of production style, however.   The

---

[6] Bertolt Brecht, "A Short Organum for the Theatre" in Brecht on Theatre, translated by John Willett (New York: Hill and Wang, 1964), 192.

[7] Martin Esslin, Brecht The Man and His Work (New York: The Norton Library, 1974), 44.

play, with its air of forgiveness, lends itself to an outlook in which the audience weeps with those who weep and laughs with those who laugh. As the crowd hears the last nail hammered into the gallows, and Macheath is lead to the place of execution a royal messenger rides onto the scene, greeted by the chant of the choir. Mack has been reprieved and he jumps from the gallows, declaring that he "knew it all the time." Polly is jubilant, Mrs. Peachum moralizes that in real life the poor rarely can expect such a felicitous ending and Mr. Peachum urges that society should not prosecute transgressions too severely.

Although there is no doubt that Brecht meant the ending to be taken satirically, the author himself understood mankind's ability to deny his own part in a violent world. In his proclamations of the inadequacy of human exertions, Peachum seeks for the inevitable spectators who cast stones only at their neighbors:

> Man lives by his head,
> That head will not suffice
> Just try it: you will find your head
> Will scarce support two lice
>
> For the task assigned them
> Men aren't smart enough or sly
> Any rogue can blind them
> With a clever lie.[8]

The plays's happy ending is indicative of what was and still is appealing to the masses. The play offers something for everyone. For some it is the daring and vicarious excursion into the dark side of the forbidden underworld of crime and prostitution. For others it is simply the brilliant cynicism of the poetry which is in keeping with the antisentimental attitudes of the day. At the same time the play is cynical enough to shock, distanced just far enough from the audience that it can deny the similarities which Mackie shares with bourgeois society and any parallels with the corruption of the underworld.

Brecht, with the writing of Three Penny, already understood what would happen when the play was assimilated into classic status:

---

[8] The Threepenny Opera, 174.

My business is arousing human pity, and I've
got to find something new. It's just too
hard, that's all. There are a few things,
of course, that'll shake a man up, a few,
but the trouble is, when they've been used
for a while, they don't work any more.
Human beings have a frightful capacity for,
um, anesthetizing themselves at will. So it
happens, for instance, that a man who sees
another man on the corner with only a stump
for an arm, will be so shocked-- the first
time--that he'll give him sixpence. But the
second time it'll only be a threepenny bit.
And if he sees him a third time, he'll hand
him over the police and not bat an eyelash.[9]

And before the opera was completed he had already
begun to develop his theories along a more stringent
path. In order for Mahagonny to have lasting gestic
effectiveness, he believed that the play needed to
offend its audience in a new way (p.2). Thus, Mahagonny relies primarily upon the text for its
Verfremdungseffekt, rather than upon breaking with
convention which over time can become its own convention.

By the time he wrote Mahagonny, Brecht was better
prepared to convey the threats of a self-cannibalizing
society and to demand action. Although his fundamental gestic principles had not changed, his
understanding of opera had matured, and his ideas
about music's relationship to epic theatre had been
clarified. Whereas the Threepenny Opera had been
initially described by its critics as indigestible,
Brecht described the form of Mahagonny as the cooking
process itself. In the notes on the opera, "The
Modern Theatre is the Epic Theatre" which he wrote
around 1930, Brecht admits that the work possesses
culinary features. However, here the kulinarish
features are brought up, not in the traditional
operatic sense, but for our inspection. It develops
by "jerks" forming grotesque contrasts: a love duet
in a brothel, a drunken escapist fantasy followed by
an electrocution for poverty. When the process itself
becomes the theme, audiences cannot be as easily

---

[9] Threepenny, 113.

overpowered by standard narcotic attractions. Furthermore, Brecht was prepared to take a more strident position against capitalism.

In the interum between the initial writing of the more primitive Mahagonnygesänge and the culmination of the collaboration of Weill and Brecht in the final opera version, Brecht had begun a new phase of development with the writing of the didactic plays and his collaboration on Happy End. His greater emphasis upon Marxism had led him to a new austerity and an even greater economy of expression. Combining Marx's functionalism and Watson's behaviorism, Brecht and Weill rejected all introspective psychology and formulated a new theory of musical drama which would teach social attitudes by "showing the highly formalized actions of abstract types."[10] These types, when placed in the context of Mahagonny's Paradise City, cut at the heart of mankind's image of his society, causing an even greater stir than Threepenny.

When the premiere of Mahagonny took place at the Leipzig Opera, on 9 March, 1930, the production was greeted with one of the most memorable full-scale riots of German theatrical history. Critic Alfred Polgar immortalized the event:

> Here, there, above, below in the electrically charged theatre contradictions flashed like lightning and aroused further contradictions which in turn gave rise to more contradictions in a geometrical progression. And soon the epic form of the theatre spread from the stage to the auditorium. . . . The woman on my left was overcome by a heart spasm and wanted to get out--only the warning that this might prove to be an historic moment kept her from leaving. . . a man behind me on the right mumbled to himself: "I'll only wait till that fellow Brecht turns up!" and licked his chops. Readiness is all. War cries echoed through the auditorium. In places hand-to-hand fighting broke out. Hissing, applause, which sounded grimly like faces being

---

[10] Esslin, 46.

slapped. . . . It was the first experiment
of Brecht's epic theatre, and the scandal
which was loosed already portended the
approaching breakup of the country.[11]

Lotta Lenya, who was to play Jenny once the play
reached Berlin, was in the audience and further
describes the volcanic atmosphere:

> I have been told the square around the opera
> house was filled with Nazi Brown Shirts,
> carrying placards protesting the Mahagonny
> performance. . . . I was startled out of my
> absorption by the electric tension around
> us, something strange and ugly. As the
> opera swept toward its close, the demonstra-
> tion started, whistles and boos; by the time
> the last scene was reached, fist fights had
> broken out in the aisles, the theatre was a
> screaming mass of people; soon the riot had
> spread to the stage, panicky spectators were
> trying to claw their way out, and only the
> arrival of a large police force, finally,
> cleared the theatre.[12]

The second days performance was given with the
houselights on. More furor.

Performances throughout the provinces were
greeted with even greater virulence than the infamous
Leipzig riot. The caucus of the National Socialists
of Oldenburg forced the cancellation of a local
performance on the grounds that it was a rubbishy work
of vile and immoral content.[13] The left was also
violently opposed to the play's negative picture of
their party and equally condemned it. Brecht was

---

[11]Alfred Polgar, "Theaterskandal" in Handbuch des
Kritikers (Zürich, 1938), 32.

[12]Bertolt Brecht, Rise and Fall of the City of
Mahagonny, translated by W.H. Auden and Chester
Kallman with an introduction by A.R. Braunmuller
(Boston: David R. Goding, Publisher, 1976), 12.

[13]Thuringia, in which Oldenburg is situated
already had a Nazi controlled government.

shocked by his failure at communicating Marxist ideas. Weill was distressed by the reception of his music. Both hastily reorganized parts of the text and were unexpectedly surprised by the successfully performance of the revised play at Kassel. The success was not lasting, however, and the opera was eventually driven from the German provincial stages.

Although negotiations to produce Mahagonny in Berlin had run into difficulties earlier, Aufricht, who had taken a chance on The Threepenny Opera, consented to form a special company for the Berlin premiere. Berlin was far more sophisticated than the cities of the provinces. A last stronghold of the liberalism it received the December 1931 performance of Mahagonny enthusiastically.[14]

It had been a very long time since an operatic work had met with such passionate opposition in Germany and even after the partial success of the opera, critics were not ready to accept Weill's genius. After the full-scale riot at Leipzig, Brecht and Weill had worked on minor changes in the hopes of alleviating the violence of the opposition. Weill's description of some of the changes describe his feelings regarding the matter:

---

[14] The success of Mahagonny, like Threepenny was cut short by the establishment of the Thousand-Year Reich. Right after the Anschluss in 1938, Gestapo agents raided the Vienna offices of Universal Edition and destroyed Weill's scores including Mahagonny. For years after the war it was believed that nothing remained of the orchestration. It was not until the mid-1950s after Weill's death in New York, that Lotte Lenya set out to record the opera and an intact orchestral score was rediscovered. A number of successful performances followed. It was not until after Brecht's death, however, that a truthful West German rendition of the work was staged in September 1963 in Hamburg. Although the reviews were generally enthusiastic, the praise was not enough to return Weill's fame of Threepenny Opera, and in Germany today his reputation stands lower than it did in the early 30s.

> For two whole days now I have worked with
> Brecht on a clarification of the events in
> Act 3. We now have a version which the Pope
> himself could no longer take exception to.
> It is now clear that the final demonstra-
> tions are in no wise 'communistic'--it is
> simply that Mahagonny, like Sodom and
> Gomorrah, falls on account of the crimes,
> licentiousness and general confusion of its
> inhabitants.[15]

Although Brecht's intentions were Marxist, thematically the play's message is broader based and it was
not simply communistic paranoia which caused opposition. The public in general felt themselves personally attacked by the piece. The violence of the
response was due to the fact that the opera was
capable of producing an even greater "shock of
recognition" than Threepenny.

In Mahagonny Brecht and Weill depict the ruthless
nature of the capitalistic system when carried to its
ultimate conclusion. Confronted face to face with
death the inhabitants of the city of Mahagonny rid
themselves of all inhibitions. In four clearly and
brutally defined visions, Brecht forces the inhabitants of Mahagonny to face the consequences of
their anarchy as they confront four typical states of
man: eating, loving, fighting and drinking. In a
series of individual unrelated scenes, Brecht amasses
more and more examples of the folly of man. Everyone
is intent upon his own foolish or evil business. Each
becomes part of an unified composition, clearly shown
by the repeated chorus.

> One means to eat all your are able;
> Two, to change your love about;
> Three means the ring and gaming table;
> Four, to drink until you pass out.

---

[15] David Drew, "Background to 'Mahagonny'" Opera,
14 Feb, 1963), 85.

            Moreover better get it clear
            That Don'ts are not permitted here.
            Moreover, better get it clear
            That Don'ts are not permitted here![16]

The pictures are so bold and vital that they contain
revolting pictures of nightmare horrors which have
not been seen since the painting of Peter Brueghel
the elder which Brecht much admired.[17]   Like
Brueghel's vast miserable types of humanity, Brecht's
characters show incredible intensity, whether horing,
eating, drinking or boxing.   There is a sense of
boundless energy.   The driving force of life itself is
one of the most effective qualities of the work.

     In the vivid eating scene Brecht and designer
Caspar Neher provide a frightening picture of a
glutton.   As the glutton stuffs himself to death
because hunger is the rule, Neher's painterly depiction   of the action looms overhead.   "We never even
hinted" writes Brecht, "that others were going hungry
while he stuffed, but the effect was provocative all
the same.   It is not everyone who is in a position to
stuff himself full that dies of it, yet many are dying
of hunger because this man stuffs himself to death.
His pleasure provokes because it implies so much."[18]

     Brecht's symbolic system helps to explain Jakes
death by overeating--a toll exacted for culinary art.

---

     [16] The Rise and Fall of the City of Mahagonny, 68,
73, 77, 100.

     [17] Brecht's interest in Brueghel probably began
when Helen Weigel gave him a book of his paintings.
Brecht immediately saw the Verfremdungseffekte in
Brueghel's work and shortly thereafter wrote Verfrem-
dungseffekte in den erzählenden Bildern des älteren
Bruegel in Bildener Kunst.   Published in Berlin and
Dresden in 1957 it was probably written in 1934.

     [18] Brecht on Theatre, translated by John Willet,
(New York: Hill and Wang, 1964), 36.

EATING

A number of the men, including JIM, are seated
at tables laden with joints of meat. JAKE is
seated at a center table eating incessantly. On
each side of him a musician is playing:

JAKE:

Two calves never made a man fatter:
So serve me a third fatted calf.
All is only half,
All is only half:
I wish it were me on my platter . . .

Watch me! Watch me! would you have guessed
How much one person can eat?
In the end I shall have rest.
To forget is sweet,
To forget is sweet.
More please! Give me more!
More please! Give me more!
More please! Give me more!

He topples over dead.

The men form a half-circle behind him and remove
their hats.

MEN: Smith lies dead in his glory,
Smith lies dead in his happiness,
Smith lies dead with a look on his face
of insatiable craving,

For Smith went the whole hog
And Smith has fulfilled himself:
A man without fear,
A man without fear.[19]

The expression on Jakes faces is like the expression
upon many of Brueghel's peasants--intense pain and
suffering coupled with a grim smile. Underneath the
satirical wit is a deeply pessimistic view of the
world. It is impossible to laugh at the robust humor
without looking beneath the surface at the tragic
implications of such folly and ignorance. Tragedy
and comedy are contained within each other.

---

[19] Mahagonny, 68-69.

In the drinking scene the visual imagery becomes
even more psychologically and physically excoriating.
Jim describes his own fate as he asks Lady Begbick to
set up rounds for all the gents.

> Everyone who gets around is sure to
>   get a skinning:
> That's the reason everybody
> Strips his own skin from his body
> And when pelts are bought on every hand
> With dollars, thinks he's winning.[20]

In the finale Jim is sentenced to the electric chair,
not because he has seduced Jenny, nor driven his
friend to death but because he cannot pay for the
drinks which he so freely has given away. He is
moneyless, the most despicable for all crimes. Here
Brecht's didactic message is brought to a powerful
conclusion. No messenger enters to save the situation. Brecht doesn't have to rely upon satire because
the imagery itself is so nakedly powerful. Romanticism is just so much merchandise appearing only as
content not as form. With the death of Jim the
inhabitants of Mahagonny must accept their fate.

H.H. Stuckenschmidt, a distinguished German
musicologist who witnessed the opening performance of
Mahagonny during the Leipzig riot sums up the importance of Brecht and Weill's masterwork:

> If a way out of the present crisis in the
> realm of opera is to be found, the only hope
> lies in the quarter where Brecht and Weill
> are carrying out their ideological renova-
> tion of the traditional genres. . . . We
> have come to the point of decision: the
> decision that there must be a new form of
> opera, a radically different way for the
> theatre. . . . It is not the originality of
> the means which is decisive, but their power
> of suggestion. . . . The work forms a climax
> in the operatic history of the present age.
> For all the occasional beery humour, its
> adolescent romanticism, it strikes a

---

[20]Mahagonny, 78-79.

powerful blow for the New Theatre, and for this very reason has aroused passionate hostilities.[21]

Without doubt, The Threepenny Opera is a masterpiece and the intense response to Brecht and Weill's "cheap music" suggests that the eventual success of the opera was self-evident. Such passions are only present when conventions have not been simply attached but have been replaced by a positive content. It is only then that a work possesses what Herman Melville described as "the shock of recognition" which distinguishes truly great and lasting works of art. However, the very nature of the operas popularity has caused it to become too familiar to alienate the audience as effectively as when it was first produced.

Mahagonny on the other hand was capable of rousing "the most violent disputation, such as has not been heard for many many years,"[22] because it resists complacency and the feeling of good cheer which inhabited Three Penny Opera. Its coarse humor, vivid imagery and robust satirical attitude still appeals to both a highbrow and lowbrow society, however the accusations against mankind are much more difficult to swallow. Magahonny charges capitalistic society with destruction of human choice and its audience with self-cannibalization. Lust for money is not a thing of the past but has been handed down from generation to generation illiciting the darkest and cruelest natures of the individual and community. Brecht provides the naked events. The message is clear. Individuals like Lady Begbick, Moses and Fatty will continue to exploit the poor offering grotesque substitutes from freedom if humanity doesn't recognize its sins. Magahonny is powerful, not simply because it attacks such a society and demands reform but because it makes us angry and makes us want to resist. such implications. The excitement of the drama comes not simply from experiencing the attack upon materialism but from the audience response to the demand. Unlike Threepenny which lives primarily by its songs

---

[21] Drew, 89.

[22] Drew, 89.

and is no longer offensive enough, <u>Magahonny</u> means
business and it will continue to do so provided that
it can survive being made classic and safe. To date,
the shock of recognition still goes beyond the
superficial art forms of the interwar years which
tended to simply "get on peoples nerves." <u>Magahonny</u>
remains a highly original opera and lasting viable
form of Brecht's <u>Verfremdung</u>.

"'Creative Vandalism' Or, A Tragedy Transformed:
Howard Barker's 'Collaboration' with
Thomas Middleton on the 1986 Version of
Women Beware Women"

William Hutchings
University of Alabama-Birmingham

A surprising number of contemporary English
playwrights have assimilated specific conventions and
plot devices of Elizabethan and Jacobean drama
directly into their own works, though their methods
and purposes in doing so are as varied as the authors
themselves. In Rosencrantz and Guildenstern are Dead
(1967), for example, Tom Stoppard uses the plot of
Hamlet as a frame for the existential plight portrayed
in Waiting for Godot; later, in The Real Thing (1985),
John Ford's 'Tis Pity She's a Whore provided a
counterpart for the romantic entanglements of Stoppard's central characteres. In Lear (1972), Edward
Bond returned to Shakespeare's sources and restored
details that his predecessor omitted, creating a new
and very powerful tragedy that differs radically from
the one which audiences have admired for centuries.
In What the Butler Saw (1969), Joe Orton adapted the
most outrageous excesses of Jacobean tragedy and
tragicomedy into a farce set in a contemporary
psychiatric clinic. Yet, despite these various
adaptations and assimilations of Jacobean plots,
characters, motifs, and themes, Howard Barker's
"collaboration" with Thomas Middleton on a "new
version" of Women Beware Women--first produced at the
Royal Court Theatre in February of 1986--is unique in
modern theatre. Whereas Stoppard's plays occasionally
include selected scenes from the earlier plays intact,
Barker has skillfully condensed the plot of the
sixteenth-century tragedy's first four acts into eight
scenes, changing its verse to prose but retaining its
diction, characters, and tone; then, however, he
discards Middleton's ending and inserts one of his
own. Using unmistakably contemporary language, he
transforms Middleton's revenge plot into an examination of subjection and liberation in both their sexual
and political forms. As on the Jacobean stage, such
dialectics are embodied in sex and violence in
extremis--but by fusing conventions of disparate
periods, Barker creates an extremely controversial,
startlingly original, and ideologically complex
analogue for current socio-political quandries.

First published in 1657, thirty years after Middleton's death, <u>Women Beware Women</u> features a typically bizarre entanglement of characters at the court of the Duke of Florence, where their clandestine lusts lead them through various illicit and incestuous relationships before their assorted betrayals and treacheries resolve themselves in a massive slaughter at the end of the play. Yet, the major characters of <u>Women Beware Women</u>--unlike those of many plays of the period--are not taken exclusively from among the aristocratic and affluent; in fact, class distinctions constitute a major basis of one of its central conflicts. Leantio, a businessman's clerk, has secretly married Bianca, who has run away from her father's house in Venice and come with her new husband to his relatively poorer home in Florence; there, the Duke, seeing her at her window, becomes enamoured of her. Through arrangements made by Livia, a wealthy woman of the city, the Duke seduces Bianca, makes her his mistress, and plans to marry her. Livia also arranges for her brother, Hippolito, to fulfill his desire to make love to his own niece, whom she has falsely told is not <u>really</u> related to him; a "cover-up" marriage to the foolish and vulgar young Ward of Hippolito's brother is used to allow the incestuous liaison to continue. Meanwhile, Livia also seduces Leantio, who has been rebuffed by his wife and, being jealous of the Duke, is attracted by the wealth that Livia owns. The Duke arranges for Hippolitio to murder Leantio, who wants to revenge his family's honor over Livia's affair with the merchant's clerk; in so doing, he enables the Duke to marry Bianca. Other disclosures-- including Isabella's incest with her uncle--lead to fatal revenge as well, which is accomplished in an extraordinarily spectacular way, even by conventional Jacobean standards for fifth-act catastrophes. At a masque held to celebrate the Duke's impending marriage, Isabella dies when she is hit with a "sign of wealth" (possibly flaming gold) thrown by Livia, who, in turn, dies by inhaling poisoned incense from Juno's altar; Hippolito is shot with poisoned arrows from Cupid's bow before deliberately running onto a guard's weapon, while one of his cohorts is dropped through a trap door on the stage for reasons that are never made clear. Finding in these events "things most fearfully ominous: and declaring that "I like 'em not" (V.ii. 185), the Duke then collapses, having been given wine that was poisoned by Bianca, though she intended it for his brother the Cardinal, who was to preside at the wedding, Bianca then kisses the Duke, drinks from the same cup, and dies, leaving the Cardinal to intone

the play's final homily: "Sin, what thou art, these
ruines show too piteously./ . . . Where lust reigns,
that Prince cannot reign long" (V.ii.114).

   In declaring himself Middleton's "collaborator"
three-and-a-half centuries after the earlier playwright's death, Barker has freely discarded both the
ludicrously contrived ending and the conventional
moralizing with which the play concludes.   Though he
has condensed the play's first three-and-a-half acts
into eight scenes and changed its language from verse
to rose (eliminating its more poetic and allusive
embellishments), he has retained the Jacobean diction
throughout Part I which ends with Livia's seduction of
Leantio...   From the outset, however, Part II is
unmistakably contemporary, and its thematic pre-
occupation with sex and violence--though no less
pervasive than among the Jacobeans--is nevertheless
markedly a product of the second <u>Elizabethan</u> age.
This segment of the play begins as Leantio enters,
"undressed," reflecting on the preceding five days of
love-making with Livia--thought his language is as
remote from Middleton's diction as the playwright's
style is from Marlowe's mighty line: "We fuck the day
to death," Leantio proclaims,

> And suffocate the day with tossing. . . .
> As for the bed, it's our whole territory,
> the footboard and the headboard are the
> horizons of our estate, rank with the flood
> of flesh. Oh, beautiful odour of the utter
> fuck! (12)

However startling the transition and however appalling
his language may be to the play's audience, the
experience that they describe is fundamental to an
understanding of the remainder of the play.   Its
language, deliberately, emphasizes the reality of the
body--in implicit contrast to the idealised but
exploitative "love" in whose name the exotic con-
trivances of the Jacobean plot are carried out.   This
experience of "the utter fuck"--and, necessarily, the
<u>language</u> with which it is described--dissociates them
from the entire tradition of "love" with all its
courtly and romantic idealizations which, as the
activities occurring in the play's Italianate court
demonstrate, have been debased both then and now.
Unlike even the conventional love that Leantio has
felt toward his wife, his relationship with Livia
brings about a transformation of the sort that D. H.
Lawrence repeatedly and ardently expounded; its

radical and revolutionary implications are proclaimed
by Livia, who exclaims that ". . . this was light and
transformation. It made me hate my [prior] life. All
hate your lives and change the world!" (20).

Whereas Middleton's version of the play presents
the characters' sexual entanglements as a perquisite
of power and wealth (as the Duke reminds Bianca in
pointing out that the opportunity to be his mistress
is an offer she cannot refuse), in Barker's version
both the Duke's politics and his various sexual
expropriations are means of subjugation in which
psychologically rooted drives for power are conjoined.
The lust and economy-based class distinctions that are
carried over from the Jacobean plot are shown to be
extension of an insatiable will to exercise power and
control over others. In its secular form, this desire
is the root of authoritarian government, including
the debauched Duke's; in its "sacred" form, it is the
basis of the authority of the Church, represented by
his brother the Cardinal. Thus, as the Cardinal
remarks in the second scene of the play's "modern"
half, ". . . There is another sex . . .[which] is not
to do with posture or with bringing off. . . . It is
politics" (20-21), and, as such, is based in similar
exploitation. Although the Duke fails to understand
his brother's insight and contends that he has "done
it all" (20), there remains still another, completely
opposite, and non-exploitative kind of sex that he has
never known--a liberating experience of the sort that
Leantio finds with Livia. Like William Blake's
symbolic figure of Orc, its energy is the natural
enemy of the dominant socio-economic and political
systems, which are based on the urges toward the
domination, exploitation, and subjugations of others.

Surprisingly, however, the general populace not
only submits to but actually revels in its subjuga-
tion--for which the impending royal wedding of the
Duke and Bianca becomes a central symbol. Specifically, the pageantry surrounding the celebration of
the royal marriage is, as the Cardinal realizes, "the
entertainment of the modern state and the proper
function of an aristocracy" (20). In a speech with
obvious topicality for an English audience in 1986,
saturated by the broadcast images of the two recent
royal weddings, the Duke in Barker's play boasts that,
despite widespread poverty and unemployment in the
realm,

My popularity was never higher, and she
dangles from me, flashing like some encrus-
ted gem, blinding discontent and dazzling
the cynic. . . . The dossers will applaud my
wedding and go home warmer than they would
be after a meal[;] there is great nourish-
ment in pageantry.   Later, the royal birth
will have them gasping who cannot conceive
themselves, and those that can will name
their brats after ours immaculate (26).

While the streets are being draped in bunting and the
(obviously anachronistic) newspapers are filled with
attestations of Bianca's virginity and disputes over
"which bonnet suits her best" (28), Livia and Leantio
contrive an act of counter-pageantry that will thwart
the planned wedding, "save" Bianca from "the acme of
artificiality" that such a fraudulent marriage would
be (30), and achieve a certain revenge against the
corrupt (and corrupting) Duke.   specifically, they
arrange for Sordido, the squalid manservant of the
Ward, to rape Bianca--an act which, they claim, will
not only "liberate her from herself [i.e., from her
pride, ambition, and inbred class-consciousness of
privilege, all of which separate her from the people]
and at the same stroke, unleash contempt on all we've
come to hate" but also "rock the state off its
foundations, which is [sic] erected on such lies as
ducal marriages" (30).   The greater "violation," they
contend, came when--as in the Jacobean play--she was
ravished (figuratively) by the allures of ducal
wealth and power and subsequently ravished (literally)
by the Duke himself; she has been, in effect, ravaged
by her greed and ambition, by her longing for the
glamour and opulence that her actual but secret (and
less than affluent) husband, Leantio, cannot provide.

    The pervasive and corrupting power of money is
also responsible for the plight of the Ward, who turns
out to be far less foolish than in the Jacobean play.
He was, he explains, abandoned in "cruel boarding
homes" by his avaricious guardian when his father
died--and he maintains that "a proper love would
[have] see[n] through a malicious schoolboy's pain"
(23).   The entire city "throbs . . . with the pulse of
money," Livia claims as she and the other conspirators
plot their subversion of the wedding, maintaining that
she and the other "stand outside it and with one
finger eliminate corruption" (30).   As a result of the
public marriage ceremony, Bianca will be no longer "a
woman at all--but a symbol of the state. . . the state

made flesh" (30); she is, in effect, marrying The People in marrying the Duke, forsaking a private life for a public (and artificial) role. Accordingly, Sordido's rape inverts the traditional <u>droit du seigneur</u>, as one of the most loathesome members of the populace preempts the Duke's sexual sovereignty. crying out "Oh, my property!" (33), the Duke bursts into the room and kills Sordido as the attempted rape is underway (just as Bonario interrupts Volpone's attempted rape of Celia, though the script is not specific on precisely what happens after Sordido "seizes" Bianca). Unlike Bonario, however, the rescuing Duke is now repulsed by Bianca and refuses to "come near such a pitch of muddy squalor"--though he insists that she must nevertheless go through with the marriage "or the government is mocked" (34). Hippolito, Polonius-like, counsels killing off all witnesses--a suitably Jocabean ending, though his methods would presumably be less flamboyant and contrived than Middleton's own--but his suggestion is disregarded. "This is real shit we're plunged in," he concludes, as the Duke considers stabbing Bianca and blaming it on the dead Sordido, thereby "convert[ing] this farce into a tragedy, and win[ning] more pity than contempt" for himself (34). However, he is moved by her beauty at the crucial moment and proves unable to act on his plan, sinking instead to his knees in sobs. Bianca still refuses to go through with the wedding ceremony and renounces her love of "power, [which] was my dream of male" (35), and she resolves to wander in quest of a true understanding of herself as a woman--though her characterization of such knowledge is phrased in astonishingly crude terms, even within the context of the play's earlier dialogue. Surprisingly, she firmly rejects the proffered "impulsive sisterhood" of Livia (36), who gained exactly such knowledge in her experience with Leantio. As unrest spreads in the streets among a populace that has grown restive in waiting for its spectacle that will not be forthcoming, the question arises of who will govern: the Ward declines the suggestion that he takes control and proposes instead that Livia should take over. She dispatches Leantio to the streets to "tell the people we have broken lies and treat the pieces," and the play ends as the Duke proclaims Leantio and Livia the new Duke and Duchess-- though the abdicating Duke's final words ("Don't love! Don't love!" [36]) provide an extremely ironic counterpart for the Cardinal's closing remarks in Middleton's version of the play, on the inherent destructiveness of Lust and Sin.

Like Brecht's literary use of history for didactic purposes of his own--and, indeed, like Shakespeare's too--Barker's expropriation of Middleton's play is the pretext for commentary on decidedly contemporary social and moral issues. Beyond the pervasiveness of "sex and violence" which, in general, conjoins the world-view of the Jacobeans and that of our own time, Women Beware Women provides a particularly effective vehicle for Barker's radical commentary on contemporary Britain-- which, like Middleton's Florence, has been preoccupied with a profligately celebrated royal wedding in a time of widespread hardships caused by the state's dire economic problems. Like many agit-prop writers in recent decades, Barker maintains that the sexualand political impulse are inextricably conjoined. As throughout the plays of Edward Bond, it is the sickness of a society based on the exploitation of economic, sexual, and class distinctions that produces individual instances of sick and violently destructive behavior; achieving a "cure' will require both a radically leftist social revolution and an equally radical sexual one as well. Politically, then, as Jonathan Dollimore pointed out in his programme notes for the original production,

> . . . This is a play which dramatises both conceptions of desire: desire at the mercy of power, desire as subversive of power. Or rather, by creatively vandalising the earlier play, Barker sets up a violent dialectic between the two. And it's a dialectic which we're living now, in a society which both incites and represses sexuality (quotes in Trotter 194).

Significantly, it is Livia and Leantio who are deemed fit to rule at the end of the play; theirs is, clearly, a triumph of the exponents of "the utter fuck," notwithstanding their earlier collusion in arranging the rape of Leantio's wife and Livia's (later-repented) arrangement of (a) the Duke' initial procurement of Bianca and (b) Isabella's seduction by her uncle. Far from the mere inclusion of such language for its shock-value, Barker's use of it is central to his social, political, and sexual views, as Kenneth Hurren has explained:

> For Barker, . . . [power and money] are virtually the enemies of sex, at least in its liberating aspect--which he is implac-

ably sold on, and keen to see incorporated
in socialist thinking. 'The Left,' he avers,
'has ignored the body. It has yielded
sexuality to the reactionaries. Middleton
knew the body was the source of politics.
He did not know it was also the source of
hope' (Hurren 24).

If, as Tom Stoppard maintained in the 1986 Cambridge
Darwin Lecture, "a theatre text is always fair game:
it is always open season on a theatre text" (quoted in
Myer 6), Howard Barker's "creative vandalism" of Women
Beware Women is as noteworthy a venture as Stoppard's
own "plundering" of Hamlet in creating Rosencrantz
and Guildenstern are Dead--even though Barker's work
is far more radical and more politically incendiary
than any of Stoppard's own. In rewriting--and/or
revitalizing--Middleton's work, which had been
unproduced from the seventeenth century until several
revivals in the 1960's, Barker has transformed a
little-known Jacobean tragedy into a provocative if
sometimes shrill and shocking affront to the com-
placencies and "received ideas" of our own day.

References

Barker, 1986:   Howard Barker and Thomas
                     Middleton, Women Beware Women.
                     (London: John Calder).

Hurren, 1986:   Kenneth Hurren, review of Women
                     Beware Women. Plays and Players,
                     March 1986:

Kerensky, 1977:   Oleg Kerensky, The New
                     British Drama: Fourteen
                     Playwrights Since Osborne and
                     Pinter. London: Hamish Hamilton.

Middleton, 1969:   Thomas Middleton, Women Beware
                     Women, ed. Charles Barber. The
                     Fountainwell Drama Texts, ed. T.A.
                     Dunn, et al. Berkeley: University
                     of California Press.

Myer, 1986:   Valerie Grosvenor Myer, "Stoppard
                     on the Bard." <u>Plays and Players</u>,
                     February 1986: 24.

Trotter, 1986:   David Trotter, "An End to Pag-
                     eantry." <u>The Time Literary
                     Supplement</u>, 21 February1986: 194.

Dramatic Time and the Production Process:
Reading for Rhythm in Miss Julie and
The Duchess of Malfi

Patrick Kagan-Moore
University of Kentucky

Defining production rhythms through the work of
the actors is one of the most difficult and delicate
processes directors enter into in producing plays. In
rehearsal, the actor must find a way to personify the
rhythms of the character, rather than imposing his own
rhythms, or allowing them to appear imposed by the
writer. In realistic plays, where style and situation
are familiar enough to draw "naturalistic" work out of
the actor, this is often an easy issue. In nonrealis-
tic plays, however, where the landscape of language
and event can seem so alien to modern actors, rhythmic
decisions come harder.

The best way I have found to direct actors toward
a unified vision and coherent acting style is by
acquainting them with the "playworld they are committed to in the work. This playworld concept assumes
an internal unity, not just to the action of the
play, but to its physical, moral, and social environments as well. Taken in this light, a playscript
exists as a small world, a complex system of forces
which governs the actions and beliefs of the characters that live within it. In this essay I discuss
analyzing textual information about time -- a part of
this system which has proven particularly helpful in
the difficult task of developing appropriate rhythms
in performance.

One script which has generated a lot of critical
confusion about performance is The Duchess of Malfi.[1]
Commentary on the play often mentions the troublesome
"evil roles" and how the critic feels they ought to be
played. As Lois Potter states the case, the modern
director "is likely to find himself forced to choose"[2]

---

[1] John Webster, The Duchess of Malfi (London,
1964), edited by John Russell brown. References are
to act, scene, line number.

[2] Lois Potter, "Realism Versus Nightmare:
Problems of Staging the Duchess of Malfi" in The
Triple Bond (London, 1975), 170.

between convention and naturalism in style, and she suggests that neither choice is entirely adequate. Despite this view, I argue here that non-naturalistic plays like the Duchess offer playworlds as coherent as naturalistic ones, and that close examination of temporal information in such plays will help actors to arrive at appropriate choices of rhythm, and indeed, of acting style. To demonstrate briefly how such analysis is used by the actor I used the opening of Miss Julie[3], and then turning attention to The Duchess, I try to shed some light on the acting demands of this difficult Jacobean play.

To begin the process of analysing time early in the rehearsal process, I ask actors to write down all reference to time that their character makes in the play. Such references obviously include information about the past and future as well as the present. They can also include more oblique references to time. "Fresh vegetables, newly picked", for instance, might be an indicator of recent action, or simply of the state of mind of the character. Verbs are often important in this context; a verb like "bustling" says a lot about a character's rhythmic patterns. It is fair to point out that no actor ever fully completes this assignment. In most plays, time so saturates the action that the references are too many to enumerate, and many are simply overlooked. What does happen, however, is that the actor arrives at a greater understanding of his character's way of inhabiting the world -- that he begins to see that his character has a point of view about time that is different than his own. And that understanding provides the first step in developing unique rhythms for the actor that are consistent with the information in the text.

The opening section of Miss Julie is remarkable in its use of time-related imagery. With startling economy, Strindberg reveals a number of things that are immediately useful to actors working on the play:

---

[3] Translation by Arvid Paulson, Seven Plays by August Strindberg (New York, 1960). Subsequent reference to this text.

an overall rhythm to the work; individual character rhythms and patterns of behavior; the direct impact which the past plays in influencing current events; and the watchful, sharp-eyed world that surrounds these characters. Much of this is revealed in the opening speeches, as Jean enters Kristin's kitchen fresh from the dance taking place in the barn:

> JEAN: Now Miss Julie's mad again -- absolutely mad!
> KRISTIN: So -- you're back again, are you?
> JEAN: I took the count to the station, and then I came back and went by the barn. I stepped inside and had a dance. And there I saw Miss Julie leading the dance with the gamekeeper. But the instant she set eyes on me, she dashed straight over to me and asked me to dance the next waltz with her; and from that moment on she has been waltzing with me -- and never in my life have I known any thing like it! She is stark mad!
> KRISTIN: She's always been crazy -- but after the engagement was broken off two weeks ago, she is worse than ever. (p. 77)

The opening illustrates several things. First of all, there is a charged atmosphere on the estate this night. The country dance provides the central metaphor rhythmically, and it is that rhythm (intense, fast-paced forward action, punctuated by brief stops for breath) which dominates the first half of the play. Secondly, action happens in the present. Both Jean and Kristin are active in the present and discuss it in precise detail. Them past events they discuss are very recent ones, and those are discussed only as they relate to the frenzy of this night. Repetitions and word choice reflect this focus on the moment: the words "now" and "again" are used liberally. Just as it is in the original Swedish, the word "now" is used nine times by Arvid Paulson in the first four pages of the translated text.[4] Additionally, there are repeated references to the shortness of time: "instant," "immediately", "is it ready",

---

[4] August Strindberg, Frøken _Julie in Naturalistiska Sorgespel_ (Stockholm: Albert Bonnier, 1920). In fact, the Swedish "nu" appears nine times from the beginning of the play to the initial "pantomime" (117-123).

"dashed straight over to me", "the next one" (pp. 77-80). The effect of this barrage of present-time words is to quicken the energy of the present. Midsummer's Night is charged with life and motion.

Additional pressure comes from the past in this play. Both Jean and Kristin are watchful and judgemental; they observe things that happen around them, and they remember such events for later use. Jean, in fact, is a storehouse of information about Miss Julie's past; he seems to have spied on her for years, and to have seen many critical events in her unhappy life. And as they watch the aristocracy, both Jean and Kristin feel that others are watching them, judging their every action; they seem always aware that they are building a history from which there is no escape. Jean worries about dancing too often with Miss Julie, fears that some might see them together in the kitchen. The peasants "are only too prone to misinterpret, to imagine things," he insists (p. 81).

Within this sharp-eyed, harried world, Strindberg invest his characters with distinct rhythmic patterns, each with a personal "clock" that allows him or her to perceive the world at a particular rate of speed.

Jean, first of all is intimately aware of the present. He doesn't seem to miss anything. He comments on the "mess" that Kristin is cooking up to abort the pregnancy of Miss Julie's dog; he criticizes Kristin for not warming the plate for his snack; insists that she provides him a crystal stem for the wine he pilfers from the Count; and he reacts instantly and indignantly when Kristin playfully musses his hair. He notices things, and he acts on them in petty, often rebellious ways. He's a compulsive man who seeks to control others, and especially to control his "presentation," his immediate theatrical image. Kristin describes him as "more of a fuss-box than the Count himself when he wants to be particular" (p. 78).

By contrast, Kristin seems to live at a distance from the frantic action around her; while she shares his attentive focus on present action, and holds strong opinions about others, she endures things rather than trying to change them. The kitchen in which the action takes place is arranged according to her tastes and needs -- efficient, clean, utilitarian; and that is the structure of Kristin's life. Strindberg illustrates her rhythmic patterns most clearly

106

when he leaves her onstage during the pantomime. In the stage directions, he specifically cautions the actress against getting caught upon the furious peace of the other characters:

> The actress must be in no hurry, as though afraid that the audience might become impatient. Kristin is alone. The faint sound of violin music in the distance, played in schottisch tempo, is heard. She hums the tune while clearing Jean's place at the table, washes the dishes and utensils in the sink, dries them and puts them away in the cupboard. Then she removes her apron, takes out a small mirror from a drawer and places it on the table supporting the mirror against the jar of lilacs. She lights a candle and heats a hairpin, with which she curls her forelock. This done she goes to the door and stands there listening. Then she goes back to the table and discovers Miss Julie's forgotten handkerchief. She sniffs of it; then she distractedly smooths it out and folds it carefully. (p. 81)

Kristin's steady, workaday rhythm is sharply contrasted by the title character, Miss Julie. As she is defined by Jean in the opening speech, Julie is rushed, out of time, travelling faster than the events around her and trying to pull them forward. Her speeches upon her first entrance support this impression strongly:

> MISS JULIE: I'll be back immediately -- you just wait there . . . Well, Kristin, is it ready?
> JEAN: Do you ladies have secrets between you?
> MISS JULIE: No inquisitiveness!
> JEAN: Is it some sort of witches' brew for Midsummer Night that you two ladies are concoting? Something to help you look into the future and see what your lucky star has in store for you -- and get a glimpse of your intended?
>
> MISS JULIE: You have to have good eyes for that. (To Kristin) Pour it into a small bottle and put the cork in tight. -- Now come and dance a schottishe with me, Jean. (p. 80)

In this exchange we see Julie trying to maintain a number of relationships simultaneously and to complete several tasks at once. She wants to hold on to whoever's at the door, to take care of her pregnant dog, to flirt with Jean, and to complete with and to befriend Kristin, all at the same time. She is travelling too fast to see things clearly, her mind racing ahead of the situation in front of her toward what goal we don't know.

Basing rhythmic choices on this admittedly sketchy reading of time information, we see three distinct voices: Kristin -- farseeing, steady and contained -- the drumbeat of fate and social condemnation; Jean -- quicker, eager to exploit opportunities in front of him, and capable of risking his future for present gratification; and Julie, erratic and impulsive, living at a tortuous pace that simply cannot last long. As these voices intermingle, changing in response to one another and the situation, the dance-like rhythm of the play is formed. We also see the unity of Strindberg's playworld. It's a world of fate, where the past will conspire to impact heavily on the present.

Time information in The Duchess is harder to grasp, but it ultimately reflects a playworld as unified internally as the naturalist world of Miss Julie. At the same time, the two playworlds are radically different on nearly all counts. Webster structures time, and his characters view time, in ways that contrast strongly with Strindberg's. We see the difference at the play's outset. As opposed to the frantic opening of Miss Julie, The Duchess begins quietly -- actually in a static "picture gallery" introduction of the play's central characters. As the scene unfolds, Antonio (a courtier to whom things happen throughout the play, but who initiates little action himself) converse with Delio (a character who survives the play's bloodshed -- a "watcher" who remains outside the action). For Delio's benefit, Antonio draws verbal portraits of the central characters as each appears before us: Ferdinand and the Cardinal, brothers to the Duchess; Bosola, the instrument of nearly all the bloodshed in the play; and the Duchess, the play's heroine, round whose life and death the other's futures are formed. Antonio's descriptions of these characters are notable in that they contain few specific references to time:

> ANTONIO: The duke there? A most perverse and turbulent nature:
> What appears in him mirth is merely outside;

> If he laughs heartily, it is to laugh
> all honesty out of fashion. . . .
> He speaks with others' tongues, and hears
>   men's suits
> With others' ears; will seem to sleep o' the
>   bench
> Only to entrap offenders in their answers;
> Dooms men to death by information;
> Rewards by hearsay.
>   (1.1.169-177)

This speech illustrates several points. First of all, the opening movement of the play, the "picture gallery," is an inactive, passive entertainment: one character describing the inner life of others. Here, Webster presents us with stasis as a dramatic choice, and he underscores that choice repeatedly early in the play. Antonio presents Duke Ferdinand, not as an active, powerful ruler, but as a deceptive man who prefers the "offstage" manipulations of hearsay and betrayed trust. Supporting this view, Bosola describes time at court as "dog days," and the Cardinal and Duke Ferdinand as "plum-trees that grow crooked over standing pools; he says his fondest wish at this point is to feed passively on these great men like "a horse leech" (1.1.30-70). And in describing Bosola, Antonio remarks that inactivity acts on him like a corrosive:

> 'Tis great pity,
> He should be thus neglected: I have heard
> He's very valiant. This foul melancholy
> Will poison all his goodness; for, I'll tell you,
> If too immoderate sleep be truly said
> To be an inward rust unto the soul,
> It then doth follow want of action
> Breeds all black malcontents; and their close
>   rearing
> Like moths in cloth, do hurt for want of wearing.
>   (1.1.75-82)

These speeches also show that few of Webster's characters notice the events happening around them. Instead of present action, their attention is generally captured by philosophical matters: issues of human nature, decorum, personal responsibility, or good and evil. As the play progresses, much of this talk concerns the "soul," and serves to frame the play in a context of eternity. Where Strindberg' numerous references to the moment gave a rushed urgency to <u>Miss Julie</u>, Webster's references suggest that life takes place within a limitless void:

> BOSOLA.   Yes, I hold my weary soul in my teeth;
>   'Tis ready to part form me. I do glory
>   That thou, which stood'st like a huge pyramid
>   Begun upon a large and ample base,
>   Shalt end in a little point, a kind of nothing.
>
> (5.5.75-79)

This melancholy "want of action" is underscored in numerous ways: by character attitudes, by the regular use of the passive voice, by images Webster employs, and by the "soft," downbeat quality of many entrances, and much of the play's violent action.

In Bosola's conversation with Ferdinand early in the play, the characters adopt passive role in the world; they take no responsibility for their actions (present or past), and they seem to regard even their own decisions as accidents that are beyond their control:

> BOSOLA.   I was lured to you.
> FERD. My brother here, the Cardinal, could never abide you.
> BOSOLA.   Never since he was in my debt.
> FERD.   May be some oblique character in your face made him suspect you.
> BOSOLA.   Doth he study physiognomy?
>   There's no more credit to be given to th' face
>   Than to a sick man's urine, which some call
>   The physician's whore, because she cozens him: --
>   He did suspect me wrongfully.
> FERD.   For that
>   You must give great men leave to take their times
>   Distrust doth cause us seldom be deceiv'd--
>   You see, the oft-shaking of the cedar-tree
>   Fastens it more at root.
>
> (I.1.232-243)

In this roundabout interchange, Bosola and Ferdinand obscure what is at heart a very simple event. First of all, the use of the passive voice makes the action appear disembodied and accidental. Ferdinand says his brother "could never abide" Bosola; for his part, Bosola feels the Cardinal "did suspect me wrongfully." Apart from the fact that all this language is oblique an inactive, it tends to deaden the impact of Ferdinand's purpose in the scene: bribing Bosola to spy on his sister. Appropriately, Ferdinand repeats the "fixed tree" metaphor in this scene, echoing Bosola' earlier characterization of the great men's inactivity.

This scene reveals that these characters live in a world where men are "made" to feel mistrustful by something as elusive as an "oblique" character of face; and where those who yearn for action, such as Bosola ("Whose throat must I cut," he asks, in response to Ferdinand's bribe), are discourage from taking it. Direct actions (securing Bosola a position at court, for instant) take place offstage either before or after this scene; what happens within it is discussion of mistrust, sadness, and human nature. Such action is repeated often in the play.

Webster's imagery often supports this view also, focusing away from decisive action and referring to a world where time moves very slowly. Bosola says the court is like a hospital, stacked with sick men, waiting to die. Ferdinand, who goes mad after the death of his sister, says that he is "studying the art of patience:"

> To drive six snails before me from this town to Moscow; neither use goad nor whip to them, but let them take their own time; the paitent'st man i' the world match me for an experiment; -- and I'll crawl after like a sheep biter.

> (5.2.45-50)

In his madness, Ferdinand sees time stretching before him into eternity. It's an exceedingly grim image, but it differs only in degree from the way the others have described Ferdinand throughout the play.

Structurally, The Duchess often reflects the same rhythms we see in the verse and character attitudes. Where entrances and exits throughout Miss Julie are strong, marked by urgent needs and rushed imagery, many in The Duchess are "soft." The Cardinal exits quietly during Bosola' speech in the first scene, so quietly that Bosola is surprised by his absence. Ferdinand apparently enters as one of an aimless

111

crowd, with no fanfare, and not especially noticed by
Delio, who says only that the chamber is beginning to
fill up with people. Later in the play, Bosola's
"apricock" conspiracy, in which he attempts to
discover the Duchess' pregnancy, is delayed by two
conversations, one about the qualities of the perfect
courtier, another in which he lectures an old woman
about the sins of the world. Even violent actions in
the play are often muted. The Cardinal dispatches his
mistress with a poisoned book in the course of a few
lines, having given no indication that he would murder
her except that she was beginning to annoy him.

It should be noted that these actions occur in a
bare-stage verse drama, rather than the cluttered
detail of a naturalist stage. The power that the bare
stage lends to the human figure might tend to
strengthen otherwise "weak" entrances. But on any
stage, entrances are made stronger by the support of
an urgent line, and weakened by the absence of
accompany speech. Certainly, Shakespeare is rightly
seen as a master of powerful entrance and exit lines
on the bare stage; and Webster's choice to design
these actions without supportive verse seems to me to
underscore the time fabric of the rest of his play.

All of this time information suggests that the
world of The Duchess is notable for its inactive
characters and dramatic structure. Having said that,
however, I think it is wise to point out that Webster's play also contains many passages that move
very quickly and that reflect powerful motivations.
It is not my intention to say that there's "no
action" in The Duchess, or that there aren't active
characters, or that the less active characters are not
often moved to forceful response. All of these things
are evident in the play, and contribute importantly to
its rhythms. And this kind of dynamic actions must be
considered in order to come up with sensible choices
for performing the play.

The strongest, most active character is the
Duchess herself. Although she hangs in the background in her first appearance, she soon begins to act
decisively. Hounded by her brothers to endure her
widowhood and forsake any attempt to remarry, the
Duchess moves directly from her conversation with them
to propose to her steward, Antonio. This precipitous
action places her at odds with her brothers wishes,
and she reveals to her servant that she's aware of the
potential danger:

DUCHESS: Good, dear soul,
    Leave me; but place thyself behind the
      arras,
    Where thou mayst overhear us; Wish me good
      speed;
    For I am going into a wilderness
    Where I shall find nor path nor friendly
      clue
    To be my guide.
$$(1.1.358-361)$$

In the action that follows, references to present time abound. The Duchess comments often upon Antonio's behavior; she notices that he trembles, that he is distracted, that he's afraid when her servant woman enters the room. She uses the word "now" seven times after she places the ring on his finger, and her speech is dotted with active verbs and present-time phrases: "quickening", "too soon", "I do here put off vain ceremony" (1.1.415-505).

The Duchess is a woman for whom time moves quickly, and that quality is repeated in her later scenes. When we see her next she is late in pregnancy, and she is onstage only briefly before she goes into labor, with "no time" left to remove her to safety. Following that, in another brief appearance she attempts to quiet her brother's suspicions. In her next scene she is betrayed, and decided to send her husband "instantly" to safety. The action around her rushes forward, and she makes decisions moment by moment trying to stem the flood. Although the Duchess expresses hope in the marriage scene that time will heal the bitterness of her brothers, Bosola indicates that time is her enemy, a tool of evil:

    ...the devil takes delight to hang at
    a woman' girdle, like a false rusty watch,
    that she cannot discern how the time passes.
$$(2.2.25-28)$$

As her situation becomes more desperate, the Duchess realizes she has little time left. Increasingly, she reflects upon the fate of her soul and prepares herself spiritually to die. Even then, however, she does not join her brother in melancholy brooding. She maintains contact with action around her. As the executioners stand before her, waiting to carry out the murder, she instructs Cariola about the children's needs:

```
I pray thee, look thou giv'st my little boy
Some syrup for his cold, and let the girl
Say her prayers ere she sleep. [Cariola
    is taken out.]
Now what you please; what death.
```
                                    (4.2.202-205)

The Duchess' repeated references to present time
show that she is a character who, more often than any
other in the play, responds to and has an impact on
the action immediately before her. She is not,
however, a "naturalistic" character to the degree that
we see in Miss Julie. Her past is sketchy, she
develops in the play through a succession of critical
moments rather than a causally linked action, and she
sees the central battleground in this drama as
eternity and the human soul:

```
Pull, and pull strongly, for your able strength
Must pull down Heaven upon me: --
Yet stay; Heaven-gates are not so highly arched
As princes' palaces; they that enter there
Must go upon their knees. [Kneels]
```
                                    (4.2.230-234)

The Duchess shows us, however, that Webster can create
"present time" characters, and that active forces like
the Duchess are not alien to the poetic drama he
writes. In fact, her active presence in the play
serves to highlight the paucity of such action on the
part of many other characters. She provides a ground
against which the stasis of other characters gains
impact.

    Taking all this information in, then, we can
begin to make acting decisions for The Duchess of
Malfi. Although one ought to hesitate before directly
prescribing an "acting style" for these characters,
several things are indicated from this reading of
time:

1. Webster's characters come out of an undefined
    past, and disappear at play's end into a void.
    To the extent that these characters brood upon
    philosophy, mortality, or other abstractions,
    they exist dramatically, as slow, powerful "mask"
    rather than psychological developed characters.
    To the extent that they observe present action
    and pursue attainable, specific goals, they move

114

away from their masklike natures, and come closer to the kind of frantic, present-tense characters we see in naturalistic works like Miss Julie.

2.   The foundation of the actor's work, then, must be the "mask"; he must develop physical and vocal characteristics that can fully exploit the powerful images Webster provides. In accordance with this, since so much of the play's action seeks to avoid direct contact with or impact on other characters, the actor must become comfortable with "playing the mask," using voice and gesture dramatically in a way that presents the character but does not necessarily advance the action of the play.

3.   To succeed, performers must learn to commit physically and emotionally to actions of spectacle. The violent deaths of such epic characters, for instance, will require elaborate pictorial treatment. To an extent, such spectacle might be provided technically through use of lighting or scrims. But the actor must possess the physical agility and strength to perform choreographed movements of some difficulty. Ronald Bryden described this style as "a circus of evil."[5] And it is appropriate to many roles, especially the "evil" characters. It requires the actor to turn off his naturalistic impulses, and invites comparison with contemporary acting styles that rely heavily upon physical and vocal technique: Brechtian theatre of alienation or kabuki, for instance.

4.   All the same, just as in Brechtian theatre, the actor must use the mask to perform more nauralistic actions where appropriate. This does not mean the character will suddenly become Freudian or contemporary in gesture. But the mask must be flexible ("natural") enough to portray the full range of the character's actions.

5.   Finally, actors must ground their work in a vision of time that looks at temporal life as a process resulting in death, and being as an

_____

[5] Ronald Bryden, The Observer, July 18, 1971.

115

eternal, spiritual history. Only in such a
vision can theactor find the truth of these
larger-than-life, curiously inactive characters.

What, then, do we get in terms of rhythm in the
two pieces? How does time information affect the
actor's work? In Miss Julie we see an ensemble of
characters, each with a different view of time, but
each connected intimately to the others and to the
things around him-- affecting and affected by other
characters continually. In The Duchess we find
characters often waiting to act, examining their inner
world, and seeking dominance over the shadowy world of
the soul.

We can also see that there is a "natural" acting
style to the playworld of The Duchess. But the
conditions of life in that world, the accepted sense
of human impotence, make its natural style a radically
different one from that in Strindberg's Miss Julie.

Life Near Death:
Art of Dying in Recent American Drama

Margot A. Kelley
Indiana University

During the late 1970's, a spate of plays with main characters who are dying appeared. The shift of focus in these works--from death to dying by terminal illness--substantiates one character's claim in The Shadow Box that "there's a huge market for dying people right now"[1]. This market is not only "huge," but also fairly new, since progressive, long-term diseases are a comparatively recent development, ironically linked with scientific advances.

This rise of science has altered not only the way we die but also the way we approach death. Although science has replaced religion as a dominant force in Western society, it does not meet the emotional and psychological needs of either the dying person or the survivors. It does not provide a new ars moriendi to replace those that religions offered. Perhaps in response to this perceived lack, Bernard Pomerance, Ronald Ribman, Michael Cristofer, and several others[2] all suggest new arts, and do so by focussing on terminal illness. By pairing the dying protagonists with at least one physically fit character in each work, the playwrights offer a newly defined art of dying, and more importantly, an art of living until the final moment, and an art of living as the sur-vivor. These arts, as presented in The Elephant Man, Cold Storage, and The Shadow Box, are primarily individualized, secularized, and interactive pro-cesses; and they are valuable replacements for the ars moriendi lost when faith became subordinate to technology--the very change which heightened the need for such skills. Quite clearly these plays offer new "mythologies of dying" which incorporate the current

---

[1] Michael Cristofer. The Shadow Box (New York: Drama Book Specialists, 1977) 44. Hereafter cited as SB in the text.

[2] Other plays which consider similar situations include Edward Albee's The Lady from Dubuque, Arthur Kopit's Wings, Brian Clark's Whose Life is it Anyway?, William Hoffman's As Is, and Larry Kramer's The Normal Heart.

fascination with death and dying, while also beginning
to overcome the concurrent reluctance to discuss death
with those who are imminently approaching it.

Although the illness which John Merrick suffers
is never ignored in The Elephant Man, the emphasis is
not initially on the deformity as a terminal condition. Instead, his disfigurement is considered as a
vehicle for social criticism, a view which subsumes
the man to the disease. However, when Merrick is
brought back to the hospital to stay, Treves begins
to realize that Merrick is a human, and deserves the
opportunity to live as one. In scene nineteen,
Treves explains to Gomm that "[Merrick's] achieved
greater and greater normality," and in doing so is
becoming "a mockery of everything we live by"[3]. The
mockery forces Treves to re-evaluate his own vision of
the world, which has been grounded in contemporary
standards. His early contentment as "a scientist in
an age of science" (EM 9) has given way, replaced by
despair because his scientific study of Merrick and of
his other patients has led first to confusion and
second to a belief that England demonstrates "daily by
the way it lives that it want do die" (EM 54).
Treves' confusion originates partly in Merrick's
ability to prompt people to confront and recognize
the limits of their outlook, thereby realizing the
need for a new vision. This capability, rooted in the
world view which his deformity has prompted Merrick
to develop, may be described as Christ-like, a
parallel Pomerance encourages the audience to draw.[4]
However, viewing him as simply an emblem of the
degraded condition of Victorian society or as a
Messianic figure neglects other features which are
equally important.

By attributing an animalistic physiognomy and an
angelic spirit to Merrick, Pomerance empowers the
cliched image of man as mediator between the animal

---

[3] Bernard Pomerance. The Elephant Man (New York:
Samuel French, Inc., 1979) 53. Hereafter cited as EM
in the text.

[4] Merrick's cruciform position during Treves'
lecture, his dying only after constructing a church,
his uncomplaining attitude throughout his suffering,
and his betrayal by Ross are among the details which
strengthen this parallel.

and the spiritual and indicates that Merrick is unquestionably human. Furthermore, by establishing Merrick's humanity, Pomerance had implicitly established Merrick's right to enjoy all the same privileges as other people, including a community, love, faith, and security. However, his illness is so disfiguring that it alienates him from conventional participation in society. Merrick is presumed to have suffered from neurofibromatosis, a non-malignant tumor disorder. In Merrick's case, the involvement was so severe that he, like Treves, would have been able to gauge his debilitation, and would have been aware of his imminent death. Merrick's deliberate preparations for death strongly suggest that he had accepted it, just as he had accepted his disease, and was preparing both himself and Treves for his inevitable departure. His final acts include finishing all uncompleted tasks, and providing Treves with the coping skills to survive alone in his newly altered world.

When Treves brought Merrick to the hospital, he gave him a home and security. By introducing him to the Bishop and Madge Kendal, Treves provided the rudiments of a community, as well as contacts to help Merrick embark upon his quest for faith and love. Before he can die well, Merrick attempts to fulfill these quests; and in scene fourteen, he confides to Kendal that he "need[s] a mistress," but that he think "it is hopeless" (EM 41). She acknowledges that it is unlikely, but generously responds to his subsequent admission that he has never seen a naked woman by baring her torso. The encounter is loving, but not erotic--rather, it is innocent, "for a moment, Paradise" (EM 43) as Kendal explains to Treves. This scene provides the most loving encounter Merrick has.

Merrick embraces religion much more easily. He prays devoutly, shares his beliefs with Treves, and builds a church. While Merrick is finishing his model of "grace flying up and up from the mud" (EM 35), Treves is breaking down, finally aware that his world view is no longer supportable. Acknowledging that science is not enough because he "apparently sees things that other don't" (EM 54) Treves begs the Bishop to help him. At this moment, Merrick places the last piece on his model, and the scene closes as he announces "it is done" (EM 55). Although literally the chapel, the "it" refers also to Merrick's life, which he has lived as fully as possible in order to be ready to die: he has had a moment of love, gained a

certain spiritual and artistic fulfillment in complet-
ing the model, and succeeded in forcing Treves to
question his old vision and begin searching for a new
one. Soon after this, Merrick lies down and dies.

One critic describes Merrick's death alterna-
tively as a murder by society and as the suicide of a
disillusioned man.[5] However, the death need not be
considered so bleakly. Before dying, Merrick deliberately lived as fully as was in his power, and offered
Treves a new perspective. In one of his final lines,
the "scientist in an age of science" states that
Merrick's greatest misfortune was having "a romantic
imagination" (EM 58). Although he retracts this
because he "is not really certain of it" (EM 58), the
more vital, humane view implicit in such an appraisal
is clearly new to Treves, and is more closely aligned
with Merrick's outlook. Merrick has demonstrated--and
therefore shared--a way of living that surpasses mere
existence, an imaginative, innocent mode which
incorporates most human needs and desire (community,
goals, etc.).

The Elephant Man affirms life in the race of
imminent death, and rejects attitudes which lead to
stagnant, death-like existences. In Cold Storage, by
Ronald Ribman, death in life and life in the face of
death are even more emphatically posed as central
concerns. In this play, two men who are patients at
a metropolitan cancer hospital meet, learn to deal
with their diseases, and learn to help one another
cope with death. Parmigian, who is dying of cancer,
enables Landau to realize at last that it is all right
that he survived and escape from Nazi Germany, even
though his parents and sister did not. Through their
interactions, both men acquire new insights and
necessary coping skills--just as Merrick helped Treves
to cast off untenable social mores and Treves helped
Merrick to live comfortably.

Because Ribman has eliminated the physician-
patient relationship, the reader's impulse to cate-
gorize one character as sick and the other as healthy
is immediately thwarted. Instead, Ribman balances
physical and psychological health, creating characters

---

[5] Janet Larson, "The Elephant Man as Dramatic
Parable," Modern Drama 26 (1983): 349-50.

who are equally debilitated, but in different ways. Parmigian, like Merrick, is physically quite ill, but has well developed coping skills. Landau, like Treves, seems healthy and successful, but is psychologically very unhealthy. While both men are clearly quite ill, their encounter teaches each how to live until he must die.

Ribman has defined the two men as opposites. Yet, he manages to undermine the categorizations and the reader's early impressions. Initially, Parmigian seems bitter, rude, and beyond hope-going so far as to urge Landau to help him commit suicide. Polite, soft-spoken Landau is horrified, and tries to persuade Parmigian that he should hold on. After defining the characters by this encounter, Ribman demonstrates that Parmigian is the one clinging desperately to life and that Landau has given up.

Landau's apathy seems incongruous at first. He seems to have enjoyed the great American dream. An uneducated immigrant, he has become an investment advisor in fine arts, with a perfect wife, two perfect daughters, a house on Nantucket, and a standing squash game two afternoons a week. The superficiality of Landau's life is highlighted, though, by Parmigian's ability to accurately describe it after knowing him only ten minutes. Further, Parmigian seems to have intuited not only the surface, but also the deeper facets of Landau's character; and he senses that Landau is emotionally almost dead. Consequently, Parmigian is surprised and pleased when Landau responds sarcastically to his vision of frozen perfection, since sarcasm and insensitivity are the means that Parmigian uses to survive, making jokes to try to stay alive.[6]

Although Landau is offended by Parmigian's cavalier attitude and angered by his pushiness, Parmigian remains undaunted in his attempts to draw Landau out of his empty world into the one of the roof garden. The effort is not purely altruistic: Parmigian needs people to survive, someone to be "interesting" for, someone to interest him. Angered and

---

[6] Ronald Ribman, Cold Storage (New York: Nelson Doubleday, Inc., 1976), 12. Hereafter cited as CS in the text.

frustrated by Parmigian's persistence, Landau realizes
that Parmigian is "interested in anything that isn't
silence" (CS 69) and finally opens up, describing his
escape from Germany, his guilt about surviving, and
his emptiness at living without a past. Parmigian
urges him to live in the present, to realize that he
has "not only survived . . . [but] triumphed" (CS 79).
This speech is undercut by Parmigian's admission that
the "analysis is from a movie [he] once saw" (CS 83).
Nonetheless, Landau does have a breakthrough. Both
men realize that Landau has spend his life waiting for
death, and that now, free from the guilt of surviving, he can actually begin living. The bonding which
occurs also gives Parmigian something to live for, and
the man who "tried to commit suicide three time this
month, and never once . . . [while] in a bad mood" (CS
18) concludes the play promising that tomorrow will be
"a very interersting day" (CS 87).

Parmigian's survival is predicated upon adherance
to a certain world view, just as Merrick's was.
Whereas Merrick offered a traditional, idealistic
vision of love, Parmigian offers a less traditonal,
but captivating outlook--that of Wallace Stevens'
Emperor of Ice Cream, with whom he identifies early in
Act Two.

When Parmigian tells Landau that he ordered ice
cream for dinner, Landau replies that he "can't live
on ice cream" (CS 53). Parmigian insists that a very
famous emperor once did, and that he can too, adding
that when he is "finished with ice cream, if all [he]
can eat is chocolate mousse, then [he is] going to
live on chocolate mousse!" (CS 53). Although this
outburst embarasses the two men, it also cleverly
reaffirms the attitude Parmigian espouses. Like the
Emperor of Ice Cream, Parigian offers a new direction
for life, advocating exuberance while we live instead
of adherence to sanctimonious rituals for death. He
wants Landau to cast away the illusions which he has
allowed to rule his life, and begin a new with self-
awareness and zest.

Just as Landau's outlook on life is improved by
his interaction with Parmigian, Parmigian's view of

death is changed and made less terrifying by Landau.[7]
Parmigian is able to articulate his fears, realize
that he is "waiting for the courage to die" (CS 61),
and remind himself of his own need to live as fully as
possible. Landau is a physical reminder that survival
without life is simply another form of death, and
assisting Landau helps Parmigian to continue.

Parigian's condition reminds us that technology
enables people to survive much longer than they
"live." Consequently, society feels a new need to
find coping mechanisms that will help the terminally
ill to truly live and will help their survivors to
accept their changed world. This new responsibility
for dealing with terminal illness that society shares
with individual families is frequently stressed in
contemporary death and dying psychology; and the
hospice of The Shadow Box represents a societal rather
than individual coping mechanism intended to help
people to die well. It allows and encourages acceptance of the proximity of death, but without the
negative associations and appearance of a hospital,
like the one Landau and Parmigian were in. However,
acceptance of death cannot be imosed either by setting
or by another person, and the tensions rising from the
conflict between awareness and denial are central to
this play.

The characters in The Shadow Box dramatize the
five stages of dying that Elisabeth Kübler-Ross
outlined in On Death and Dying: denial, anger,
bargaining, depression, and acceptance.[8] While the
stages can overlap, the prevailing emotion must be
acceptance in order for the individual to live fully
at the end, and for the survivors to retain emotional
equilibrium. Of the three characters who are dying,

---

[7] Gerald Weales, "Ronald Ribman: Artist of the
Failure Clowns," in Essays on Contemporary American
Drama Eds. Hedwig Bock and Albert Wertheim (München:
Max Hueber Verlag, 1981), 83.

[8] Elisabeth Kübler-Ross, On Death and Dying (New
York: Macmillan, 1969). Donald Duclow makes a similar
observation in "Dying on Broadway" Contemporary Drama
and Mortality," Soundings 64 (1981), 207.

Joe and Brian have accepted death; the third, Felicity, is angry and still bargaining for time. Consequently, she is not able to live as the others do.

Joe is a simple, open character who explains that "you get scared at first. Plenty. And then you get pissed off" (SB 6). But he then concludes that "it happens to everybody, right?" (SB 7). Because he has reached this point, he regards the stay in the hospice almost as a vacation, which his wife Maggie will love. The early part of their time together is marred, though, by her inability to accept his approaching death. She refuses to discuss his condition with Joe or their son, and will not even enter the cottage--as if staying outside will insure that Joe will not die. She feels abandoned and frightened, and she begs Joe to come home. When he refuses, saying that he is going inside to tell Stephen that he is dying, she makes him tell her first. Hearing it enables her to finally accept it, and she agrees to go inside, so that Joe does not have to struggle alone. Maggie is the least independent of the survivors, and needs the most guidance from the dying person. The role-reversal is carried to an extreme to show that coping is an interactive process--both parties need help, and both must be able to offer some strength.

Agnes and Felicity show a similar reluctance to confront and thereby cope with imminent death. Although Felicity realizes she is dying, she remains angry--telling the interviewer that she's a "corpse [with] one lung, one plastic bag for a stomach, and two springs and a battery where [her] heart use to be" (SB 36). She fluctuates between this aggressive hostility and a pathetic docility, waiting for letters from her daughter Claire. Trying to give meaning to the remainder of Felicity's life, Agnes began writing letters ostensibly from Claire, who had run away as a teenager, and died shortly thereafter. However, the Interviewer attributes Felicity's unanticipated longevity to a bargain that she has probably made with herself to live until Claire comes to visit.

The result of this kind deception is an inability for either Felicity or Agnes to live. Since Felicity will not accept her death in a meaningful way, she cannot come to terms with it. Further, Agnes endures the difficult task of caring for her mother, and loses her own energy and vitality in the process. The failure to cope underscores the sadness of a death without new life.

Brian, by contrast, lives more fully in the time shortly before his death than he had up until that point. In his opening interview, he expresses not only acceptance of his approaching death, but also goes on to say that it is "a relief--if you think about it . . . if you think clearly about it" (SB 16). His resignation allows him to live in his last few weeks. He explains to Beverly that he is writing again because "when they told me I was on my way out. . . I realized that there was a lot to do that I hadn't done yet. So I figured I better get off my ass and start working" (SB 43). Approaching death intellectually, he reasons that "the only way to beat this thing is to leave absolutely nothing behind" because if it is "all used up" he can "happily leap into [his] coffin and call it a day" (SB 46).

While Brian explains his preparations and upcoming death sometimes calmly, and sometimes almost exuberantly, neither his lover, Mark, or his former wife, Beverly, can entirely cope with Brian's disease. Mark is horrified and disgusted by the illness itself, and frightened at the thought of Brian actually dying. He clings to "a bad case of the hopes" (SB 87), and Beverly is afraid that this hope will hurt Brian, realizing as Brian does that living now begins with acceptance of death. Both Mark and Beverly are frightened; and while they believe in Brian's ability to cope, they can not completely share his acceptance of the inevitable.

Even though Maggie, Beverly, and Mark have not reached the same degree of resolution about their fate that Joe and Brian have, they share in the final affirmation of life and death in the closing line of the play. These characters enumerate all that they have, and Brian observes that "they tell you you're dying, and you say all right. But if I am dying . . . I must still be alive" (SB 101). Given that, each of them affirms that what remains are "this smell, this touch," "this taste," "this breath," and lastly "this moment" (SB 102). The moving affirmation of the need to embrace "this moment" epitomizes the art of living that this play advocates. Only Felicity and Agnes do not participate in the affirmation; instead, Felicity repeatedly asks "what time is it?" to which Agnes replies "I don't know." because they have not reached

125

any resolution about their fates, they remain locked in a temporal framework, unable to transcend the fear of finitude that the others are beginning to escape.

While the definition of a new art of dying is obviously crucial to these works, developing an art of living is equally-- if not more--important. All three plays describe the coping skills that the dying employ and offer to their survivors; and all three stress that these skills must be defined and refined by the individuals. The few techniques offered by society are not, finally, sufficient.

Merrick in The Elephant Man offers a positive, rather innocent outlook which Pomerance does not make identical to traditional religious faith. This attitude is characterized by love and honesty, in contradistinction to Treves' analytical scientism and the aristocrats' shallow belief that money and power are central. The coping mechanism in Cold Storage is even less concretely defined, yet it provides a valuable secularized mode for living and for approaching death. Parmigian wants life to be "interesting," a nebulous way of describing all that moves daily live beyond mere existence. Further, he demonstrates to Landau that survival is predicated upon the rejection of superficiality and empty routine, with the subsequent replacement of those by the "Emperor of Ice Cream" attitude that his struggle with"the emperor of diseases" (CS 65) has foregrounded. Similarly, the characters in The Shadow Box embody certain approaches to life and death which are not merely dramatizations of Kübler-Ross's stage of dying. Brain lives frantically, with the same need for completion that Merrick exhibited, and with both an intellectual and an emotional acknowledgement of his imminent end. These provide some comfort and reassurance for Beverly and Mark. Joe's acceptance helps Maggie to realize that his death is not her end; if he can face death, then she can face life without him. Both men's modes of acceptance are largely extensions of their ways of facing life. Through her failure to cope with life or death, Felicity counterpoints all the characters who do manage.

Each of the characters who "lives" does so by using his usual coping mechanisms to the limit, urging the survivors to acquire the same skills.

Hence, the actual art of living remains a highly individualized and personal effort. In the absence of strong religious foundations, or of viable socially or scientifically defined methods, Pomerance, Ribman and Cristofer maintain that people must define this art by relying upon themselves and those immediately around them to live, to die, and to survive.

The Reappearance of Chaerephon in Aristophanes' Wasps

Bruce H. Kraut
University of Georgia

The cameo appearance of Chaerephon in the Wasps is a difficult scene to interpret. To comprehend the purpose of this unexpected entrance we must recognize a certain type of comic allusion in which the playwright requires his audience to recall his previous opera and thus follow the dramatic tradition established by the poet.

Aristophanes' Wasps focuses on the character of Philocleon, the epitome of the litigation-crazed Athenian juror, who must be physically restrained by his own son to keep him from making his daily pilgramage to the Law-Court in anticipation of entertainment from the anxious defendants, a few pennies from the government, and the satisfaction of exerting some control over the lives of others. In the course of the play, Plicoleon's son succeeds in dissuading the old man from his inveterate habits, and tries as best he can to prepare his father for life with the so-called "better" elements of society. His training takes the form exclusively of the proper manners for a cocktail party concentrating on the most appropriate sorts of stories to tell when in the company of the elite. The final episodes of the drama concern the disastrous results of Philocoleon's foray into "higher" society, and it is one particular moment from those episodes that concerns us here.

The scene is as follows: After the dinner party at which Philocleon has wreaked such havoc,[1] three plaintiffs appear successively on stage to demand satisfaction from the old man. The second plaintiff is a bread-seller, Myrtia (1396), who claims that Philocleon owes her recompense for striking her with a torch and stealing "ten-obols' worth of bread and an additional four loaves" from her basket. In response to Philocleon's flippancy (he fans the fire of her anger by relating an "Aesopic" story in which he overtly depicts the bread-seller as a "bitch",

---

[1] This is offstage action, described by the slave, Xanthias, in lines 1299-1325.

1401ff.) she vows (1406ff.) to drag him into court with "this fellow Chaerephon" as her summons-witness:

> So you deride me?! I shall summon you--
> whoever you are -- before the market clerks
> for damaging my wares, using as my witness
> this fellow Chaerephon here."

Chairephonta toutoni, in the Greek, indicated that Chaerephon is actually on stage at the time. This is certainly the person she was addressing as she entered at line 1388: "For the Gods' sake, please, come and stand by me!" That this is the Chaerephon whom we know as the crony of Socrates becomes clear from Philocleon's description of his as yellow, the common comic depiction of the sallow-complected Chaerephon, at 1413.[2] This is a rare, if not the only, instance in the extant plays of Aristophanes where the poet bothers to name a witness,[3] and we must conclude that there is a point to the physical appearance of Chaerephon on stage at this juncture. Is he brought on solely for the purpose of mocking his sallow countenance, or is there perhaps a more fitting purpose to his role as summons-witness here? Mac-Dowell[4] (ad loc) expresses the frustration felt by many commentators on this problem:

> But why does Aristophanes select him to be
> the Bread-seller's summons-witness? There
> must have been something funny about
> linking him with a bread-seller or with a
> summons..Although he says nothing, a good
> deal may be made of his appearance and
> behavior. No doubt the actor wears a

---

[2] Cf. Clouds 503f. and Eupolis frg. 239.

[3] Plutus 499 may be another exception. Other instances where a witness is called for: Clouds 1218, 1416 (and note the general use of martyromai without a person specified), 1222; Acharnians 927; Wasps 1436; Peace 1119; Birds 1031; Frogs 528; Plutus 932; frg. 245.

[4] Douglas M. MacDowell, Aristophanes: Wasps, text with introduction and commentary (Oxford, 1971).

grotesque yellow mask, and he may ape the Bread-seller's gestures of perform other antics not mentioned in the dialogue.

It is no doubt possible that Chaerephon is meant to clown around on stage and thus ad to the bomolochic humor of the situation, but the role of the mimicking clown is already taken up by Philocleon throughout this scene, and to introduce a secondary bomolochus at this point would rather detract from the humorous antics of the protagonist than add more mirth to them; and it still does not explain the selection of Chaerephon for this purpose in this play.

There is one possible explanation for Chaerephon's presence which is suggested by an appreciation of the uses and importance of comic allusion in the plays of Aristophanes. Allusion is understandably a staple of comic expression, for it is the basic of parody. Parody of al kinds provides inexhaustible fuel for the comic playwright, and the recognition of the various forms of parody provides plentiful research for the scholar interested in comic techniques. The more obvious form of parody operates by allusion to the playwright's environment, borrowing (and altering) notable institutions, individuals, and dramatic scenes with which the audience would be familiar through the prevalence, frame, or notoriety of the object being parodied.

Yet, there is also a subtler form of parodic allusion; one which functions by back-referencing the tradition established by the playwright himself, that is, a kind of self-allusion in which the poet can reach back to his own productions with more or less reminiscence and remind the audience (with then necessary mnemonics) of material from one of his earlier plays. Such self-reference in the play of Aristophanes ranges from the obvious to the highly-subtle (and at time highly-speculative). Measuring from the meager remains of Old Attic Comedy, we see that self-allusion tends to be strongest between plays performed closer together in time, with the play alluded to still well within the memory of the audience, as we might naturally expect. Certainly, self-allusion in comedy reflects the distinct assertiveness of the ego of the poet within this genre, an assertiveness which reveals itself most clearly in the anapaests (the parabasis proper) of the earlier extant drama,[5] but with varying degrees also in other portions of all of the extant works of Aristophanes (and even with some frequency in the fragments of his own and his contemporaries' productions). In the Acharnians of 425, for example, Aristophanes uses his protagonist, Dicaeopolis, as his mouthpiece quite explicitly at the introduction to the play's agon when he recalls the litigious reaction of Cleon to Aristophanes' previous play, the Babylonians:

> Cleon cannot attack me this time on the grounds that I speak ill of the city in the presence of foreigners. (Ach. 502f.)

Self-allusion compels the audience to recall the previous works of the playwright and to string them together in a theatrical biography of the playwright, thus admitting and accepting a continuity in the poet's work, as though one central thread of genius tied all this diverse plots together.

Aristophanes composed several plays which bear the same titles as previous plays of his. We know, for example, that he wrote another play entitled Peace. In 408 he produced a play called Plutus and in 388 another play by the same name. There is also a second version of Thesmophoriazuase, of which several fragments survive. One cannot always tell whether duplicated titles signify two plays loosely based on the same theme or a reworked version of essentially the same plot. In the case of Aristophanes' clouds, however, we are fortunate to have what is undoubtedly a revised version of an earlier play, changed in some scenes, identical, or nearly so, in others. Allusion to the first version of this comedy plays an important role in the second version, especially concerning the failure of the original (it took the third prize); in fact, the impression left by the parabasis of this second attempt would have us believe that the whole purpose of composition of another version of Clouds was to reaffirm the worth of the first version and give the judges a second opportunity to acclaim it. If we had more of the original for comparison, I suspect we would find that this "obsession" pervades

---

[5] The parabases of Acharnians, Knights, Clouds, Wasps, and Peace comments heavily on this tradition, recalling the worth of Aristophanes as well as the worthlessness of his adversaries.

not only that section which typically defends the artistry of the poet but also other portions of the play which are more obviously part of the plot, in lines which are spoken more clearly in character.

Whether or not this second version was actually performed is a difficult question to answer, but the most acceptable range of dates for its composition falls between the years 420 and 417.[6] That would place this second version at least three years after the production of the original, which was put on at the City Dionysia in 423 B.C. Awareness of this interval may help to explain the need for the numerous "overt" references to the audience is likely to have forgotten details of the first performance in the intervening years, and after so may other dramatic productions. Since Clouds II does indeed drive substantial meaning from the text and failure of the original version of clouds, and due to the identity of the titles of the two plays, we are apt to draw a comparison between those two plays alone, while failing to observe that another play, produced directly after the first Clouds, actually contains our earliest commentary on the play; I am referring of course, to Wasps. And one should note that although it is not as "obsessed" with the outcome of that first performance of Clouds, Wasps does openly comment on Clouds in the parabasis and does also, I believe, demand of the audience that it compares certain portions of the two, consecutive plays.

With Wasps we are dealing with a different situation in terms of the mnemonics of allusion, for Wasps was Aristophanes' first performance after the original Clouds (Wasps was produced at the Lenaean festival of 422. The Lenaea took place sometime in January, the City Dionysia toward the end of March). The parabasis proper of Wasps, like that of Clouds II, draws its raison d'etre from the dramatic context itself; and like the corresponding passage from Clouds II it relates closely with those portions of the drama which reflect on the poet and his art. These anapaests present a strong statement in defense of the dramaturgical powers of Aristophanes. Part of this defense springs from the failure of his entry at the City Dionysia of 423, Clouds:

---

[6] Cf. Kenneth Dover, <u>Aristophanes' Clouds</u>, p. xxviiif.

Now then, people, pay close attention, if
you want to hear the real thing. For the
poet is anxious to chastize is audience,
because he says that in return for the many
good things he did for you before, you have
done him wrong (1015-17).

Since in the second version of Clouds Aristophanes
returns to this topic, we are not surprised to find
that he expresses his dissatisfaction with the
reception of Clouds in terms similar to those he
penned in Wasps:

I was routed underservedly, beaten by a
bunch of clowns. I blame the sophisticated
spectators for that, since for you I was
always concerned.

That is to say, in composing Clouds II Aristophanes
resumed the thread of criticism begun in his first
commentary on Clouds I.

Despite the difference in subject matter of
Clouds and Wasps, between philosophy on the one hand
and law on the other, Aristophanes pictured the plays
as at least similar enough in some respect to warrant
similar comments concerning his abilities as a
dramatist and poet. The most striking point of
contact between the Clouds plays and Wasps, outside
the parabases, is to be found in the characterization
of the protagonists, Strepsiades and Philocleon' and I
think that with Clouds only months behind them the
spectators would have recognized these similarities:
of age, of disillusionment, of role-reversal with a
son, of general uneducability and incorrigibility, and
of certain "poetic" qualities which both of these
characters share with the playwright himself, mainly
in terms of the use of parody and the object of the
parody (whom we recognize as favorite victims of
Aristophanes' wit). The ego of the poet thus emerges
on stage both in the aforementioned section of the
play, which invites us to trace numerous similarities
from one protagonist to the next; these similarities
are particularly illuminating between plays of
chronological proximity, where the audience might well
be expected to have the protagonist from the poet's
previous work still fresh in mind. Philocleon reminds
us of Strepsiades not only in his general behavior and
social status but also in that we find too in Wasp
this correspondence between the poet and the protagonist, particularly in the episodes, those scenes which

follow the parabasis. The spectator watching the performance of Wasps would have been struck by certain points of comparison between it and Cloud (from the previous dramatic festival, a matter of only months before). He is likely to have easily kicked up on larger similarities of characterization (specifically between the protagonists, Strepsiades and Philocleon) as well as on subtler allusions. This recognition of the close identity of Strepsiades with Philocleon along with an understanding of the principles of self-allusion in Aristophanes helps us, I believe, to solve the puzzling reference to Chaerephon in Wasps.

Although he does not appear on stage in the second version of the Clouds, there are several tantalizing references to Chaerephon in that play which intimate that in the original version he actually did appear, and probably played an extensive role. Dover's assessment is logical:

> In view of the prominence given to Chaere-
> phon 'offstage' in 104, 144ff., 156ff., and
> 1465, it is also legitimate to wonder
> whether he had a part in the original
> version or in an early (but superseded)
> stage of revision.

In some mss. there is also the attribution of one of the final lines of Clouds (1505) to Chaerephon, at the point when Strepsiades is incinerating the Phrontisterion. Even though that attribution may be the result of scribal error, the error itself may have been inspired by a text in which Chaerephon did, in fact, play a larger part, namely the first version of the play. If the reference to Chaerephon in Wasps is intended to recalled a dramatic scene from an earlier play in which the sallow-faced philosopher played a larger part and perhaps was abused by the comic hero of the play, that play, I suggest, was Clouds I.

The identifiable points of contact between Strepsiades and Philocleon, the parallelism between the episodes in these two temporally proximal plays, in which both protagonists turn away adversaries with twisted parodic usage of a new kind of knowledge or training, and the insistent connection toward the end of each play between the hero and poet make the Chaerephon allusion both comprehensible and humorous. He steps out of the pervious play and into the present one to bring his mocker (Strepsiades/Philocleon/Aris-tophanes; remember the words of the Bread-seller:

"whoever you are!", "hostis ei", 1406) to trial.
Aristophanes achieves his joke by using the com-
monality of his comic hero, the natural extension of
his own genius, to take yet another swipe at Chaerephon, and at the same time to fashion a tighter link
within his personal theatrical tradition. Just as
Aristophanes stepped forward to remind us in the
parabasis, "in his own voice," of his previous play
so now in the episodes a character from that very
play enters and meets the projection of the poet
outside the parabasis, the comic hero, the one who
achieves time and again all of those "beneficent
deeds" which the poet claims to continually accomplish
in and through his dramas for the sake of his audience
and his society, giving the hero and Aristophanes
("whoever you are!) yet another chance at winning our
applause.

Lorenzaccio and the Drama of Narration

John W. MacInnes
New College of University of South Florida

For a number of years I read this "armchair" play as a film scenario ahead of its time or as the French say: avant la lettre. The thirty-eight scene changes, which sometimes follow upon each other at a staccato pace, result in a stage play that is unwieldy in practice but which at the same time offers the armchair reader of our century a vivid, filmic spectacle to the imagination. To my mind Lorenzaccio was a cinema script written, now to distort the French phrase, not so much avant la lettre but avant l' image. When I learned that a cinematic adaptation of the play had in fact been done in the 1950's, my sense of Musset as a proto-cinéaste was only confirmed. But later readings of the play have caused me to reconsider this line of thought. Despite the rapid shifts of setting and the punctuation of the drama by breathless little scenes, Lorenzaccio ultimately fails as a film scenario for one family obvious reason: too many characters--especially the hero--talk too much. Lorenzaccio is no more a scenario awaiting the advent of its proper technology than is Richard II, and perhaps--given the bulk of its prose--even less so.

One might, at this point, sigh--thinking of the récit de Théramène that bring Racine's Phèdre to its end--and conclude that discursive theater is merely an inherit French convention, or even curse. More sympathetically one might point out that Lorenzaccio is an historical tragedy whose genre requires a good deal of narrative exposition in order to make clear the setting and conflicts against which the more persona drama of Lorenzo is set. I quite agree with this sympathetic defense of the play's discursivity: the elaborate plotting between the Marquise and the Cardinal, for example, or the heroic call to revolt by the elder Strozzi, need a good deal of explanation in order to be situated in the context of the play. I would call all such passages which function thus first-level narratives. I would not wish to demean them by that categorization; in fact, I am merely reiterating a distinction made by John Dryden in his "Essay of Dramatic Poesy" in 1668. But I want to suggest that these are narratives of contextualization, and can be distinguished from a second level of narration whose source and focus are Lorenzo alone. On this second level, Lorenzo is engaged in narrating himself--in the telling of his self--because, as he puts it: "The world has to know a bit about who I am, and what it is."[1] This second level of narration, this self-presentation and self-representation, constitute as much of Lorenzo's personal drama as do any of his acts on stage: whether or not he kills the Duke is secondary to our appreciation of just who it is who might kill the Duke, and of the ultimate absurdity of that act. It is the telling, not the doing, that gives Lorenzo his fascinating texture, and that makes him less than a mere cinematic actant and more, perhaps, and enterprise, as Nietzsche's Ecce Homo is an enterprise, to be contemplated from the comfort of an armchair.

Lorenzo must tell himself because he cannot act himself. In order to win the confidence of the Duke whom he wants to assassinate, he must fawn and feign, becoming the Duke's procurer and dissembling his own virility to the point of fainting at the sight of an unsheathed sword. The play opens with a scene at night in a garden, where Lorenzo and the Duke accomplish a rendez-vous with a young Florentine--a tryst that Lorenzo has not only arranged, but over which he now gloats. The scene is interrupted when the girl's brother happens upon the Duke, Lorenzo, and their guards. He decrys the corruption of Florence by the pandemic lascivity which thrives under the Duke's rule. He announces that Florence has become "a forest full of bandits, full of poisoners and dis- honored girls" (336), and is about to take his complaint to the Duke when it is revealed to him that the Duke stands before him, disguised in a cloak. The outrage brother can only desist, and the scene ends. This scene is only two pages long and runs only a few minutes, but it evokes a pair of themes that will govern the rest of the play.

First, there is that theme so dear to Neo- classical French theater: the disparity between appearance and being. While they await the girl 's

---

[1] Théatre I, Garnier-Flammarion, Paris, 1964, p. 397. The translation is my own, as are all other translations from French texts cited. Further refer- ences to Lorenzaccio will be from this edition of the text, and given in parentheses following the citation.

arrival, Lorenzo recounts to the impatient Duke the true character he had espied beneath her appearance or morality:

> Bourgeois mediocrity personified! Moreover, she's the daughter of solid folk, whose lack of wealth has not allowed her a solid upbringing; no depth to her principles, nothing but a thin veneer; but what a violent current of a magnificent river running beneath that layer of thin ice that cracks with each step! Never has a flowering bush promised rarer fruits, never have I sniffed in so childish an air a more exquisite odor of whoredom (334-5).

This theme is echoed visually by the cloaked disguise both Lorenzo and the Duke are wearing, of course, and is further reinscribed in the possible excess of Lorenzo's florid language. We are led to wonder from the start whether this vile procurer, so clearly witty and bright by contrast to his fellows, does not also have some raging torrent hidden beneath his icy amorality.

But this first theme, though evoked with economy and complexity--since it not only calls in to question the truth of the world's appearance but that of our protagonist--is linked to a second one right from the start, which is the decline of patriarchal authority. The rule of the old laws, we are told by the brother, may no longer exist; scoundrels, he says, are cutting the throats of families and dishonoring their daughters; and the brother himself is shown to be impotent in the face of the Duke's armed guards. The danger that has been loosed upon the world of Florence under the reign of Duke Alexandre is clearly not limited to the political decline of a republic toward militarily-enforced tyranny: beyond the question of which form of government might best rule the city lies the issue of the law, the family, and the virtue of maidens, or--in Lacanian terms--the issue of the father's name and its authority. One of the guards announces to the bewildered brother: "Ta soeur est dénichée..." (336), which we can translate as "your sister has flown off from the nest," or even, to reflect better the brutal level of discourse, "Your sister has flown the coop." Your sister, in other words, is no longer a procreative being under your patriarchal control. Beyond-- but not far beyond--the question of equality among men lies the question of the pleasures and powers of women who are no longer under paternal guard. The political institution that is at stake, as numerous allusions and metaphors throughout the play make clear, is not just the republic, but the patriarchal order itself. The alternative to that order is the chaos of harlotry.

Two themes, then, have been evoked in parallel: the theme of appearance versus being, and that of the threat to patriarchal security imposed by libertinage. Those themes will not remain in mere parallel, but will ultimately become entwined in Lorenzo's attempt to tell who he is in contrast to who he only appears to be. The height of that telling occurs in the third scene of the third act, in a long conversation between Lorenzo and Philippe Strozzi--the patriarch sans pareil in the play. The scene begins when two of Philippe's sons are arrested and taken to tribunal by a horde of German officers. As the crowd that had been witness to the arrest dissipates, Philippe is left alone, seated on a bench, when Lorenzo suddenly appears to ask with mocking insolence whether Philippe has taken to begging in the street. Philippe replies that he is indeed a beggar--an old man reduced to begging for justice. Musset has recreated, we might note, the scene of Le Cid in which Don Diègue must enlist his young son's aid in reestablishing the family's name. Philippe repeats to Lorenzo, in effect, that famous question: "Rodriguez as-tu du coeur?" But he does not receive in return the proud answer of a Rodriguez.

The actual question that Philippe puts to Lorenzo runs:

> You are a Medicis yourself, but only in name; if I know you at all, if the hideous comedy you play has left me an impassive and faithful spectator, then may the man now distinguish himself from the histrion. If you have ever been anything that I deem honest, then be so today. Pierre and Thomas are imprisoned (388).

It takes Lorenzo ten pages of text to respond to Philippe's urging. In the course of his response he reveals his secret dream of entering the annals of history by murdering a tyrant, his initial desire to assassinate Clement VII before being bannished from Rome, and his present plunge into debauchery in order to gain the confidence of Duke Alexandre so as to murder him. The entire reply to Philippe forms one of the great document of nineteenth-century French literature, and clearly paves the way to much of the literature off our century that is classed under the rubrics of Existentialism and Absurdity: I do not intend to do it justice in a few minutes here. I would like briefly to focus on its climactic moment however, in which Lorenzo's self-narration gets to the heart of things, reaches its rhetorical apogee, and shows the extent to which the themes of being and of sexual threat have become inextricably intertwined.

In the course of his narration to Philippe, Lorenzo tells of how he conceived a quasi-Sartrian to project for himself one night:

> My youth was as pure as gold. During twenty years of silence thunder piled up in my breast, and I must now in reality be a spark of lightning because, suddenly, one night when I was sitting in the ruins of the Colosseum, I stood up for some unknown reason, I stretched toward the sky my arms soaked with dew, and I swore then that one of the tyrants of my country would die by my hand. I was at the time a peaceful student whose only concern was the arts and sciences, and I cannot tell you how it was that this foreign promise happened within me. Maybe it is the same kind of thing one feels upon falling in love (391).

Lorenzo has indeed fallen in love--with an image of himself as a great man in the service of humanity, or what he describes as:

> A statue who would step down from his pedestal to walk among men in the public square is something like what I was the day I began to live with the idea that I had to be another Brutus (3902)

But to fulfill this desire, he goes on, he has had to become vile, and yet despite al the viscious acts he has committed to gain the Duke's trust he still walks the streets with impunity His very existence, therefore, has become scandal in which is fellow citizens are implicated by virtue of their approbation.

141

As he puts it:

> And here I am in the street, me, Lorenzac-
> cio? and children don't toss mud as I pass?
> The beds of girls are still hot with my
> sweat and their fathers don't take their
> knives and brooms to assail me as I walk
> by?... Poor mothers shamefully lift their
> daughter's veil when I stop at their door;
> they show me the girl's beauty with a smile
> more treacherous than Judas' kiss while I,
> pinching the little one's chin, clench my
> fist in anger and shuffle in my pocket four
> of five stinking pieces of gold (394).

Lorenzo's project to become a second Brutus has led
him, then to observe an aspect of humanity that has
shaken his faith in the value of the project itself.
His narration continues toward a lurid climax:

> ...all masks fell before my gaze; humanity
> lifted its dress and showed me, as it might
> to an connaisseur worthy of her, its
> monstrous nudity. I saw men as they are,
> and I asked my self: for whom, then, am I
> working? (394-5).

As I said earlier, the themes of true being and of
sexual threat become intricated throughout the play;
in this moment of Lorenzo's self-narration they are
solidly bound together. That Musset should have
Lorenzo formulate his disillusion in this particular
way is an event we might well take time to consider.
The general metaphorizaiton of truth as nudity
appealed to Musset as a general rule. We read in his
Confessions, for example:

> This baneful idea that truth is nudity came
> to me in relation to everything. The world,
> I told myself, calls its make-up paint
> "virtue," its rosary "religion," its
> trailing cloak "suitability." ... It goes to
> church, to balls, to assemblies; and when
> evening has come it unknots its dress, and
> one sees a naked bacchant with a pair of
> goatfeet.[2]

---

[2] Confessions d'un enfant du siècle, Gallimard,
1946, p. 149.

This is not the occasion to speculate on how "the world" or "le monde," a masculine noun in French, becomes surprisingly transformed into a "bacchant," nor on the additional complexity of the image of a goatfooted celebrant of Bacchus. It is more to the point to note that such problematic confusions of gender disappear from Lorenzo's narration, in which the feminine noun "humanité" lifts her logically consistent skirt to reveal her naked truth to a shocked and frightened Lorenzo. In the dramatic narrative, the scene is simple and consistent: feminine nudity is perceived as monstrous because it is "read," so to speak, as the simultaneous reality and threat of castration. "Humanity" plays the role of the Medusa, as Freud outlined it in his essay in 1922. But Lorenzo, being already a statue who has stepped off his pedestal--and an old mutilator of statues as well, we might recall--is not turned to stone in the face of the Medusa. Whereas Feud had read the stoniness as a phallic erection, to be brandished as a denial of fear and awe, Musset's Lorenzo might be said more to melt or shrivel, when confronted by humanity's truth. if we follow the phantasmatic logic of the narrative's imagery, the truth of humanity appears as the fact of castration, which intervenes to disrupt the project of a narcis-sistic erection of the self as a reified, statuesque construct.

One might interpret Lorrenzo's narrative sequence in terms that are fairly strictly Lacanian, at this point. That is to say, one might stress the extent to which the sexual-political climate that reigns in Florence under the Duke has raised to the point of verbal intrusion all the anxiety that habitually underlies patriarchal systems--anxieties concerning the mythic, cultural, contingent nature of the forces that determine the Symbolic order. The rule of the Name-of-the Father depends, after all, on a kind of patriarchal stability that has been undermined by Lorenzo in his dealing for the Duke: it is not then surprising to find him reacting with hysterical rhetoric to the collapse of an order upon which his own identity depends. The drama of Lorenzo's self-narration, in this case, would be the story of a man first engaged in a narcissistic infatuation with a phallic representation of the self, but who, in pursuit of that representation, comes to discover in humanity a form of generalized lack in being: the truth behind the appearance would turn out to be what Lacan calls a failure-to-be-there, or a failure to find oneself present, as presence, in the symbolic, patriarchal order of the world. And that reading of Lorenzo's story is certainly justified by the hysterical register of his language, and ought to be taken into consideration.

But there is another, equally compelling, psychoanalytic account of the dynamics of human situations that is lately being foregrounded in the reading of Freud. Recent readings by Derrida, Deleuze, Lacoue-Labarthe, and Borch-Jakobsen have increasingly stressed the role played by identification in the continual formation of any human subjectivity. As Borch-Jakobsen puts it in his book, Le Sujet freudien, desire operates at a primary level not as the desire for an object, but as the desire to be or become a subject. Implicated in this desire is the role of a model who is construed as having that mode of subjectivity that the non-subject wants for himself. In Jakobsen's terms:

> We can then reach the following conclusion about the relation between identification and desire. Desire does not work by means of dissimulation, of deformation or dis-placement; it is not a matter of Enstellung (Freud's term for dream distortion). To present things in this way would be yet again to suppose that the subject of desire precedes his mask, precedes his phantasmatic places (his Stellen). It would be to suppose the subject, the servitor of representation (the subjectum, the hupokeimenon). And while that supposition would lead us back to the ineradicable problematic of subjectivity itself, it would also satiate once more the ineradicable megalomania of desire--which is nothing less than a desire-to-be-a--subject (a desire-to-be-close-to-oneself, a wanting-to-be-free...). And that would be to go on dreaming.[3]

Jakobsen's point is this: the desire of all desire is not to have, for instance an object; it is to be, to experience one's subjectivity as whole and unique. But because being is an object of desire, or

---

[3] Paris, Flammarion, 1982, p. 65.

we might even say the function of desire, rather than an inherent component of existence, the sense of being must be appropriated through some model-- through some double with whom I identify because he appears to <u>be</u>. And so I cannot help but live my being in the mode of some other, who serve me a model of subjectivity, which I appropriate as my own "self": a self that is always a duplicate of a "me" that I see elsewhere, and that I want to annihilate and replace by virtue of my identification with him. After all, if he is me then I must come to stand where he now is; the object of identification is always a rival.

This post-Lacanian reading of Freud sheds a clearer light on the dynamics that determine that second-level narration by which Lorenzo tells the truth of his self behind its appearances. The drama of Lorenzo's telling is the revelation of an "abyss,"[4] as Philippe calls it, that is the self. When Lorenzo claims that the lifting of a skirt revealed to him men as they really are, we must take him at his word, but we must also hear him out, for he goes on to say that his play-acting is no longer an act. "Vice, he says, was at first a mere cover; now it is glued to my skin" (396). What he has come to know is the extent to which identity as the murderer of Alexandre is based upon his identification with Duke, or his desire to stand in his place. Lorenzo is, in a sense, the man he abominates; and he hates his double precisely because Alexandre is his double-- standing there where he, or they, ought to be.

<u>Lorenzaccio</u> is, then, a play about the tensions inherent in the telling one's real self; in order that "the world know a bit about who I am" I must talk about others, ineluctably, and, finally to prove my point, I must murder them, then die.

---

[4] During this crucial attempt to tell his self, Lorenzo elicits a telling response from Philippe Strozzi, who remarks "Quel abîme! que tu m'ouvres!" (397). That is precisely Musset's point, I believe: the attempt to tell one's unicity can only open on to a narrative abyss, an endless soliloquy, and an ontological quicksand, precisely because one cannot "be" oneself without the mediation of others.

O'Neill's Servitude, Shaw's Candida, and the
Comic Vision

Ronald R. Miller
Western Maryland College

Eugene O'Neill, like modernists such as Chekhov
and Pirandello, was inclined to reappraise the
essentially tragic condition of man through a comic
lens. One factor that contributes to O'Neill's
reputation as a modern dramatist was his capacity to
construct dramatic situations which are at once
explicitly tragic and implicitly comic, a tendency
which contrasts to that of Chekhov and Pirandello, who
were drawn to the opposite view; that is, toward
situations explicitly comic and implicitly tragic.
O'Neill developed this comic capacity throughout his
career in a series of modern "satyr plays"--among
them Anna Christie, Welded, Ah, Wilderness! and
Hughie--which take a point of view diametrically
opposed to that of his tragedies. In these comic
works, he conceived dramatic situations in which the
inevitability of tragic suffering is refuted by social
reconciliations that imply the possibility of lasting
happiness within marriage, friendship, family or
community.

The first of these "satyr plays," and the model
for those which followed, is Servitude.[1] It is one of
several works composed during O'Neill's first year as
a practicing dramatist. After his release from the
Gaylord Farm Sanitarium, where had been treated for
tuberculosis, he returned to his home town of New
Lord, Connecticut, and wrote eight one-act plays and
two longer works over a period of a year. Of these
Servitude was the last to be written, in the summer of
1914. (Tornqvist: 259)

---

[1] Most critics have regarded Servitude as a
substandard work without critical significance (i.e.,
Floyd 84). Among those who have thought the work to
be one of relevence to the interpretation of the
O'Neill canon are Travis Bogard and Doris Alexander.
Bogard has noted the influence of Shaw's interpreta-
tion of Nietzsche on O'Neill's play. (315)
Alexander argues that the work anticipates Days
Without End in demonstrating O'Neill's inability to
reconcile love with social reform. (403-5)

What is striking about Servitude, in the context
of the other naive plays written during this period,
is that it is comic in both intent and effect. In
contrast to "pretragic" works such as The Web and
Bound East for Cardiff, Servitude conceives of human
suffering as neither the consequence of socioeconomic
factors nor of larger patterns of fate. Rather,
O'Neill seems in this play to regard suffering as
following from limitations in personal ideology and
behavior. The crises of the play develop from the
inabilities of his characters to recognize social
situation which are implicitly dangerous or to develop
ways of thinking appropriate to their reconciliation.
This comic idea--that suffering is neither socially
nor metaphysically inevitable, but rather the consequence of human folly--is notable in Servitude because
it represents O'Neill 's first attempt to affirm man's
capacity for avoiding tragic suffering through
personal transformation.

O'Neill's play describes instead a process of
"comic suffering"--a process of psychological and
ideological self-transformation--which defuses the
potential for physical violence at the end of the
play. The conflict which emerges in Servitude is
between two ideologies concerning marriage: a
"conservative" notion of feminine self-abrogation and
a more "radical" belief in a woman's right to persona
sovereignty. This traditional theme of domestic
drama, treated provocatively by Henrik Ibsen in A Doll
House some four decade earlier, is reappraised by
O'Neill.[2] His principal characters, the writer David
Roylston and his admirer Ethel Frazer, discovering the
curse of the play that the principle of self-
abrogation, while less intellectually compelling than
what Roylston calls "self-realization"--seems more
appropriate to the nurturing of domestic harmony and
personal satisfaction.

Roylston is a successful American playwright and
novelist, a composite of muckraker--he has written an

---

[2] Several critics of O'Neill have noted the
connection to Ibsen's A Doll House. Doris Falk was
perhaps the first to address this relationship. (15)
More recently, Bogard has written on the triangular
relationship between Ibsen, Shaw and O'Neill in her
shared concern with the status of women within
marriage.

expose of Wall Street entitled The Street--and social dramatist. In every aspect of his life he has apparently excelled. He lives in an exclusive community on the Hudson, is married and has two children, and is attended by a manservant: He has authored a number of works which have achieved both critical and popular acclaim. He is, moreover, a man who seem to have value and convictions; wealth has apparently not been for him an impediment to social criticism and philosophical insight. At the core of his personal aesthetic ideology is the notion of personal freedom, of liberation from social and domestic conventions, which he terms the principle of "self-realization." (I:238)

The crisis of the play is precipitated when one of his admirers, a beautiful women named Ethel Frazer, appears on his doorstep late at night. Roylston's wife and children have gone in to the city for an overnight trip. Although the visitor is unknown to him, she presents herself as his most devoted follower. She has endeavored to live her life according to the precepts drawn from her reading and viewing of Roylston's works. The woman has recently abandoned her wealthy husband, a financier, and has taken lodgings in a depressed area of the city in order that she might live without obligation to him. She tells Roylston that her decision to leave her husband has been taken in consideration of his argument for the duty of the individual "to assert its supremacy and demand the freedom necessary for its development." Unable to find appropriate work, and nearly broken with despair, she has come to him for reassurance that her quest for "self-realization" has not been in vain. She contrives to stay the night in Roylston's house as a test of his capacity for integrity and truth to self. His decision to allow her to remain compromises him in the eyes of his wife, who interprets Mrs. Frazer's presence in the house as evidence of her husband's philandering.

Mrs. Roylston's return gives Mrs. Frazer the opportunity to gain insight into other aspects of Roylston's personality. Mrs. Roylston has determined to leave her husband, not out of reproach for his apparent infidelity but in order to free him from any obligation to her. Nevertheless it becomes clear to Mrs. Frazer that Roylston has exploited his wife's affections, using her as a source of income and secretarial labor, then neglecting her in favor of other admirers. Mrs. Frazer is convinced that

Roylston's ideals are contrived justifications for his self-indulgence, and she berates him in a subsequent scene:

> ...you 'were on such a high pedestal--I thought of the superman, of the creator, the maker of new values. This morning I saw merely an egotist whose hands are bloody with the human sacrifices he has made--to himself! (III:280-1)

Mrs. Frazer's attacks transform Roylston's vision of himself; he begins to perceive his complicity in the failure of his family life. He determines, moreover, to be reconciled with his wife, having recognized her devotion to him. Indeed, he begins to regard her as important of his professional success. Mrs. Frazer, significantly, is also transformed. Disillusioned by Roylston's ethics of self-realization, she adopts his wife's virtue of self-abrogation, and determines to live once again with her husband. Soon, however, the latter pushes his way into Roylston's home with a pistol, intent on revenge for what he too wrongly perceives as a case of infidelity. But he is quickly disarmed, mistaken assumptions are corrected, and both marriages are reclaimed.

If O'Neill had Ibsen in mind when he conceived the ideal for Servitude, it is evident that he turned to Shaw's Candida as a model for the construction of both the work's dramatic progression and its comic resolution. Whereas Ibsen endows Nora with a measure of tragic dignity because of her decision to leave her husband, O'Neill seems to regard Mrs. Frazer's decision to leave her husband as an act of folly which she is permitted to recognize through the workings of Servitude's plot. In placing the focus on the folly rather than heroism, O'Neill follows the lead of Shaw, who saw the process of reconciliation between the self and the world as following from the "debunking" of foolish ideals rather than from acts of personal courage.

Like Candida, O'Neill's play concentrates on a process of personal transformation, in which a male "authority figure" comes to understand the truth of his personal pretensions and to acknowledge the contributions of his wife to the creation of his

domestic harmony.[3]   Both the reformist cleric Morell
in <u>Candida</u> and the writer Roylston of <u>Servitude</u> are
well-to-do, comfortable with their positions of
intellectual authority, and content in their marriages.   But the ideologies which have gained them
renown in their respective fields are belied by the
realities of their domestic situations.   The actions
of both plays describe the process by which these men
are confronted with challenges to the validity of the
world they have created, and accordingly, to their
right to the emotional luxuries--love, respect and
celebrity--which each has assumed to be his due.
Their personal values, held to be deep truths, are
revealed as pretentious projections of personal ego,
the offspring of their wives willingness to eclipse
their own potentials in domestic and professional
service to their husbands.   In each play an intruder
into the family circle initiates the process of
disillusionment.   Shaw employed a young poet, Marchbanks, whose love for Morell's wife Candida enlightens
him to the cleric's fraudulent presumption that his
preeminent position in the household and his right to
Candida's affections are due to his stature as a man
and a thinker.   Marchbanks recognizes two truths which
have never occurred to Morell: that Candida is a free
woman, and that she is capable of loving another man.

O'Neill modifies Shaw's approach.   His intruder
is a woman rather than a man, but one whose entrance
into the family circle similarly, creates sexual
tensions within the family.   Her function is similar
to that of Marchbanks; as an outsider, Mrs. Frazer
retains an objectivity which allows her to recognize
the essential inauthenticity of Roylston's pose.
These intruders initiate a process of transformation
within the men whose domestic power they challenge.
The processes are similar to those described by
Aristotle in his analysis of plot: that is, comprised
of scenes involving reversal, suffering and recognition. However, they are comic in intent.   Instead of
articulating man's incapacity to reconcile elements
of his own nature with the metaphysical challenge of
"being"--a tragic theme that O'Neill would later probe

---

[3] Shaw described the "pleasant" plays of <u>Plays
Pleasant and Unpleasant</u>, of which <u>Candida</u> is one, as
concerned with the "romantic follies" of society and
the "struggles of individuals against those follies."
(<u>Plays</u> 8:xxv)

in considerable depth--the process of "comic suffering" is directed towards the recognition and
correction of flaws in social thinking and behavior.
Consequently, it may be seen as a process of psychological "wounding" which leads to personal transformation.   This transformation undercuts the need
for suffering or more profound effect--mortal
suffering of body or soul--in order to restore harmony
between man and the cosmos.

In the case of Candida, the reversal of fortune
begins late in the first act, when Marchbanks confronts Morell with the fact of the former's love for
Candida, and suggests that she may return his love.
This initiates the process of "comic suffering" on the
part of Morell, which culminates in final scene of
recognition.   In this scene Candida, obliged by the
men to choose between them, identifies Morell as the
weaker of the two, and determines to stay with him not
as an act of romantic love, but in a spirit of
motherly self-abrogation.   She declares that it is
Morell, despite his apparent competency, who his the
weaker of the two, and consequently needs her more.

The dramatic structure in Servitude is similar.
The reversal of fortune occurs when Mrs. Roylston
returns, discovering the apparent impropriety.   The
process of comic suffering is initiated when Mrs.
Frazer confronts Roylston, who expresses profound
discomfort at the ephemeral nature of what he had
regarded as a dependable marriage.

> ...your visit has stirred up the depths with
> a vengeance--the muddy depths....I feel as
> if the world were turned topsy-turvy. When
> you have taken a thing for granted for
> years, when a faith in it has been one of
> the main props of your life, although you
> might not have realized its importance at
> the time--and suddenly you make the dis-
> covery that you trusted in a sham, that you
> prop in worm eaten! It is rather a tough
> tumble, isn't it? (III:278-9)

The process of "comic suffering," in turn, leads to
Roylston's recognition of his own culpability.

> I see, I see! Poor Alice! What a woman she
> is! And I--good heavens! You threatened to
> open my eyes--I've lived with her all these
> years and forgotten how much I owed to her.

152

She has protected and shielded me from
everything--made my opportunity for me, you
might say--and I took it all for granted--
the finest thing in my life!   Took it all
for granted without a thought of gratitude,
as my due.   Lord, what a cad I've been!
What a rotten cad!   (III:293)

In both plays the drama is brought to climax by a
threatened act of violence, an aborted act of passion
which serves as contrast to the intellectualized
agonies of the male protagonist.   In Shaw's work,
Candida worries that Marchbanks may take his life; in
Servitude, the estranged husband of Mrs. Frazer
bursts into Roylston's house with a revolver,
incensed over his wife's apparent infidelity.   These
threats of violence, while soon defused, invoke the
implicit potential for tragedy in apparently comic
works.

That O'Neill should have turned to Shaw as a
model for his first "satyr play" is not surprising.[4]
Of the modern playwrights with whose work O'Neill was
familiar, none was more concerned with invoking
implicitly serious themes within explicitly comic
structures.   In his critical writings, Shaw argued
that comedy and tragedy sprang from the same source.
"The tragedy and comedy of life," he wrote, "lie in
the consequences, sometimes, terrible, sometimes
ludicrous, of our persistent attempts to found our
institutions on the ideals suggested to our imagina
tions by our half-satisfied passions." (Shaw, 1965:
90-1)   For Shaw, the "comic suffering" brought about
by verbal lacerations--generally by women towards men,
as demonstrated in Mrs. Warren's Profession and
Heartbreak House as well as in Candida--permitted the
kind of "ludicrous" recognition of self which fore-
stalled the more "terrible" consequences which
resulted when men were permitted to indulge their
follies to the point of tragic calamity.

For O'Neill, the model provided by Shaw was
appropriate to his own intention of finding a comic
approach to an issue he was inclined to view tragically.   In Servitude he suggested the possibility that
personal follies might be corrected through a painful

---

[4]O'Neill was an early student of Shaw, having
read his "The Quintessence of Ibenism" while still in
high school.

process of self-recognition. This notion of dramatic progression, whole perhaps not comic in the conventional sense, followed from shaw's idea of comedy as a form capable of revealing the passions of man without recourse to tragic denouncement. Servitude suggests that while the young Eugene O'Neill had experimented in his first year of dramatic composition with works of tragic sensibility, he had by no means settled on such a world view. Instead he seems to have followed the lead of Shaw in regarding the consequences of human folly as neither inevitably tragic nor comic. In Candida, he found a model for dramatic structure which permitted tragic undercurrents to the action to be redirected into a progression of reversal, suffering and recognition which, while it mimicked tragic form, nevertheless allowed for the reconciliation of potentially dangerous conflict within the social universe.

It is significant that, at this point in his career, O'Neill had not yet fully conceived of redemptive moments of spiritual insight which would provide tragic catharses to his protagonists. In a sense, Servitude is the culminating work of his first year of dramatic composition, a play that affirms the possibility of the epistemological mind to grasp meaning within the social context.[5] It was not until Beyond the Horizon, written in 1917, that he would develop a fully tragic work in which self-realization, unachievable in the world of domestic and economic reality, would be seen as available in the triumph of the spiritual self through suffering. In this later play, self-recognition and self-transformation are regarded as possible only in a metaphysical universe beyond social consciousness.

Despite his success with tragic subjects, O'Neill never fully abandoned the comic perspective, the ideal that life might be perfectible within the social cosmos. His series of "satyr plays"--works such as Ah, Wilderness! and Hughie--were complemented by other works which O'Neill labeled "ironic tragedies." In these plays, which include The Hairy Ape and Dynamo, the search for metaphysical meaning through suffering

---

[5] A recent production of the play has been documented by Paul Voelker. In his report he argues that the play, despite its low critical repute, is worthy of stage performance.

ends ambiguously and at time ludicrously. In a third
set of plays, dramatic "epics" such as <u>Marco</u> <u>Millions</u>
<u>Strange Interlude</u> and <u>The Iceman Cometh</u>, O'Neill found
forms appropriate to the reconciliation of tragic and
comic perspectives within a single work. It is this
"epic" juxtaposition of dramatic genres which represents O'Neill's most advanced effort to integrate the
social vision which he inherited from Shaw with the
metaphysical view of reality that he shared with
modernists such as Strindberg, Checkov and Priandello.

While <u>Servitude</u> is by no means a major work, it
nevertheless has considerable significance in the
development of the O'Neill canon. It is in effect
the work of an "apprentice" seeking forms appropriate
to the representation of a nascent world vision. The
play suggests that, at this point in his career,
O'Neill was not a determinedly tragic writer. His
exploration of the potential of Shavian comedy represents but one of several experiments in comic form
which were to appear throughout his career, functioning as "satyr plays" within the generally tragic
thrust of his dramaturgy.

LIST OF WORKS CITED

Alexander, 1961:   Doris Alexander, "O'Neill as Social Critic" in <u>O'Neill and his Plays</u>, edited by Oscar Cargill, N. Bryllin Fagin and William J. Fisher (New York: New York University Press).

Bogard, 1972:   Travis Bogard, <u>A Contour in Time</u> (New York: Oxford University Press).

Falk, 1982:   Doris V. Falk, <u>Eugene O'Neill and the Tragic Tension: An Interpretive Study of the Plays</u>, 2nd ed. (New York: Gordon Press).

Floyd, 1985:   Virginia Floyd, <u>The Plays of Eugene O'Neill: A New Assessment</u> New York: Frederick Ungar).

O'Neill, 1964:   Eugene O'Neill, <u>Servitude</u> in <u>Ten "Lost Plays"</u> (New York: Random House).

Shaw, 1965:   Bernard Shaw, <u>A Prose Anthology</u>, selected with Introduction and Notes by H.M. Burton (Greenwich, Conn.: Fawcett Publications).

Shaw, 1931:   Bernard Shaw, <u>Plays</u>. Vol. 8. <u>Plays Pleasant and Unpleasant</u> (New York: Wise & Company).

Sheaffer, 1973:   Louis Sheafer, <u>O'Neill: Son and Artist</u> (Boston: Little, Brown).

Tornqvist, 1969:   Egil Tronquvist, <u>A Drama of Souls: Studies in O'Neill's Supernaturalistic Technique</u> (New Haven: Yale University Press).

Voelker, 1982:   Paul Voelker, "<u>Servitude</u>'s American Premiere (?): A Report by the Director" in <u>The Eugene O'Neill Newsletter</u> 6:2 (Summer Fall 1982) 457.

Black Man-White Woman
The "Lynch Pattern" as Morality Play

Marcia Press
Indiana University

A popular joke from the black community depicts a black man standing outside St. Peter's Gate, seeking admittance to heaven. When asked what brave thing he has done in order to deserve getting into heaven, the man answers: "I married a white woman in Bilox, Mississippi." "When did you do this," asks the gate-keeper. "About two minutes ago," the black man answers. The joke refers, of course, to the black man-white woman taboo, violation of which often meant death by lynching for the black man. The taboo is still with us, and the historic lynch ritual, while no longer an actual mechanism for social control as it once was, has lived on also, symbolically embedded in our literature. While there have been a number of interpretations of the psychology of lynching, its social intent is certainly clear. Officially jus-tified as punishment for the crime of rape against white women, in reality the charge against the black man was usually not rape -- if there was a charge at all. The subtext here is obvious; lynching was a terrorist tactic designed to control the behavior of blacks, and in particular black men.

Realistically depicted lynchings, often rendered in gruesome detail, appear frequently in American novels, but usually as ancillary materials, not as the central vehicle of the plot. The subtext of social control, however, does appear as a central theme, and it achieves a particular dynamism in drama. In a theatrical setting, literary representation is also actual representation. Because of the continue cultural currency of the black man-white woman taboo, such liaisons, when depicted on stage, take on an emotionally charged ichnographic quality. The real life visual image of an actual black man and an actual white woman, in close physical proximity on a stage, provides an effective theatrical situation and not surprisingly, the structural underpinnings of several twentieth-century American plays are formed by the motif elements of taboo violation and the subsequent consequences. This structure can be seen, for example, underlying James Baldwin's <u>Blues for Mister Charlie</u> (1964), and variation of it is also present in Imamu Baraka's <u>Dutchman</u> (1964).

In a study of literary and historic lynchings, Trudier Harris suggests that the lynching of black men served the psychic purpose of a "ritual exorcism." The black man-white woman relationship, is not simply outside the realm of cultural norms, it is taboo in the most primitive sense of the word, that is to say, it violates our modern-day equivalent of the sacred, i.e. the status quo. We must remember that American culture denies its interracial reality. Despite several centuries of racial mixing, Americans persist in viewing race, both figuratively and literally, as a black and white issue. Interracial liaisons, particularly those involving black men and white women, threaten our cultural sense of identity. Once our traditional concept of how things should be-- according to a white male view of the universe -- has been disturbed, there must be a ritual sacrifice in order to "exorcise the evil" and thus make the world all-right again. Lynching was one such mechanism, for by punishing taboo violators, it reaffirmed the taboo's validity. In symbolic terms, the literary "lynch pattern" carries this same message. Interestingly, dramatic punishment does not necessarily come at the hands of an angry public mob as is the case with the historical ritual, nor is the punishment restricted to the black man. In Howard Sackler's The Great White Hope (1968), for example, it is the white woman who dies, at her own hands. In terms of the "lynch pattern" what is important is the symbolic ritualism with which this punishment is carried out: a signal of danger, a violation of the taboo, and then the inexorable destruction of the taboo violators and their forbidden relationship.

Once the "lynch pattern" is set in motion a human sacrifice is required in order to neutralize the chaos unleased by the breaking of the taboo. Such a sacrifice can only be avoided through a nullification of or atonement for the taboo violation. Thus, renunciation of the taboo relationship serves to lessen the severity of the punishment. When the taboo is not heeded, however, punishment which is equal to that of death, at least metaphorically, is demanded. Insanity represents one such equivalent, as does castration, whether real or symbolic.

Eugene O'Neill's All God's Chillun Got Wings (1924), provides an interesting example of such symbolic punishment. O'Neill punishes both members of a black-white marriage through a self-inflicted psychological annihilation. Ironically, while there is no public attack on O'Neill's interracial couple within the play, O'Neill himself was barraged with hostile and threatening letters condemning the play.[1] Also, the New York City Police Department, acting in the role of symbolic lynch mob pro tem, sought a quick demise of O'Neill's black-white couple by attempting to bar the play from opening. Although New York's "finest" were unsuccessful in their efforts, the Mayor's Office succeeded in holding up the permits necessary to allow the play's child actors to perform. As a result, the first scene had to be read to the audience by the stage manager. This practice continued almost until the end of the play's New York run, at which point the permits were finally granted.

Even without the four black and four white child actors, the first scene would still call attention to a sharp dichotomy between the black world and the white. The first scene opens onto an intersection of two streets. In one the faces are all black, in the other all white. O'Neill also stresses the cultural difference between the two worlds by using different sounds, such as distinctive laughter, which can be heard from the two streets. Only the children playing marbles at the intersection where the two worlds meet are able to transcend this racial division. In the innocence of childhood, black Jim Harris and white Ella Downey become sweethearts. Here we see a foreshadowing of the play's taboo violation. It was, in fact, because Ella and Jim hold hands in this first scene that the Mayor's Office refused to allow the child actors to perform. Typical of O'Neill's characters, both Jim and Ella are outsiders who, in an attempt to "belong," seal their devotion to each other by pretending to swap racial identies.

After the passage of years, during which time Jim and Ella grow into adolescent maturity, Jim is still smitten with Ella. She, however now seeks to find her friends "among my own kind." When Jim asks her why she avoids speaking to him, she responds arrogantly "What would we speak about? You and me've nothing in common anymore" (29). When Jim presses her to remember their past feelings, Ella grows indignant and

---

[1] A similar fate befell the white actress, Jane Alexander, in 1968 when she appeared opposite James Earl Jones in Sackler's The Great White Hope.

rebuffs him saying "Of all the nerve! You're certainly forgetting your place!" (29). By now Ella has learned what it means to be white and to be black in America. Ella's sense of pride, however, expressed in the language of racial superiority, is broken by the passage of more years. She has been seduced and abandoned by the neighborhood bully. The child which resulted from the union has died of diphtheria. Throughout the ordeal, Jim has been a loyal friend. Feeling alone and desperate, facing the alternative of suicide or prostitution, Ella consents to marry Jim.

The wedding scene which closes Act I is the briefest scene in the play. By bringing to fruition the foreshadowed taboo violation of scene one, this scene sets the "lynch pattern" in motion. Not coincidentally, the scene stands at the play's direct center and separates the lives of Jim and Ella into a before and after of their taboo violation. In this scene, O'Neill brings to bear the devices of dramatic expressionism to call attention to the cultural meaning of this marriage. Importantly, O'Neill does not actually depict the wedding ceremony. this fact combines with O'Neill's somber imagery to give the overall effect, not of a wedding, but of a funeral. The scene opens to reveal "stern, forbidding" looking buildings with drawn shades, including the church at center stage. The only sound is that of a melancholy voice signing a funeral dirge. The music fades to a silence that is broken abrupt by church bells, which like a signal, summon forth two streams of people, white from the left and black from the right. Mechanically, the "form into the two racial lines ... unyielding, staring across at each other with hostile eyes" (42). There are no smiling well-wishers surrounding Jim and Ella as they are joined in marriage, only these two separate row of people.

As the couple emerges from the church:

> The doors slam behind them like wooden lips of an idol that has spat them out. ... They stand in the sun light, shrinking and confused. All hostile eyes are now concentrated on them. ... They hesitate and tremble. (42)

The fact that the church "spits" them out suggests that even God is not pleased. The whole scene is designed to reinforce the ominous message that the universe has been disturbed. The taboo has been violated; the furies have been unleased.

Act Two opens with Jim and Ella's from France, where they have been living in order to avoid social ostracism. Ostensibly, they have returned "to face things." In reality, they have come back because there is no longer any reason to stay away. For a while, during which time the couple had lived platonically, they had been happy. Once the marriage is consummated, however, "the menace of ...ingrained racial complexes" (Block 149) begin to destroy Ella's mind. O'Neill emphasizes the fact that it is the taboo of interracial sex which triggers the disintergation of Jim and Ella, both as individuals, and as a couple. Ella had been able to accept her marriage to Jim so long as they were husband and wife in name only. The beginning of a sexual relationship, however, forces Ella to confront all the cultural messages which she has internalized about black and whites. For Ella, acceptance of Jim, a black man, as a real husband is a great humiliation. Evidence of this is seen in her response to seeing an old friend on the street. Ella calls to him and when he fails to respond, she has a paranoid episode in which she imagines that she is being rejected because of her marriage to a black man:

> He never heard a word I tell you! He did, too! He didn't want to hear! He didn't want to let anyone know he knew you! Why don't you acknowledge it? ... It's true, and you know it. ... He doesn't want to know you anymore. ... Why? You know well enough! Because you married a-a-a- . . . (61).

Ella's racial paranoia comes to focus on the bar exams for which Jim is constantly studying and which he constantly fails, not out of ignorance, but because of his own self-consciousness at being the only black amidst a sea of white faces. Jim's failure to pass his exams becomes for Ella "the symbol of his inferiority, which she must preserve at all cost" (Block 148). Having taken Jim as her husband, Ella prevents Jim from studying. When at the play's end, he has again failed his exam, Ella is delighted:

> Oh, Jim, I knew it! I knew you couldn't [pass]! Oh, I'm so glad, Jim! I'm so happy! You're still my old Jim ... The devil's dead. See! It couldn't have lived in you.

161

> Then I'd have to kill you, Jim, don't you
> see -- or it would have killed me. (73-74)

The devil is blackness and all that it represents
for Ella -- her beliefs about black inferiority and
her shame at having entered the black world. The
symbolic incarnation of this devil is a hauntingly
beautiful Congo mask given to Jim and Ella as a
wedding present. Ella becomes obsessed with the mask
and imagines that it is trying to destroy her and
turn her black. Lacking any real sense of identity,
Ella clings desperately to the myth of white superiority. Jim's blackness, as symbolized by the Congo
mask, comes to represent for Ella the evil unleased by
her taboo violation, a pollution of her "superior"
white world, and the reality of her own diminished
status. She has mothered a child out of wedlock, lost
the child, been rejected by that child's father, and
finally, she has been, in her view, "reduced" to
marrying a black man. Ella's own self-hatred and
tenuous hold on reality get transformed into the more
comfortable feelings of racial superiority, all of
which she projects onto the inanimate mask:

> What're you grinning about, you dirty nigger
> you. How dare you grin at me! I guess you
> forgot who you are! That's always the way.
> Be kind to you, treat you decent, and in a
> second ... you're all over the place putting
> on airs, why it's got so I can't even walk
> down the street without seeing niggers,
> niggers everywhere. Hanging around ...
> going to school -- pretending they're white
> -- taking examinations... It's you who're to
> blame for this! Yes you! Oh, I'm onto you.
> But why d'you want to do this to us? What
> have you got against me? I married you,
> didn't I. Why don't you let Jim and me
> alone? (73-74)

Though the symbol of the mask, O'Neill establishes a stereotypic connection between blackness and
the primitive and elemental forces of life, of which
sexuality is clearly one. Ella, who is unable to
deal with interracial sexuality -- it is at this point
in her marriage that her breakdown begins -- manages
in her insanity to separate Jim from his blackness and
also from his masculinity. Be ensuring that Jim is
neither able to sleep nor study, and thereby prevent-
ing him from passing his exam, Ella strips Jim of his
manhood. In this way, she can cast Jim in roles with

which she is comfortable, and in doing so, she brings about the final motif element of the "lynch pattern," that of human sacrifice. Ella pretends that Jim is white, "the whitest man that ever lived," thereby destroying his black identity and consequently his selfhood. She also regresses back to childhood, and casts Jim as either a little boy or her "old Uncle Jim who's been with us for years and years." (77-78) Through both these roles, Ella symbolically castrates Jim, thus achieving the intent of the more brutal rituals often associated with actual lynchings. And through her insanity, Ella is, of course, also destroyed.

Ironically, O'Neill was quite surprised when the public response to this play centered around its theme of interracial marriage. But even so eminent a critic as T.S. Eliot, who thought the play more successful than Othello at universalizing issued of racial difference (Cargill 168), cannot neutralize the "peculiar" nature of American racial dynamics, particularly as they operated in 1924. O'Neill, like others, is part of the tradition he seeks to transcend. It is O'Neill as playwright, not just Ella and her delusions, who invests the Congo mask with a stereotypically "primitive" symbology. And it is O'Neill as playwright who sets up the stereotypic dichotomy between blacks and whites, depicting the former as "participants in the spirit of Spring" and the latter as "awkward natural emotion" (15). Also, by having Jim accept the emasculation with Ella demands, O'Neill seems to be suggesting that Jim's tragedy stems from his cultural ordained willingness to suffer such humilation, that being black he would gladly give us his manhood and his identity for the "privilege" of having a white wife. He also seems to be operating within the mythic tradition which holds that a white woman who sleeps with a black will be "ruined." The myth implied an actual physical rending of the white woman caused by the stereotypically enormous genitalia of the black man. While Ella suffers no physical damage as a result of sleeping with Jim, their sexual relationship does destroy her mind. This is not to imply that O'Neill's play was intended to be about the danger of intermarriage. However, placed in the context of American racial mythologies, as well as historic reality, the play's message clearly is about intermarriage. the message is one of doom, played out according to the structure of the "lynch pattern." Ultimately, the play's message is voiced by Mrs. Harris, Jim's mother, who says: "Dey's o'ny one should. De white and de black shouldn't mix dat close. Dere's one road where de white goes on alone, dere' anudder road where de black goes on alone--" (49).

This is the symbolic content of the "lynch pattern," that black and white should not mix and that violators of this taboo will pay with their lives. This symbolism is directly related to the social control intent of the actual historical ritual of lynching. O'Neill not only projects this message, but he also suggests that love between a black and a white woman cannot exist. Jim and Ella are not a modern-day Romeo and Juliet. Romero and Juliet lost their lives, but not very essence of their individual beings and not the affirmation of self as expressed through sexual love. In O'Neill's play, not only do both Jim and Ella become the asexual children of scene one, but through the stage directions which progressively lower the ceiling and shrink the apartment size in each subsequent scene in Act Two, we quite literally watch the walls closing in upon and suffocating this ill-fated couple.

Another play in which the edict of the "lynch pattern" is also expressed is <u>Deep are the Roots</u> (1945) by Arnaud D'Usseau and James Gow. More openly stereotypic than the O'Neill play, <u>DATR</u> demonstrates, in a more obvious way, the social control intent of the black man-white woman taboo. Just as O'Neill establishes the dichotomy between black and white, so too D'Usseau and Gow portray a world in which the rules of racial separation and appropriate conduct are deeply ingrained. Early in the play, the rules governing appropriate relations between a black man and white woman are violated. When this occurs, we have a signal of danger, not unlike the opening scene in <u>AGCGW</u>, in which Jim and Ella hold hands, inno-cently, but with foreshadowed meaning. Brett Charles, a black soldier, has returned home after having served with honors in World War II. Bella Charles, his mother, is on her way to meet her son's train. Genevra Langdon, youngest daughter of the wealthy white family for whom Bella works, insists on accompany her, despite everyone's protestations that a white woman "does not go to the station to meet a colored man" (D'Usseau and Gow 96). When Genera dismisses the warning and goes with Bella to meet Brett, her childhood friend, there is a clear fore-shadowing of the "lynch pattern."

164

Once Brett arrives at the Langdon household, it becomes apparent to all that he is much changed. No longer is he willing to accept the patronizing role that Southern culture demands of a black man. When his mother questions him about his behavior, he explains that in Europe he had been treated like a man. During the conversation, Bella learns that in England Brett had dated with women. Again, the danger signal is sounded. Bella's response harkens back to Mrs. Harris's warning in AGCGW that black and white should travel separate roads. Social mixing of the races, Bella proclaims, is "written on the book of what is and what ain't," it makes "the earth ... split open and you're standin' on the edge looking down" (106). She reminds Brett that "Black's black and white's white."

Senator Langdon, aging Southern aristocrat and father of Genevra, not only has noticed the changes in Brett, but does not like them. In his view, Brett has "gone off to war and come back with a lot of foreign theories." In drawing the stereotypic conclusion "that over there he slept with white women" (109), Senator Langdon echoes even more loudly the signal of danger which has already been sounded. Whatever the reality of Brett's relationships with white women in Europe, however, he is well aware that he is now back home in the American South and he remembers well his lessons in "the facts of Southern life." As children Brett and Genevra had been best of friends until their early teens when they were forbidden to play together any more. Ironically it had been the occasion of an amateur back-yard version of Othello that resulted in a switching for Brett and a tongue-lashing for Genevra. Consequently, upon his return, Brett keeps his distance from Genevra. She, however, chides him for being unfriendly and formal and eventually convinces him to take a moonlight stroll with her. When Genevra seeks to continue this practice, Brett begs off and in the ensuring conversation Genevra realizes that Brett is in love with her. Genevra also knows the "fact of Southern life" and immediately stops pursuing Brett's friendship.

Despite the innocence of their stroll, however, they have violated the taboo. Senator Langdon, even without knowledge of this infraction of the Southern code, perceives Brett as a threat to his way of life and accuses him, without any evidence, of having stolen his watch. Here it becomes clear that the black man-white woman taboo is actually a symbol for

165

the broader prohibition of any manly assertion on the part of the black man, just as lynching themselves, publically justified as a "protection of white womanhood," were actually a mechanism for controlling black behavior, employed in retaliation for any infraction of the racial code, no matter how minor, no matter whether real or imagine. Senator Langdon insists that Alice, his older daughter, call the police to have Brett arrested. Alice, knowing that Brett is innocent, refuses -- that is until she learns of the moonlight walk. At that point, Alice does call the sheriff, whereupon Brett is beaten into unconsciousness for not confessing the theft.

Regardless of Alice's knowledge that Brett is of good character, she nonetheless turns on him when she discovers his violation of the black man-white woman taboo. Within the play's structure, Brett's beating is clearly due to the transgression against the taboo and its discovery. Stereotypically, Alice assumes that it was Brett, not Genevra, who initiated the walk in the moonlight. She is convinced that Brett must have forced himself upon an unwilling and repulsed Genevra who must have fended off his sexual advances. She is disbelieving when Genevra tells her "I didn't try to stop him, because, he didn't try to touch me."

Despite Alice's incorrect assumptions, the relationship between Brett and Genevra remains pure and chaste. While the two clearly care for each other, they both accept the fact that there is no possibility for them to act on the feelings. At the play's end, they not only agree to go their separate ways, but both decide they must leave their hometown because of their disgrace. Brett's punishment for the moonlight walk is rather minor within the context of lynching, but this is directly related to the fact that the relationship is renounced, thereby affirming the taboo's validity. Brett and Genevra pay for their transgression against the taboo but not with their lives since the renunciation of the relationship serves to "exorcise the evil" and to set the universe to right again.

The "lynch pattern" is but one aspect of the mythos associated with the black man-white woman taboo, part of the intent of which is clearly to inforce a separation of the races. Other structures, more often than not, are found in narrative genres.[2] But the ceremonial nature of the "lynch pattern," as a symbolic form of ritual exorcism, is inherently theatrical and calls out for performance. It is hardly surprising, therefore, that the phenomenon of lynching, a unique form of American ritual drama even in its historical reality, should surface in symbolic form on the American stage. The "lynch pattern" transforms an historic ritual of taboo, social transgression, and punishment into a kind of twentieth-century morality play which, like the actual historic ritual, imparts high-stakes lessons about how blacks and whites in American can, and should, relate to each other.

References

Block, 1939:

Anita Block, The Changing World in Plays and Theatre (Boston: Little Brown & Company; reprinted edition, Da Capo Press, 1971).

Cargill, 1961:

Oscar Cargill, et al., eds., O'Neill and His Plays: Four Decades of Criticism (New York: NYU Press).

D'Usseau and
Gow, 1946.

Arnaud D'Usseau and James Gow, Deep are the Roots in The Best Plays of 1945-1946, Burns Mantle, ed. (New York: Dodd, Mead & Company).

---

[2] Other mythological structures which define the black man-white woman liaison are the rape archetypes such as the "beast" rapist, the "falsely accused innocent," and the "militant" rapist, as well as what this writer had termed "the myth that the myth is real" in which the black man-white woman attraction is viewed as an inherently hostile socio-historic imperative.

Harris, 1984   Trudier Harris, Exorcising
                      Blackness: Historic and Literary
                      Lynching Rituals (Bloomington, IN:
                      Indiana Univ. Press).

O'Neill, 1924:   Eugene O'Neill, All God's Chillun
                      Got Wings (News York: Boni &
                      Liveright).

Pinter's Ruth, Duras' Véra

Judith Roof
Illinois State University

Desire governs the theatrical economy revealed in Harold Pinter's The Homecoming and Marguerite Duras' Véra Baxter. Constructed from the point-of-view of the male characters and apparently focussing on them, both plays enact a gender politic of desire similar to that set forth by Luce Irigaray in her critique of Freud and in her Marxist analysis of woman as commodity[1] While both plays are complex and rich, one way to view the over commerce which structures the plays is as an exposure and feminist analysis of how the theatrical spectacle of women on stage functions to reassure the male's "relation to the phallic terms."[2] Motivated by a desire for the other, male characters in both plays attempt to purchase the women, Ruth in The Homecoming and Véra in Véra Baxter, whose desire certifies males wholeness and potency as a "truth" displaced onto and mirrored back from them.

---

[1] Luce Irigaray, This Sex Which Is Not One, trans. Catherine Porter (Ithaca, N.Y.: Cornell University Press, 1985). Though the entire collection generally treats the aforementioned topics, essays particularly focussed on woman as commodity are "Women on the Market," pp. 170-191, and "Commodities Among Themselves," pp. 192-197.

[2] Juliet Mitchell and Jacqueline Rose, eds., Feminine Sexuality: Jacques Lacan and the école Freudienne, trans. Jacqueline Rose (New York: Norton, 1985), 162. The phrase cited comes from an explanatory preface to Jacques Lacan's "Seminar of 21 January 1975" in which he discusses the difficulties of the situation of woman as "fantasy object" in a representation which "serves to ward off the unconscious." Luce Irigaray both echoes and critiques Lacan's observations about the function of woman in representation, reducing lacan's more complex inquiry into topology to a question of gender politics. However, her analyses, while not representative of Lacan's thought, are suggestive feminist insights into the operation of representation in culture.

Premised upon an "exchange of women,"[3] theater is generated by a transaction of looks--a look at the desiring woman and an imagine inviting glance of desire from her--both on stage and between the stage and the audience. In their market in female desire, these plays operate from a prostitution economy in which ontology is economics; death is a sale of the woman, her transformation from subject to object, from seer to seen. As tokens of exchange, Ruth and Véra are the unstable and potentially uncontrollable currencies whose representation traces and reveals the workings of the mechanism. Consciously consenting to their prostitution--in fact, seeming to benefit by it--Ruth and Véra knowingly play the system. However, while Ruth's actions reveal and confirm the function of woman in theater, Véra chooses to escape the formula, refusing to become the spectacle of female desire, suborning the theatrical economy, and suggesting the possibility of an escape from this commerce.

The Homecoming present a sardonic image of reunion and refound wholeness accomplished by the family's capital investment in Ruth, the wife of the eldest son, Teddy. When Teddy takes her home for a visit, she is offer a position as family matriarch/tart, taking the place of the family's dead matriarch/tart, Max's wife, Jesse. The currency of this exchange is her desire, revealed in her apparent willingness to fill their need not only for a mother figure, but also for a mistress for themselves and for

---

[3] Both Luce Irigaray and Catherine Clément hint at the exchange equation suggested in this paper. In "Women on the Market," in This Sex Which Is Not One, Irigaray connects sexual difference, sexuality, and commerce as crucial parts of a male desire economy. In her exploration of the magic of marginal role in The Newly Born Woman, Clément links theater and spectatorship to the exchangeability of women: "There is no doubt that woman might speak by herself, from herself; at least she is recognized as a producer of signs, whereas the other function alloted to her, like the linguistic function, strictly concerns the exchange between the groups. Duet, song, representation of a relationship as spectacle exchange object and theatrical object; object of theater, woman in the initial exchange" (28). Catherine Clément and Hélène Cixous, The Newly Born Woman, trans Betsy Wing (Minneapolis: University of Minnesota Press, 1986).

other men (as Jesse might also have been, suggested by her affair with MacGregor). The exchange is material, accomplished as a business arrangement. Though Ruth is a "tease" (p. 68),[4] offering drinks to Lenny and not "going the whole hog" with Joey, her sexual authenticity stimulates an otherwise sluggish economy; she assumes the place of Jesse as well as the female roles filled since Jesse's death by Jesse's husband, Max, and his brother, Sam. Ruth's desire is the presumed, but necessary, element of the exchange. When Max begs for her attentions at the end of the play, he is begging for her confirming glance and for her kiss that will assure him that he is "not an old man." Her preference for Max and his at-home sons over the successful, but distanced son, Teddy, proves to them their desirability. Though she seems to acquiesce to their plans, Ruth manipulates them emotionally and sexually, holding over them the assurance that their economic prowess is also sexual potency, and that a beautiful woman such as she wants them and wants to work for them.

The purchase of Ruth is an exercise in masculine vigor which allows the family tow swing a deal, get the best of her, and place themselves in a status of illusory control. In exchange for getting the "gravy," certain household services, and the cost of her support, the family must set her up in a flat with a maid, clothe her, and provide an allowance. The deal is, of course, skewed economically; the men get the best of Ruth as a capital investment, since she must provide her own support, bring a few bob into the household and fulfill their sexual needs. Their financial dominance is enhanced by Ruth's business acumen; a though negotiator, Ruth capitulates only after a rough skirmish on the fiscal battlefield. The portrayal of Ruth's choice as an independent action is crucial: as an autonomous agent--as a Ruth who chooses ruthlessly --she provides a disinterested confirmation of their success and strength in the image of her voluntariness. As their "objective" mirror, Ruth is the truth of their lost potency, the illusion of its recovery, and they buy this truth with a business proposition which markets the illusion of wholeness as the commodity of Ruth's desire. The return on their investment comes in her willingness to bargain and to

---

[4] This and all subsequent references from Harold Pinter, The Homecoming (New York: Grove Press, 1965).

continue to allow their illusion of dominion. She must work for them, as money works, without consideration for her pleasure; their pleasure is her pleasure.

The play The Homecoming peddles this truth, this promise of the return glance of desire which makes the faily whole again at the expense of Ruth. In this sense, Pinter's characterization of the exchange of women is a brutal objectification of theater as a marketplace of desire; conscious of the mechanisms at work in the stage representation of women, Pinter's treatment of Ruth is an exposé and analysis of the posture of woman as the mirror of male desirability. The play's off-cited immorality is a bare revelation of the operation of theater and the place of women within it. She is an instrument posed as a character, an agent to fill a need in play about need.

Reverberating beyond the boundaries of the play, Ruth also becomes a product of a critical commerce as revealing as is her role. Criticism of The Homecoming comforts the disturbance created by Ruth, by appealing to stereotypical representations of woman which function as reassuring mirrors. Interpretations of Ruth replicate her status as commodity, soundly replacing her in her "proper" role, correcting her, reentering her into the fantasy from which she escapes in her matter-of-fact acceptance of the business arrangement. While establishing her free will, critics take it away, situating her as a position, a function mistaken as a person in revealing terms. Martin Esslin calls her a "nymphomaniac,"[5] the complement of endless potency. "The center of their collective consciousness,"[6] she is clearly the mother/whore' the "modern bitch-goddess,"[7] who "comes home to

---

[5] Martin Esslin, "The Homecoming: An Interpretation," in a Casebook on Harold Pinter's "The Homecoming", ed. John Lahr (New York: Grove Press, 1971), 5.

[6] James Hollis, Harold Pinter: The Poetics of Silence (Carbondale, Southern Illinois University, 1970), 103.

[7] 7Margaret Croyden, "Pinter's Hideous Comedy," in A Casebook on Harold Pinter's "The Homecoming", ed. John Lahr (New York: Grove Press, 1971), 49.

herself, to all of her possibilities as a woman,"[8] where she "fulfills their needs" to "fulfill her own needs," [9] since "their need is her need to,"[10] and she is "thirsty for return to fulfillment of animal needs."[11] "Appearing to promise more than she ever intends to deliver,"[12] she nonetheless wins the struggle for power, but simultaneously fulfills their wishes.[13] Assuming the "patriarchal chair,"[14] "she is wife, mother, daughter-in-law, sister-in-law, whore, and eternal feminine. She is al things to all people,"[15] though the play is "Ruth's process of self-

[8] Hugh Nelson, "The Homecoming: kith and Kin," in Modern British Dramatists, ed. John Russell Brown (Englewood Cliffs, NJ: Prentice-Hall, 1968), 149.

[9] Steven Gale, Butter's Going Up: A Critical Analysis of Harold Pinter's Works (Durham, NC: Duke University Press, 1977), 155.

[10] Augusta Walker, "Why the Lady Does It," in A Casebook on Harold Pinter's "The Homecoming", ed. John Lahr (New York: Grove Press, 1971), 119.

[11] Lucinda Gabbard, The Dream Structure of Harold Pinter's Plays: A Psychoanalytic Approach (Rutherford, NJ: Farleigh Dickenson University Press, 1976), 194.

[12] Austin Quigley, The Pinter Problem (Princeton: NJ: Princeton University Press, 1975), 223.

[13] Gabbard, The Dream Structure of Pinter Plays, 185.

[14] Gabbard, 186.

[15] Hollis, Harold Pinter: The Poetics of Silence, 106.

discovery."[16]   While she is critically portrayed as the self-satisfying complement, she is also titillatingly dangerous. Making "no distinction between body and mind,"[17] and "more interested in power,"[18] she has the sexual "whip hand,"[19] caused by her "rapacity" and the "craving of her nature,"[20] and her "forwardness' and "sexual aggression."[21]   In other words, Ruth's function is repeated in a critical commerce where she again returns a reassuring reflection, characterized as whatever is necessary to complete an interpretation, Ruth is still the malleable mirror who reveals the needs and biases of those who purchase her. Even in criticism, she is trapped as a commodity.

Like Ruth, Véra Baxter's desire is a spectacle to the purchased and traded in an economy where money and desire are posed as equivalents. Duras' five-scene play, re-adapted from her earlier play Suzanna Andler (1968) and her film Véra Baxter (1976), recirculates the commodity of the unknowable Suzanna/Véra one final time. By refusing to be the spectacle and the mirror, Véra finally subverts this economy at the end of Véra Baxter and in so refusing, both exposes the mechanism

---

[16] Nelson, "The Homecoming: Kith and Kin," 147.

[17] John Russell Taylor, "Pinter 's Game of Happy Families," in A Casebook on Harold Pinter's "The Homecoming", ed. John Lahr (New York: Grove Press, 1971), 63.

[18] Steven Aronson, "Pinter's 'Family' and Blood Knowledge," in A Casebook on Harold Pinter's "The Homecoming", ed. John Lahr (New York: Grove Press, 1971), 84.

[19] Irving Wardle, "The Territorial Struggle," in A Casebook in Pinter's "The Homecoming", ed. John Lahr (New York: Grove Press, 1971), 44.

[20] Walker, "Why the Lady Does It," 120.

[21] Katherine Burkman, The Arrival of Godot (Rutherford, NJ: Farleigh Dickenson University Press, 1986), 146.

of this play (and perhaps all of theater) as an exchange of the spectacle of female desire and escapes herself from endless circulation. To the accompaniment of unlocated noise and light Duras denominates "Outside turbulence," Véra's story is told in a hotel bar by Michel Cayre, her ex-lover, to a total stranger, the Bar Customer while Véra is out trying to rent a summer villa. After hearing the history of the Baxter's marriage, the Bar Customer becomes implicated in the exchange of desire and goes to the villa to acquire Véra, who refuses his proffered identification, rejecting finally her mirroring function.

That Véra, like Ruth, is a commodity exchanged for her desire is clearly established in the play's recital of Véra's history as a series of economic exchanges. Véra is married to Jean Baxter, who is desirable to women mainly because he is able to make huge amounts of money. Baxter pays for his infidelities by sending his wife checks for each of his extra-marital affairs. Wanting to regain desire for Véra, he sell the rights to her to Michel Cayre for two million francs. Since Véra Baxter can "only be known through desire ... outside of marriage" (p. 29), Jean hopes that her seduction by Michel will renew her desirability as the object of desire of another.[22] However, Jean can only generate desire for Véra vicariously through the report of her stage infidelity; to have desire for her he must identify with Michel's desire for her. The story of Véra's seduction is extracted from Michel by the Bar Customer and by Monique Combès, one of Jean's ex-lovers in the first two scenes of the play. Both the Bar Customer and the play's audience overhear the history; both become implicated as consumer of Véra's desire.

The middle man in Jean Baxter's money/desire economy, Michel Cayre has a fiscally-generated infatuation for Véra. In his narration to the Bar Customer, he reveals his uncertainty about his own role as a commodity purchased by Jean Baxter, but he also discloses that for him, too, money and desire are interchangeable. While Michel admits that Véra "isn't even beautiful," (p. 25) the combination of money and

---

[22] This and all subsequent citations from Marguerite Duras, <u>Véra Baxter</u>, trans. Phillpa Wehle in <u>Dramacontemporary: France</u>, ed. Philipppa Wehle (New York: PAJ Publications, 1986).

desire is too heady for him, knowing he has lost her from the first, he is seduced by her lack of desire for him and by the balance of the commodity value of two million francs owing in desire, in performance, in suffering. Describing his affair with Véra, he comments: "desire catches up with you, you know, it takes over..." (p. 25). Though he says that he "tried to make up" for his exchange of money and desire, he confesses that his effort were probably attempts to "Get power" (p. 25).

At Michel's admission of his desire for power, the Bar Customer takes his place in the economy by literally finishing his sentence for him, contributing the words "Get power". Now a part of the commerce, the Bar Customer seek Véra at the rental property at the end of the play, offering an identification with her that Véra refuses. In response to his advances Véra appears to recognize in the Bar Customer her own death with brought to light in her discovery in Scene IV that her marriage to Jean is finally completely over because she doesn't "love anybody any more" (p. 32). However, when the Bar Customer, the last representative of Jean Baxter's economy, tells her "that's one possible identity (pause) I might hold on to, for you" (p. 41), Véra chooses not to respond, observing instead that "The electricity's been turned off" (p. 41). Véra's function as the tradeable mirror of desire ceases; one step ahead of Ruth, Véra exits the economy which provided her financial gain. Véra's recognition of her desirer for death, "the easiest of all desire" (p. 40), is a recognition of the extinction of her desire. As she tells the Bar Customer: "I don't know how to want anything any more" (p. 40). Her value as a desiring mirror extinguished, the commodity of her desire disappears.

Both of these play suggest a view of theater as a prostitution economy which is not a new idea as the historical exclusion of women from the stage, the attitudes of Church father, and Zola's novel Nana can testify. However, the exposure in The Homecoming and Véra Baxter of precisely the components and mechanism of this economy, as well as their foundation in sexual difference reinforces a model of theater as a search (like that of Oedipus) constructed from an essentially male point-of-view. If female characters serve to reassure male wholeness, the identity at issue is the male's. In a Freudian scheme, the woman, though necessarily an independent character, is also and primarily a fetish, the displaced visible evidence of castration anxiety at its appeasement. Despite the liveliness of her characterization, the woman is still an object, a tool in the search for male self-verification that takes a particularly specular form and which more importantly, is tradable--is in a castration commerce--by definition. Women can be purchased. The woman stands in as the fetish. The fetish stands in for the phallus; the phallus is the signifier of wholeness.

The revelation of the mechanisms of a theatrical prostitution economy also suggests a way to interpret ostensibly woman-centered plays which takes into account representations of sexual difference as they relate to the often self-referential politics of theatrical performance. The frequent identification of a female "star" with a strong female role (or even male in the case of Sarah Bernhardt) and her subsequent currency as a theatrical led is not only testimony to habitual typecasting, but evidence of a commerce in the image of woman itself which comes to signify desire in a short-hand semiotics derived from her mirroring function in the theater.

The mechanics of a prostitution economy might also help to explain the relative absence of active women protagonists in drama as well as the frequent portrayal of strong female characters as hysterical or at least mysterious. The lack of women exists because women are objects, positions serving mainly as complements. However, as tradable fetishes, women also gauge male anxiety about identity: the stronger and more enigmatic the female character becomes, the greater the anxiety she allays, the greater her commercial value. The working of the spectacle in representation as suggested by Irigaray, makes it difficult to escape this fetish function connected to spectacle. Though women can be authentically strong, lays with strong and somewhat misunderstood female protagonists such a Shaw's Saint Joan and Ibsen's Hedda Gabler can be seen profitably as masked capitalizations on the spectacle and enigma of female desire, both of the character and of the actress circulated in the role. Their economic leverage lies in their tremendous power which precedes their predictable and reassuring fall. The binary oppositions inherent in the representation of sexual difference require a return to supplementary. And object-blood on the part of the woman character.

177

In this context Pinter's portrayal of Ruth and Duras' treatment of Véra reflect and subvert the typical rendering of women in a theatrical economy. Pinter's work reveals and analyzes this economy while still relying upon it, but in so doing also creates the paradox of Ruth, deliberate escape from objectification in her cold-blooded assumption of the term of exchange. The refusal of Duras' Véra introduces the possibility of escape from the economy suggesting that a feminist theater might establish its own terms by means of its rejection of an economy dependent upon seeing desire. In Véra's rejection of the Bar Customer, Véra joins the sea of non-individuate voices which constitute the Outside Turbulence playing throughout the piece. The commodity of Véra is lost. Her refusal of identification makes her invisible, but brings to the fore the Outside Turbulence which resists commerce because it cannot be located or defined. As Cixous has suggested, feminist theater is a theater of noise and presence. Duras rejects the commerce, the narrative decoy of the play, and connects Véra with a sea of women who have made noise all along.

Fictional Response to Political Circumstance:
Martin Walser's The Rabbit Race

Jürgen E. Schlunk
West Virginia University

A fundamental question about a piece of literature concerns the writer's motivation for writing it.
Although it is impossible completely to explore the
motivating forces behind a literary work, this
question is most productive for the purpose of opening
up discussion and further examining a particular work.
I would like to demonstrate the validity of this
approach with Martin Walser's early play, The Rabbit
Race (Eiche und Angora), first produced in 1962.[1] In
addition to discussing the play and reviewing its
production history, I will draw for Walser's theoretical essays on the nature of writing and dramatic
literature in postwar Germany as well as from statements he made in various interviews. Such personal
statements are sometimes thought to have only limited
value for the purpose of analyzing a literary text;
however, they frequently reveal an author's motives
more directly than the literary work itself and should
therefore not be dismissed. In Walser's play I
discern three levels of motivation: the personal
level, motivated by a sense of deficiency prompted by
Germany's political status; the symbolic level,
motivated by Walser's view of the artist;and a
general level, motivated by his understanding of the
individual's struggle to assert his innermost desires
facing an indifferent, intolerant, and restrictive
society.

The Rabbit Race is a natural choice for demonstrating the validity of this approach because it
represents Walser's first serious effort to grapple
with the dramatic form (Rischbieter, 1962, I), and
although another play--The Detour (Der Abstecher)--
came out a year earlier, The Rabbit Race, subtitled "a

---

[1] Eiche und Angora, originally published in
Theater Heute in November 1962, was revised in 1963
and included in: Walser, 1971, 53-113.

German chronicle in eleven scenes" and first in a dramatic trilogy, is a much more ambitious work.[2]

As a chronicle of the postwar period, the play starts during the final days of the war prior to the German capitulation in 1945 and ends with the Wirtschaftswunder in full swing in 1960. Walser depicts the behavior of the inhabitants of Brezgenburg ("Pretzelville"), a microcosm of the society at large, who eagerly and opportunistically adapt to every political change, with the exception of Alois Grübel who, as his name (from the German for 'to brood') suggests, is very slow in discarding the Nazi ideology that had been hammered into his brain. Formerly a communist, he had been subjected to brainwashing and torture-- including involuntary sterilization--during the Third Reich. Just when he has finally adapted to the new ideology, the war is over, the political climate changes, and his clinging to Nazi ideas leads to new punishment and victimization. While everyone around him concentrates on the present and blocks out memories of the past, Alois's "relapses" (e.g., scenes 5, 6, and 8) embarrass the community. They finally rid themselves of him by sending him off to a sanatorium.

The play's reception in Germany has been uneven. Whereas its premiere on September 23, 1962 in Berlin's Schiller-Theater, directed by Helmut Käutner, drew mostly negative reactions both from the audience and from West German critics, East German critic Ernst Schumacher was favorably impressed by the play's message and formal experimentation (Beckerman, 1970, 104-106). But of the twenty theatres that had intended to produce the play more than half decided not to do so after the Berlin failure although Walser supplied a revised, tighter version. Only a few West German critics (e.g., Hellmuth Karasek) recognized the significance of the play's political theme and elaborated on its merits. Later productions in Vienna and Zurich were considerably more successful, suggesting that one reason for the Berlin disaster was Käutner's naturalistic direction. The play's oblique political message was also perceived in other European countries, as major productions in England (Edinburgh, 1963) and France (Paris, 1968) prove. The British

---

[2] The other two plays in the trilogy are Überlebensgroß Herr Krott and Der Schwarze Schwan, both 1964 (Walser, 1971, 155-272).

production was based on an adaptation by Ronald Duncan (Walser, 1963). Jean Jacques Gautier's favorable review attests to the success of the French production at the Théâtre National Populaire (Beckermann, 1970, 106-107), based on Gilbert Badia's excellent translation which beautifully renders the meaning and tone of the German original. Between 1969 and 1974, the play was also staged in Holland, Belgium, Czechoslovakia, Italy, Spain, and Greece. Whereas the publisher lists no German production of The Rabbit Race during the 1970s, five theatres performed it during the mid-1980s, giving evidence of renewed interest.

A very effective production of the play I saw in Stuttgart's "tri-bühne" in 1985 aroused my interest in the question of Walser's motivation for writing this play. Martin Walser never hesitated to express what makes a writer write. His frequently quoted essay, "Who Is a Writer?," begins: "I have repeatedly tried to express that only he who lacks something has something to say" (Walser, 1979, 36).[3] By writing, Walser claims, the writer responds to a deficiency of his damaged identity. He writes not by choice, but by necessity. In regard to this necessity, Walser comments in another essays:

> When I notice [the writer] has defended himself by writing, his words have grown out of necessity and this carries over to me. . . . Attack and defense are closely related in literature, but the defense seems always more believable to me; it profits stylistically from its urgent necessity. (Walser, 1965, 106-07)

The urgent necessity, the very prerequisite to Walser's functioning as a writer, is a strong sense of national identity--something which he, through political circumstances beyond his control, has always lacked.

What was Walser's motivation for writing drama after first having established himself in the short story and novel? In an interview shortly before The Rabbit Race premiered in 1962, Walser explained his turning to the writing of plays:

---

[3] This and all subsequent translations are mine.

After having written prose for many years, I
simply enjoyed it. Beyond the perhaps
somewhat presumptuous intention of wanting
to meet the audience more directly, I also
had the feeling, you know, like a farmer who
practices crop rotation: if one has always
grown wheat on a field, or rye, one simply
wonders what else could be produced from the
same soil. (Rischbieter, 1962, I)

This statement reveals the sheer excitement of a
writer experimenting with his medium. The dialogue
form attracted Walser because it suited his interest
in concrete issues: "In the theater I have always had
the feeling one joins the contemporary public debate.
consequently, my dramatic writings have always had a
more topical motivation than my novels, my prose
writings" (Reitze, 1986). Interviewed by Horst Bienek
in early 1962, Walser stressed the challenge of
writing plays: ". . . for a time I felt as if I had
to readjust and tighten every tiny screw in my
language control center, switch to another frequency,
a different voltage" (Bienek, 1962, 251-252). But
Walser turned to the dramatic medium for one more
reason: between the end of the war and 1960, hardly
any plays had been written by German playwrights. Of
those produced in Germany during the first decade
after the war, many had been foreign. Even those by
the Swiss dramatists Frisch and Dürrenmatt, though
written in German, did not actually reflect the German
experience. The early plays by German dramatists like
Tankred Dorst, Wolfgang Hildesheimer, or Günter Grass
gave evidence of foreign influences, imitating Ionesco
and the theatre of the absurd.[4] Seldom did a German
dramatist, therefore, have a better opportunity for
steering the theatre in a new direction and making a
fresh start. And although The Rabbit Race may have
fallen short of most critics' expectations, the play
was innovative and historically relevant. Walser used
his unique opportunity by focusing on an important
sociopolitical issue and trying out new ways of
presenting reality on stage. He also discussed his
concept of stage realism in his theoretical essays
"About Expected Theatre" (1962) and "Imitation or
Realism" (1964) (Walser, 1965, 59-93).

---

[4] For a list of plays written by German dramatists
prior to The Rabbit Race see: Arnold, 1977, 276-283.

Walser's specific kind of realism does not preclude invention; in fact, he was convinced that German drama needed new ways of reflecting reality and predicted in 1962 that more "invented" plots would appear. Invention, rather than detracting from current reality, might actually reveal it:

> One cannot invent anything. Imagination is a production chamber in which nothing occurs which does not have a cause outside itself. The product of imagination must be measurable by this cause. From this comes its necessity and plausibility. The writer's arbitrariness has its limits at the point where the plot must bring forth scenes, must cause human beings to speak and walk. (Walser, 1965, 61)

The prophecy concerning invented plots, however, was not fulfilled. The dominant dramatic style of the mid- to late 1960s, the "Dokumentartheater," experimented with a direct representation of reality on stage. Walser expressed his disappointment over this development in his essay "A Further Daydream Concerning the Theatre" (1967) (Walser, 1968, 71-85). For his own dramatic writing, however, the invented plot ("Fabel") remained of central significance.

The challenge for German playwrights in the early 1960s lies in the need for accuracy, by which Walser means historical accuracy: "A German writer must deal exclusively with characters who either conceal or reflect the period from 1933 to 1945; who either conceal or reflect Germany's East-West situation. Every sentence of a German writer who is silent about this historical reality, conceals something" (Walser, 1965, 64). It is Walser's intention to write a play which reflects all of Germany's historical reality-- hence his ambitious plan for The Rabbit Race, a "German chronicle."

Walser's motivation is best reflected in the play's main character, Alois Grübel. On the most basic level, he had a practical reason for making him the protagonist of his play. The original idea for writing The Rabbit Race came from an account about a Polish prisoner hanged in 1945 by local residents of the Lake Constance area for having made love to a

German girl.[5] Whereas this still remains a subplot of the play, Walser did not feel confident enough to make his protagonist a Pole, and concentrated instead on Alois Grübel (Rischbieter, 1962, I).

This character, hopelessly out of step with the times, serves various functions. As someone who subjects himself to the authority of others, he is--as Walser himself stated--"a kind of representative of the anonymous nation as a whole." And in explaining why Germans have been mostly followers, Walser continued:

> . . . our people always go along; we are a pious nation and easy to control. . . . Therefore easy to lead astray to act our worst. Which means, however, I believe, that we could also be led to act our best. but that depends on those in charge, those who set the tone. (Rischbieter, 1962, I-II)

Wolfgang Böth's recent interpretation of The Rabbit Race convincingly argues that the motivations for Grübel's behavior have been misinterpreted by most critics. Alois's readiness to adapt to restrictions imposed on him by society have often been considered the focus of Walser's criticism, but actually Walser depicts adapting as the survival strategy of his dominating opportunists (Kreisleiter Gorbach, Professor Potz, Dr. Zerlebeck, Studienrat Schmidt), rather than of those dominated (Alois, Maria, the Pole) (Böth, 1983, 132). Böth finds Alois more resolute in resisting adaptation than other critics have given him credit for (e.g., Rischbieter, 1962, I). Investigating Walser's less obvious motivations for inventing Alois Grübel makes it possible to go even beyond Böth's argument.

Alois's greatest joy consists in singing and his strongest desire is to be allowed to join the Brezgenburg men's choir. Whereas his falsetto voice, result of Nazi torture, had once caught the choir conductor's interest and helped him escape execution, a few years later when everyone is trying to block out their

---

[5] For another treatment of the same theme in recent German literature see Rolf Hochhuth's Eine Liebe in Deutschland (Hamburg: Rowohlt, 1978). Hochhuth's novel was also made into a film.

memories of the Nazi period, the same voice is perceived as a disturbing reminder of Germany's dark past. Yet hoping against hope to gain admission to the choir, Alois patiently tolerates the most painful restrictions Potz, Schmidt, or Dr. Zerlebeck impose on him.[6] He even gives in to the demand to kill his beloved rabbits. As Böth carefully documents (124-130), the liberating self-expression of musical performance is a goal which remains permanently out of Alois's reach. However, through the very futility of his struggle, the complacency and corruptness of the other characters are revealed. The discrepancy between what society keeps promising but never grants him impresses on the reader that Alois is morally superior to those manipulating him.

The obvious sympathy Walser demonstrates for his protagonist suggests that Alois serves yet another function. Walser frequently makes his protagonists his personal spokesmen and Alois Grübel, like several other protagonists of Walser's novels and plays, can also be seen as an extension of the author himself.[7] Walser clearly uses Alois with his passion for music as a vehicle for presenting his concept of the artist in society. Alois's stubborn insistence on his right to sing parallels that very necessity (Walser, 1965,

---

[6] In this regard, Alois Grübel has striking similarities with Büchner's Woyzeck.

[7] In support of a close autobiographical link between Walser and his protagonists, several of his theoretical essays could be quoted. Also of interest is Walser's concept of "Dividuum," a play on words, opposing the notion of unity implied in the term "Individuum," which appears in his novel Das Einhorn (Kreuzer, 1970, 485). Other Walser protagonists who might be said to function as extensions of the author himself are Hans Beumann, Anselm Kristlein, the Zürns, Franz Horn, or Helmut Halm. The closest relative of Alois Grübel among Walser's protagonists and equally convincing as an image of the artist's role--this time in the West German society of the 1970s--is the chauffeur Xaver Zürn of Seelenarbeit whose devoted but frustrating service to the unresponsive Dr. Gleitze reflects Walser's personal skepticism regarding the insignificance of the artist in a capitalistic society.

107) which drives the artist to perform his art--regardless of obstacles encountered. His sterilization during the Third Reich is a particularly graphic way of demonstrating the cost of insisting on one's right to artistic--or any other--self-expression under a totalitarian regime. But most importantly, what first appears to be naiveté--Alois's slow adjustment to the changing political climate--may also be seen as a disguise for a deliberate act: his refusal to forget. Art is a nation's memory, and the artist preserves memories lest they be forgotten. By deliberate maladjustment, by refusing to forget, Alois bears witness to the German past, which makes it more difficult for others to suppress their recollections.

Alois's love of music which has become a political statement suggests the most significant function of this figure for Walser. Naive as Alois may appear, he is still a vehicle for Walser's own political sentiments. Hiding behind the very simplicity of his character, Walser acts out a deep personal desire: that the Germans would freely give testimony to the continued presence of their historical -past. This is what Alois represents and what lends him his depth. and it is for this reason, I believe, that this otherwise simple character has often been compared to Brecht's much more cunning Good Soldier Schweyk.[8] Critics and audiences alike obviously recognize Walser's serious intent behind Alois's seeming naiveté.

On the basis of what has been explored so far, it is possible to take a final look at The Rabbit Race and Walser's statement regarding the writer's prime motivation for writing, that predominant sensation of lack or deficiency. The immediate cause for the sense of deficiency which motivated Walser to write The Rabbit Race is Germany's fragmented history itself. Most importantly, disrupted German history has prevented him from developing a firm sense of national identity which writers seem to need more than others. Referring to Heine, Walser once wrote: "Heine achieved two identities in his life: the identity of

---

[8] See for example two early reviews on Walser's play: Kurt Honolka, "Schwejks blasses Abziehbild," Stuttgarter Zeitung 25 Sept. 1962; and 'Werner Wollenweber, "Der brave Zivilist Schwejk," Zürcher Woche 10 May 1963.

a German poet and that of a Jew. But two identities
are less than one. And what makes this situation even
more precarious: poets depend more on their national
background ["das Nationale"] than even soldiers or
generals" (Walser, 1983, 183). Yet Walser refuses to
bow to any limitation of his historical memory. He
defends himself against such restriction through his
fiction and his fictional characters. Alois Grübel
is an appropriate vehicle for an act of liberation.
This, after all, is a basic function of literature,
which ". . . is from the beginning a liberating
energy; as such it serves by itself to dismantle
power" (Walser, 1973, 132). The individual's consciousness is permanently besieged by a restrictive
reality, and writing is Walser's most effective
strategy against further encroachment. Fiction allows
him to depict an individual's consciousness in its
totality, including its vulnerability, its most
intangible desires--even its frequent triviality.
Thus, Walser's play is a counter proposal to reality:
not in the sense of utopian fiction, which proposes an
impossible ideal, but rather in the sense of engaged
literature which, by suggesting what might be possible, challenges the limits of reality. What prevents
Walser from writing utopian fiction is his passion for
historical accuracy, for detail, and all-
inclusiveness. His works are firmly grounded in
reality and even his most remote fictional inventions
still reflect this fact: ". . . the conditions of the
invented plot clearly inform about their relationship
to reality" (Walser, 1965, 60).

In conclusion: personal as the motivation for
The Rabbit Race may originally have been, the play's
intent is much broader. In portraying Alois's modest
desires and the unresponsiveness and intolerance of
his environment, Walser reveals the permanent discrepancy between an individual's justified desires
and society. This permits the reader to see Alois as
a representative of a common predicament. More
importantly, Alois' unwillingness to adapt or to give
in to political expediency is a deliberate act of
resistance demonstrating the need to defend the
individual's consciousness against the encroachment by
a restrictive reality. Alois is a precise fictional
response to Walser's own innermost need: to keep
striving for a sense of wholeness--even if his goal
remains permanently out of reach because of the events
of German history, political circumstances, and the
unwillingness of Walser's contemporaries to integrate
the effects of the past into their present.

References

Arnold, 1977: Positionen des Dramas, ed. Heinz Ludwig Arnold and Theo Buck (Munich: C.H. Beck).

Beckermann, 1970: Über Martin Walser, ed. Thomas Beckermann (Frankfurt: Suhrkamp).

Bienek, 1962 Horst Bienek, Werkstattgespräche mit Schriftstellern (Munich: Deutscher Taschenbuch Verlag, 3rd ed., 1976).

Böth, 1983: Wolgang Böth, "Anpassung und Widerstand: Zum Prozeß der Bewußtwerdung Alois Grübels in Martin Walsers Eiche und Angora," Amsterdamer Beiträge zur Neueren Germanistik 16:117-139.

Kreuzer, 1970: Ingrid Kreuzer, "Martin Walser," Deutsche Literatur seit 1945, ed. Dietrich Weber (Stuttgart: Kröner) 484-505.

Reitze, 1986: Paul F. Reitze, "Walser: Ich werde mich nicht an die deutsche Teilung gewöhnen" and "Es gibt keinen Schriftsteller, der nicht am liebsten Lyriker wäre," Die Welt 29 and 30 Sept.

Rischbieter, 1962: Henning Rischbieter, "Gespräch mit Martin Walster," Theater Heute 11: I-II.

Walser, 1963: Martin Walser, The Rabbit Race, trans., Ronald Duncan, Martin Walser: Plays I (London: Calder), 7-99.

------, 1965: ---, "Vom erwarteten Theater" (1962), "Freiübungen" (1963), and "Imitation oder Realismus" (1964), Erfahrungen und Leseerfahrungen (Frankfurt: Suhrkamp) 59-110.

------, 1968:   ---, "Ein weiterer Tagtraum vom Theater," Heimatkunde: Aufsätze und Reden (Frankfurt: Suhrkamp) 71-85.

------, 1971:   ---, Eiche und Angora, rev. 1963, Gesammelte Stücke (Frankfurt: Suhrkamp) 53-113.

------, 1973:   ---, "Wie und wovon handelt Literatur" (1972), Wie und wovon handelt Literatur (Frankfurt: Suhrkamp) 119-138.

------, 1979:   ---, "Wer ist ein Schriftsteller?" (1974), Wer ist ein Schriftsteller? (Frankfurt: Suhrkamp) 36-46.

------, 1983:   "Heines Tränen," Liebeserklärungen (Frankfurt: Suhrkamp) 175-207.

The Dead March in <u>Lear</u>: Folio Confusion,
Stage Direction, or Multi-leveled Sign?

Carolyn H. Smith
University of Florida

Philip McGuire has recently pointed out how
performances of Shakespeare's plays can differ because
of the way acting companies vary the timing of
silences between words and movements. Acting companies can also differ in their staging of sound
affects and ceremonial movements, as for example in
the closing scene of <u>King Lear</u>. In the Folio version
of <u>Lear</u>, the last words are Edgar's; then comes this
stage direction: "Exeunt with a dead march." In most
modern performances, this march is eliminated (Rosenberg, 123). It may seem non-essential since it is
only in the Folio. However, even if we do not agree
with Steven Urkowitz that the Folio is based upon
Shakespeare's own revised text, we can agree with him
that the Folio has been carefully edited. Therefore,
its stage directions, including the dead march, are
not textual confusions. Furthermore, from a semiotic
and psychological standpoint, this dead march is
important because it is a sign bearing three significant functions beyond its function as a means of
exiting: it marks the state of affairs; it initiates
the process of mourning necessary for an acceptance of
death; it locates political power.

The dead march marks the state of affairs in
several ways. First, by involving the bodies of King
Lear and his three daughters, it recapitulates the
concluding situation, namely, the death of Regan by
poison, Goneril by self-inflicted dagger, Cordelia by
hanging, and Lear by shock. The dead march also
creates a ceremony appropriate for the movement of the
bodies of a royal family from the place of death. It
thus parallels the dead march at the end of Kyd's <u>The
Spanish Tragedy</u>, when the bodies of the King of
Spain's brother and the King of Portugal's son are
taken away. Similarly, Hamlet is taken from the
throne room by a dead march, called by Fortinbras the
"soldiers' music and the rite of war."

Such stage directions imply a common understanding of the term "dead March." At least one drum was
apparently assumed. In his codification of music for
the English army in 1622, (in <u>Five Decades of Epistles
of Warre</u>), Francis Markham says that "when any [sic]
dies, the <u>Drumme</u> with a sad solemnitie must bring him

Cordelia by hanging, and lear by shock. The dead
march also creates a ceremony appropriate for the
move of the bodies of a royal family from the place of
death. it thus parallels the dead march at the end of
Kyd's The Spanish Tragedy, when the bodies of the King
of Spain's brother and the King of Portugal's son are
taken away. Similarly, Hamlet is taken from the
throne room by a dead march, called by Fortinbras the
"soldiers' music and the rite of war."

Such stage directions imply a common understanding of the term "dead March." At least one drum was
apparently assumed. In his codification of music for
the English army in 1662, (in Five Decades of Epistles
of Warre), Francis Markham says that "when any [sic]
dies, the Drumme with a sad solemnitie must bring him
to his grave, for it is the only mourner for the
lost, and the greatest honor of Funerals. . . the Drum
performing the last dutie" (Long, 6). Like Markham,
who says that the dead march's drum should have "sad
solemnitie," Aufidius at the end of Coriolanus says
that the drums should speak "mournfully" in the dead
march for Coriolanus. Today J.S. Manifold concludes
that the drum for the dead march achieved its effects
because muffled (Long, 22).[1]

For the dead march in Lear, the Globe probably
used only the mournful drum since this would more
obviously signify the tragic state of affairs--not
only death, but plural deaths and by horrible causes.
As in Coriolanus' dead march, the soldiers may have
trailed their steel pikes. Banners may have remained
aloft as in such heraldic funerals of the time as
Queen Elizabeth's, in which the standards, banners,

---

[1] Other instruments could be used. From Long's
1955 Shakespeare's Use of Music, we can conclude that
the march in The Spanish Tragedy had trumpets and that
they sounded a "mournful Cynet [sennet]," or fanfare,
as do still Flutes (recorders) accompanying a coffin
in Marson's Antonio and Mellida, Part I, V (Long, 37).
In Beaumont and Fletcher's The Mad Lover (ca. 1618) a
dead march as "sackbuts and drums" (III.iv). whether
muffled or not, the drum was beaten very slowly since,
according to Sir John Hawkins' history of music in
1766, the ordinary "English march of the foot" of
this period was "characteristic in dignity and
gravity," differing from the French, which was "brisk
and alert" (Farmer, 21).

and bannerols were prominently displayed (Fritz, 65; Greaves, 723-729). Such ceremonial movement is in accord with the ceremonial movement added elsewhere in the Folio's version _Lear_, as for example in Cordelia's fourth act entrance. The Folio's stage direction says that the enters with "Drum and Colours," and with other "Souldiours" and the Doctor (IV.iv), whereas in the Quarto she enters only with the "Doctor and others."

The way _Lear_'s dead march is acted can both mark and interpret the final situation. If the march is disorganized, with the characters uncertain as to who should do what and in what order, if the drumbeat is erratic, and if the bearers of the biers stumble because of the weight of their burdens, then the ceremony can signify the collapse of man and society under the weight of physical and moral evils. This can reinforce the theme of the power of evil suggested earlier in the cruel blinding of Gloucester, Lear's mental collapse, and the hanging of Cordelia. Even an orderly dead march can reinforce the idea of collapse because its suggestion of order is ironic in a world that has just had its social order collapse with the death of a king and his three daughters, two of whom were disloyal to him and to each other. Paradoxically, an orderly dead march, especially one with loyal mourners, can also signify that order is possible even in the disorder of political collapse and death. It can also signify the idea that while individuals suffer, collapse, and die, moral ideals such as loyalty and service remain permanent and give order and stability. The ceremony can thus reinforce the themes of love and order suggested earlier in the way Edgar helps Gloucester, and the Fool, Kent, and Cordelia help Lear.

Commentators tend to see the last scene as implying _either_ collapse _or_ transcendent order. However, in her recent study of tragedy Susan Letzler Cole joins such commentators as Norman Rabkin in seeing paradoxical meanings as a feature of tragic drama. As Cole explains, such drama is paradoxical because it is like a mourning ritual, which is performed on behalf of an absent presence, with mourners ambivalently wishing to maintain the presence and yet also wishing to sever and redefine this presence. _Lear_'s dead march thus encapsulates the tragic drama because it is a mourning ritual and, as such, facilitates severance, yet, even if hurried, it maintains presence through its ordering and slow beat.

The dead march in Lear can further signify presence if
the mourners delay the exit of Lear's bier until the
last and if, as in public funerals of the time, they
place signs of Lear's earlier presence on the bier,
such as his sword or gloves. Trailed pikes would also
signify both former public activity and the separation
from them.

In addition, the movement of the dead march helps
in the process of mourning because it suggests the
three actions which, according to contemporary
studies, are needed for recovery from mourning: a
review of the causes of death; admission of the
reality of this death; and adaptation to the state of
loss (Parkes and Weiss, 155-161). Cole perceptively
shows how the psychic impoverishment in Hamlet is
caused in large part because Claudius prohibits review
and forestalls admission of death by fusing funeral
and marriage rites (Cole, 41-60). Lear's dead march
is like other Renaissance funeral rites, which,
according to Philippe Aries (164-68), offered review,
admission of death, and identity adaptation though
ritualistic movements, music, display of symbolic
objects (such as the dead person's sword or family
colors), and placement of mourners, especially the
chief mourner. According to Aries, in this period the
chief mourner achieved prominence in several ways.
One was by ordering funeral ceremonies. Also, as
early as The Song of Roland and the King Arthur
stories, it was the responsibility of the chief
mourner "to pronounce the farewell" in such a way as
to help the survivors, "whom the deceased has left
helpless and bereft" (Aries, 143-4). According to the
Folio, Edgar is the one who says the farewell in Lear.
As Cole argues, Edgar is appropriate for this task
because he is Lear's godson and because Lear identified with him on the heath. Also, Cole adds, in the
first two lines of his four-line farewell, Edgar is
properly ambivalent because he reviews the past yet
looks to the future with "a new, feeling, voice; a
new, yet experienced, vision" (Cole, 133-35).

In his first two lines of the farewell, Edgar
says: "The weight of this sad time we must obey,/
Speak what we feel, not what we ought to say." Cole
does not explain what except for feeling is "new" in
Edgar's voice. Other commentators see little feeling
or meaning in Edgar's two lines. However, his words
make sense if heard in the context of mourning
established by the dead march. In his study of
Elizabethan elegies, G.W. Pigman has found that until

194

about 1600, the main precepts on mourning were those of Erasmus, who argued (in De conscribendis epistolis, 1522) that grief over death should be rebuked because it signifies an irrational abdication of rational self-sufficiency and an impious questioning of God. Even Spenser, in such poems as Daphnaida (1590) and his "November" eclogue, while admitting the need to express grief, implies that a mourner should suppress grief to avoid loss of reason and faith. In his elegies, Ben Jonson more rigorously chastises any display of grief. However, the view that expression of grief is necessary was defended in other elegies of the period, such as in some for Sidney and in some of Henry King's. Edgar's farewell is like these elegies. Instead of arguing that grief be suppressed in order to maintain self-sufficiency and piety ("what we ought to say"), Edgar asks the mourners to express grief ("Speak what we feel") because it is a natural reaction when the news of death first comes ("The weight of this sad time we must obey"). In his last two lines he also honors the oldest of the dead, Lear and Gloucester, by speaking of them in a brief but telling contemptus mundi eulogy as those who had to endure the burdens of life beyond an acceptable time: "The oldest hath borne most: we that are young/ Shall never see so much, nor live so long." Edgar's final words are thus appropriate because they do what a chief mourner's farewell should do prior to a funeral rite: honor the dead and help the mourners with advice on how to manage their grief.

By having a dead march follow Edgar's words, the Folio allows the necessary process of mourning to begin not only for the characters but for the viewer-reader. In addition, the movement of the march signifies a process that, according to recent studies, has to move from one state (from numbing, anger, and grief) to a second state (despair and disorganization) before a final recovery state can take place (cf. Bowlby). Whether the final state will be reached by Edgar and the others is not disclosed and is thus problematic; but by being public, social and traditional, the dead march links the mourners with all in the past who did recover as well as with those who did not. The link with those who did not recover can be stronger if Claudius-like characters despoil the rite by cutting it short, hurrying it before it can become ordered, or neglecting signs of honor and identity. Such despoiling can also reinforce nihilistic interpretations of the final state of affairs. Conversely, if the dead march lives up to its name and honors the dead by a procession kept in order by the beat of the drum, it can offer the mourners what it is has offered mourners in the past--an aid in recovery from grief.

Paradoxically, the mourners can be helped because the ceremony honoring the absent one as if present also helps sever that presence by its various reminders of absence: the bier, mournful sounds, movement away from the present space, and displacement of grief by both the performance of the ritual and by its formation. This formation can also help reorder the power structure because whoever assigns places or orders the assignments assumes power that can last beyond the time of the march. Ironically, the power may be undermined by the ceremony granting it if the ceremony is seen as theatrical and, hence, illusory, and self-fashioning. According to Stephen Orgel, such undermining occurred in the Elizabethan period because of the association between royal ceremonies in real life and their imitations in the plays. Leonard Tannenhouse sees the ceremonies in Elizabethan plays raising the same questions about the source of a sovereign's power that were being raised by political tracts of the time. Frank Moretti finds the Elizabethan tragedies especially subversive because they show how a sovereign's right to power can arouse his will to power beyond the bounds of reason, leading him to self-destruction and leading his court into a power vacuum. To Moretti, this destruction occurs in Lear. To Moretti, Edgar's final words reveal the "blind mediocrity" typical of a power vacuum.

However, Jack Goody has found from his anthropological studies that in most societies, there is a "double-edged nature of funeral ceremonies" because they "deliberately eliminate the dead man" from the midst of those whom he can no longer serve and they also "reaffirm the solidarity of the living members of the group in the face of death" (Cole, 21). Clifford Geertz has argued further that ceremonies of any kind as well as insignia are symbolic forms that "mark the center as center" because of "the ingenerate tendency of men to anthropomorphize power" (152-53). Thus, Edgar's final words can be seen as initiating the rituals of mourning needed not only psychologically but also politically as a means of confronting a power gap and relocating the political center.

Lear's dead march can be acted to signify either solidarity, collapse, or ambivalence in the political as well as in the psychological realm. Disorder may be signified if words and actions are hurried and disjointed. Even if Edgar speaks with strength and dignity, those he orders may indicate resistance, weariness, or obtuseness. Or if Lear's crown, Edgar's armor, and the solider's banners and pikes are obviously from a theater's costume room, then Edgar's power might seem illusory and transitory. Even so, if he is center stage, he can signify the new political center and the source of that power--belief transcending fact. Or if he is slightly off-center, he can signify the humility he experienced as the beggar Poor Tom; this in turn can suggest that as beggar-king, Edgar will recognize mercy as well as justice.

However interpreted, the dead march should be performed. Even though disparate interpretations are possible, the person who added the dead march to the Folio implies by the addition what Francis Markham said about the dead march, namely, that it honors with "sad solemnitie" those who have once lived. Such honoring both affirms the significance of the person now dead and it also emphasizes the reality of loss of the mourners. As Van Gennep has observed it is the function of rites of passage "to reduce the harmful effects" of such emotions as fear of change, grief over loss, and terror before the finality of death (13). Like other funeral rites, the dead march offers symbolic language through which the mourners can try to overcome adverse emotions and resolve the contradictions between life and death. The drum's beat, the bier, and the procession of mourners admit human mortality, yet the journey-like movement, the sounds, and the group formation offer consolation in the face of death's stasis, utter silence and final separation what has been said of other death rites can be said of Lear's dead march--it enables an individual "to go on living in society after the death of significant others and to anticipate his own death with, at the very least, terror sufficiently mitigated so as not to paralyze the continued performance of the routine of everyday life" (Berger and Luckmann, 101). By suggesting the paradox of sound in silence and presence in absence, it can also signify that paradox Shakespeare refers to in his sonnets--in living, we die, but in an artistic (or ritualistic) representation of that dying, there is life.

Works Cited

Aries, 1981:   Philippe Aries, <u>The Hour of Our Death</u>. Trans. Helen Weaver (New York: Alfred A. Knopf).

Bowlby, 1988:   John Bowlby, <u>Attachment and Loss</u> (New York: Basic Books, Inc.).

Berger and
Luckmann, 1967:   Peter Berger and Thomas Luckmann, <u>The Social Construction of Reality</u> (New York: Anchor Books).

Cole, 1985:   Susan Letzler Cole, <u>The Absent One: Mourning Ritual, Tragedy, and the Performance of Ambivalence</u> (University Park and London: The Pennsylvania State University Press).

Farmer, 1921:   Henry George Farmer, <u>The Rise and Development of Military Music</u> (London: Wm. Reeves).

Fritz, 1981:   Paul S. Fritz, "From 'Public' to 'Private': the Royal Funerals in England, 1500-1830," in <u>Mirrors of Mortality: Studies in the Social History of Death</u> Ed. Joachim Whaley (New York : St. Martin's Press): 61-79.

Geertz, 1977:   Clifford Geertz, "Centers, Kings, and Charisma: Reflections on the Symbolics of Power." In <u>Culture and Its Creators: Essays in Honor of Edward Shils</u>. Ed. Joseph Ben-David and Terry Nichols Clark (Chicago and London: The University of Chicago Press).

Greaves, 1981:   Richard L. Greaves, <u>Society and Religion in Elizabethan England</u> (Minneapolis: University of Minnesota Press).

Long, 1971:   John H. Long, <u>Shakespeare's Use of Music: The Histories and Tragedies</u> (Gainesville: University of Florida Press).

Long, 1955:   John H. Long, <u>Shakespeare's Use of</u>
                           <u>Music: A Study of the Music and</u>
                           <u>Its Performance in the Original</u>
                           <u>Production of Seven Comedies</u>
                           (University of Florida Press).

Moretti, 1982:   Franco Moretti, "'A Huge Eclipse':
                           Tragic Form and the Deconsecration
                           of Sovereignty." In <u>The Power of</u>
                           <u>Forms in the English Renaissance.</u>
                           Ed. Stephen Greenblatt (Norman,
                           Oklahoma: Pilgrim Books): 7-40.

McGuire, 1985:   Philip C. McGuire, <u>Speechless</u>
                           <u>Dialect. Shakespeare's Open</u>
                           <u>Silences</u>. (Berkeley: University of
                           California Press).

Orgel, 1982:   Stephen Orgel, "Making Greatness
                           Familiar." In <u>The Power of Forms</u>
                           <u>in the English Renaissance</u>. Ed.
                           Stephen Greenblatt (Norman,
                           Oklahoma: Pilgrim Books): 41-48.

Parkes, 1972:   Colin Murray Parks, <u>Bereavement:</u>
                           <u>Studies of Grief in Adult Life</u>
                           (New York: International Univer-
                           sities Press, Inc.).

Parkes and
Weiss, 1983:   Colin Murray Parkes and Robert S.
                           Weiss, <u>Recovery from Bereavement</u>
                           (New York: Basic Books, Inc.).

Pigman, 1985:   G.W. Pigman, <u>Grief and English</u>
                           <u>Renaissance Elegy</u> (Cambridge and
                           London: Cambridge Unviersity
                           Press).

Rosenberg, 1972:   Marvin Rosenberg, <u>The Masks of</u>
                           <u>King Lear</u>. (Berkeley: University
                           of California Press).

Shakespeare, 1963:   William Shakespeare, <u>The Tragedy</u>
                           <u>of King Lear</u>. Ed. Russel Fraser
                           (New York: New American Library (A
                           Signet Classic).

Stermfeld, 1963:   F.W. Stermfeld, <u>Music in Shake-</u>
                    <u>spearean Tragedy</u> (London: Rout-
                    ledge and Kegan Paul).

Urkowitz, 1980:   Steven Urkowitz, <u>Shakespeare's</u>
                    <u>Revison of King Lear</u> (Princeton,
                    NJ: Princeton University Press).

van Gennep, 1960:   Arnold van Gennep, <u>The Rites of</u>
                    <u>Passage</u>. Trans. Monika B. Vizedom
                    and Gabrielle L. Caffee (Chicago:
                    University of Chicago Press).

Pinter's Plays in Performance:
An Evolution Mirrored in Reviews

Michael Swanson
Ohio State University

The story of Harold Pinter's achievement of great status and popularity among contemporary playwrights has much to do with the education of the audience and especially the critics about his particular and various dramatic techniques. In twenty years, Pinter went from rejection as a puzzling and unclear dramatist to widespread acceptance as one of the greatest living playwrights. Examining major newspaper and magazine reviews of Pinter's full-length plays from 1958 to 1978 allows us to examine: 1) the confusion of critics as they were exposed to his particular and various techniques in such early works as The Birthday Party and The Caretaker; 2) the development of a critical response to his plays and performances and the identification of a Pintersque norm in plays such as The Homecoming, Old Times, and No Man's Land; and 3) the vehement response of the "educated critics" when Pinter deviated from that identified norm in Betrayal. While it is possible, incidentally, the critical response to the performances of Pinter plays improved as directors and actors learned to stage them, that is not my focus here -- rather, I am looking at how critics responded to the first performances of Pinter plays and major revivals and how a critical response evolved as Pinter wrote more plays.

The Birthday Party opened in Cambridge and played the provinces for a month before its May 19, 1958 London opening. Most London critics were confused by Pinter's "essay in surrealistic drama" which, the Times reviewer wrote, "gives the impression of deriving from an Ionesco play which M. Ionesco has not yet written" (20 May 1958: 3). In what was a relatively generous evaluation, this reviewer continued:

> . . . the third act studiously refrains from the slightest hint of what the other two may have been about. This sort of drama is all very well if the writer is able to create theatrical effects out of his symbolic dialogue. Mr. Harold Pinter's effects are neither comic nor terrifying: they are never more than puzzling, and after a while we tend to give up the puzzle in despair.

201

This is almost half of a short review, which is buried under a longer article hailing the Oxford production of the first play by promising playwright Bernard Kops -- probably the last time Kops received higher billing than Pinter.

J.C. Trewin of the Illustrated London News felt "obliged" to write about The Birthday Party "for reasons beyond my control" (31 May 1958: 932) in that it was a slow week in the West End. Trewin also made the comparison to Ionesco, and was also confused about the play's meaning: ". . . your guess about the play's significance is as good as, if not better than, mine." He admitted that "Mr. Pinter is a natural dramatist [with] . . . a quick sense of the stage. . . . He can write theatrically acute dialogue. The trouble is that he has been quite unable to clarify his play." Trewin came close to understand Pinter's mode, but rejected it: "He may hold that it does not need clarification, that it is the duty of an alert listener to catch every nuance, unravel every thread. If so, then I admit my dire failure." In a later review of The Caretaker, Trewin expressed his anger with Pinter for his "refusal to explain, his insistence on complete freedom of movement" (14 May 1960: 850). Trewin thus implied that the middle-class audience for which he wrote would fail to understand and become angry as well.

As if to disagree with Trewin, one of the two London critics who saw Pinter's significance noted the warm reception given The Birthday Party in the "narrow, illiberal" provinces. In a piece written a month after Pinter's first short London appearance, Harold Hobson of the Sunday Times reported that critics in Wolverhampton "gave the local theatre 'grateful thanks' for staging so 'exciting' a play" (15 June 1958: 11). Hobson noted that other provincial newspaper critics, in Birmingham, Oxford, and Cambridge, among others, were "enthralled" and "fascinated" and spoke of the great numbers of people that would see the play. An Oxford reviewer may have been the first to write about Pinter's "demonic control of suspense," according to Hobson. Hobson compared these notices with the "brutal sneers, cheap jokes or apathetic bewilderment" of the London critical coterie.

Hobson's first piece on the play in the Sunday Times was the only favorable notice given by a London daily. He noted the bevy of unfriendly reviews for

the show, and wrote, "I am willing to risk whatever
reputation I have as a judge of plays by saying that.
. . Mr. Pinter, on the evidence of this work, possesses the most original, disturbing, and arresting
talent in theatrical London" (25 May 1958: 11). He
berated those critics who demanded clear meaning from
the play, defending entertainment -- holding attention
and giving pleasure -- as the only quality essential
to a play, and finding that quality in The Birthday
Party. He also noted the play's contemporary rele-
vance: "Mr. Pinter has got hold of a primary fact of
existence: We live on the verge of disaster."

Irving Wardle of Encore also found worth in
Pinter's play. He put blame for the production's
financial failure on the critics:

> Nowadays there are two ways of saying you
> don't understand a play: the first is to
> bowl it out with the word "obscurity," once
> so popular in poetry reviews; the second way
> is to say that the seminal influence of
> Ionesco can be detected. Mr. Pinter
> received the full treatment. . . . it is his
> very instinct for what will work in the
> theatre that has prompted hostility (July-
> August 1958: 39-40).

The Caretaker was the next of Pinter's dramas to
play in London, opening in April 1960. some critics
sincerely attempted to analyze this work, while still
admitting to confusion. The Times' anonymous weekday
reviewer, in writing on Pinter's use of communication
failure, commented on "the dazed and pleasurable
confusion in which Mr. Pinter's writing leaves one"
(28 April 1960: 6). He admitted to not having any
answers, but his sense of theatricality overcame his
concern: ". . . strangely enough, while the play is
on it never occurs to us to worry about not knowing."

While The Caretaker was the first Pinter piece to
be staged on Broadway, The Birthday Party was the
first Pinter staged in America. As in England, it was
first staged in the provinces -- at the Actor's
Workshop in San Francisco, opening on July 18, 1960.
Like the British provincial critics, the San Francisco
Chronicle reviewer, Pain Knickerbocker, found the play
"moving and fascinating ... disquieting and compelling" (19 July 1960: 31). His interpretation of the
play was quite clear -- he was, perhaps, too willing
to see Pinter's characters as symbols. He did,

however, attempt to analyze the play, and did not claim that the play was obscure or confusing.

The San Francisco production was so successful that it was revived in May 1961 and reviewed by Howard Taubman of the New York Times. Taubman noted the "elusive quality of Pinter's writing," and made the observation that "He is an actor's playwright in that his laconic dialogue requires the performer to do a great deal to fill in the space between the lines" (15 May 1961: 34).

The first staging of Pinter in New York was a production of The Caretaker, opening on October 4, 1961. Most of the daily critics reacted favorably, but also echoed London's doubts about Pinter's oddness. Most used much of their space to deal with the play as a character study. The most negative review, by Robert Coleman of the New York Mirror, included an objection that the play dealt with "the lowest strata of humanity" -- We like our slices of life cut from the top. . . ." (5 Oct. 1961; reprinted in New York Theatre Critics' Reviews 22 (1961): 250; hereafter abbreviated as "in NYTCR"). Coleman also wrote that the play "began to lose us almost from the beginning."

Certain concepts were beginning to be identified as Pinteresque. In the New York Herald Tribune, Walter Kerr wrote of "a poetry of the unspecific, a use of language that is in itself devoid of concrete texture or logical sequence" (5 Oct. 1961; in NYTCR 22 (1961): 247-48). John Chapman of the Daily News wrote that The Caretaker "is filled with silences. . . and these silences are compelling in their excitement" (5 Oct. 1961; in NYTCR 22 (1961): 248). The New York Post's Richard Watts, Jr. saw Pinter's "gift for sly and unexpected humor a shrewd relish for raffish characters of even the most malignant sort, a talent for sudden revelation of personality, and a capacity for hinting darkly of sinister things to come even if they never arrive" (5 Oct. 1961; in NYTCR 22 (1961): 248). And Normal Nadel of the New York World-Telegram and Sun praised Pinter's use of a small cast to create "strength ... by the absence of ... attractive distractions: and to "achieve the greatest dramatic unity" (5 Oct. 1961; in NYTCR 22 (1961): 250).

A piece in the Sunday Times Arts section by Howard Taubman and a long, thoughtful, and favorable article in The Nation by revered critic Harold

Clurman, the longest periodical articles printed on
Pinter to that date, made a leap toward the legitimiz-
ing of serious PInter criticism.   While Clurman made
no major new observations (21 Oct. 1961: 276),
Taubman called Pinter "one of the important playwrights of our day," dealt with Pinter's progress from
The Birthday Party to The Caretaker, and made com-
parisons to Samuel Beckett (15 Oct. 1961: sec 2, 1).

Considering Pinter's growing reputation, it is
not surprising to find critical reevaluation and
revisionism in a review of the 1964 London revival of
The Birthday Party. In the Sunday Times, J.W. Lambert
claimed that Pinter had show "immense development ...
between" The Birthday Party and The Caretaker, in a
rather transparent attempt to adapt to the new
understanding of Pinter and the different receptions
given the two plays. He also implied that, had he
been able to see the firs production of The Birthday
Party, he would have been able to "discern its merits"
(21 June 1964: 33).

The appearance of The Homecoming in June 1965 in
London as a Royal Shakespeare Company production found
reviewers referring to Pinter -- who had, at this
point, staged two full-length productions and a
handful of one-acts -- as if he were a dramatic
monolith. The Times critic wrote of "all his old
cunning," "one of his finest principles," his "equivo-
cating idiom," and his "familiar motifs" (4 June 1965:
15).

This Times critic, however, may be the first to
criticize Pinter for being to obvious. The critic
wrote that the disclosure of expository information in
The Homecoming breaks Pinter's principle that "...
audiences had no right to demand indisputable facts
about characters." This is the most common complaint
of those who believe that Pinter's early works were
his least obvious, freest of artifice, and, therefore, his best. The chief exponent of this belief was
Martin Gottfried, then-reviewer for Women's Wear
Daily. His review of The Homecoming found that play
to be weaker than Pinter's earlier work (6 Jan. 1967;
in NYTCR 28 (1967): 397). Gottfried later recalled
The Homecoming as one of Pinter's better efforts (New
York Post, 10 Nov. 1976 ; in NYTCR 37 (1976): 112).
This kind of revisionism betrays a selective nostalgia
that undercuts many of Gottfied's comments.

Despite these complaints, most reviews of The
Homecoming were favorable. Only John Chapman of the
Daily News, who had raved about The Caretaker, turned
in a completely negative notice. He called The
Homecoming "a weirdy" -- he later called The Birthday
Party a "whatsit" (4 Oct. 1967; in NYTCR 28 (1967):
28). The play, he said, demonstrated Pinter's lack of
"good taste ... one other gift which might make him a
really important dramatist" (6 Jan. 1967; in NYTCR 28
(1967): 394). He dealt with the play's plot and
nothing else, he derided the playwright, play, and
cast (calling the cast "limey Gary Coopers"), and he
made the error of attributing Pinter's pauses -- which
he had liked in The Caretaker -- to director Peter
Hall, and calling them "affectations."

When The Birthday Party finally came to New York
in October 1967, critical reception was generally
good. In a reflective piece for the Sunday Times,
Walter Kerr attempted to put Pinter's output and
promise in perspective, because "we have just now
arrived at the Moment of Pinter" (15 Oct. 1967: sec.
2, 1 & 5). He explained that every new playwright
goes through "a trail period of resistance and doubt,
followed by a time of advance rumor." The importance
of off-Broadway productions of Pinter's one-acts in
developing Pinter's audience, from sparse for The
Caretaker to heavy for The Homecoming, was stressed.
Kerr also noted another of Pinter's unique effects:
"making us listen to what is going on now. Now only!
... It is important because it is taking place. ...
all intensity is rooted in the instant." Kerr said
his only objection to Pinter's work was Pinter's
inability to "sustain his unique command of the
absolute 'now' over two and one-half hours."

When Pinter's next full-length play, Old Times,
appeared in 1971, six years had passed since The
Homecoming opened. Old Times received long, respect-
ful reviews in all major British and American newspapers. Irving Wardle, now of the London Times,
called the play a "marvellous . . . theatrical poem,"
and praised Pinter for repeatedly reaching "a dead-end
perfection beyond which no other refinement or
advance seems possible," and finding "the means to
burrow forward into the stoney mass of silence that
surrounds and oppresses the work" (2 June 1971: 6).
This new means, according to Wardle, is to examine
memory, a "completely logical extension of Pinter's
methods," placing Pinter's use of ambiguity in its
"natural sphere" in memory, "where people may be lying

206

or misled and where the solitude of the human animal can find expression in widely differing recollections of the same event."

The critical response to No Man's Land in London in 1975 and in New York in 1976 was as near favorable unanimity as Pinter has ever received. The only major dissenter was Douglas Watt of the New York Daily News. Watt had "only the slightest idea what the play was about" (10 November 1976; in NYTCR 37 (1976): 116), a faint minority voice in the vast majority of critics who found No Man's Land to be Pinter's most clear play.

In the London Times, Irving Wardle's only complaint was that Pinter, "having located his territory and got to know its inhabitants, ... is now trying to extract meaning from them" (24 April 1975: 15). However, Wardle also wrote, "No Man's Land remains palpably the work of our best living play-wright in its command of language and its power to erect a coherent structure in a twilight zone of confusion and dismay."

In Newsweek, Jack Kroll took advantage of the occasion of No Man's Land's New York opening to write a long retrospective on the playwright and his works. While Kroll's new observations were few, he offered a solution to those still looking for meaning in Pinter's plays:

> The real answer is to have it both ways-- to appreciate Pinter's plays for their theatrical and verbal dynamics, their stunning sheer presence, and at the same time to luxuriate in the quiet questioning of their mystery (29 Nov. 1976: 77).

Betrayal, Pinter's most recent full-length play, threw most British critics for a loop when it opened in 1978. Wardle of the Times was the strongest voice among many who found nothing compelling in the play. Instead, wrote Wardle, "... the total gesture of the play is a blank endorsement of the obvious, conducted by characters who seem curiously anaesthetized against common human feeling" (16 Nov. 1978: 11). As a corollary, Wardle criticized Pinter for not evoking his usual ambiguity. And Wardle also wrote that "the fallibility of subjective memory finds no expression in the play." This claim is one of the most difficult to understand in the entire canon of Pinter criticism, in that the exploration of the twisting of subjective memory by time, events, and emotion is one of the major results of the chronologically backward structure of Betrayal.

Neither Wardle nor his British colleagues who disliked Betrayal discussed the backwards structure in great detail, tending to concentrate on the emptiness they perceived in the characters. The most purposeful ignorance of this device, new to Pinter and generally innovative, coupled with the sarcastic and almost bitter tone of the majority of the reviews, leads me to believe that the critics were unprepared by Pinter's experimentation and reflexively reacted against it. The reaction also led critics to criticize such Pinteresque techniques as the use of banal dialogue, which they had previously praised.

Response to Betrayal on this side of the Atlantic was radically different. American reviewers were more enthusiastic and more unified in their reviews of this play than of most of Pinter's work. A number of the critics, including Kerr, Barnes, and Kroll, found the unique structure to be just what was needed to tell the story of the rise and fall of an extramarital affair. As Kerr wrote, "It moves forward to where the emotion is" (7 Jan. 1980: C13).

Perhaps the American reviewers were more agreeable to Pinter's experiment because the basic context of the play is more clear -- we know more about Pinter's characters in Betrayal than ever before-- while the London critics desired continued ambiguity. Kroll offered another explanation why Betrayal got bad London notices: "Although a success in London, Betrayal was victimized by a current critical infatuation with leftist cliches: some critics professed lack of interest in the adulterous affairs of the chic publishing and art crowd" (21 Jan. 1980: 86). Another possibility is that the British response was simply a case of unfulfilled expectations. British reviewers expected a typical Pinter outing, and, instead, got something new. American reviewers, being warned ahead of time by the British notices, went to the theatre expecting something unusual for Pinter, which is what they found.

There was some disagreement in New York as to the ultimate worth of Betrayal. Barnes, in the Post, summed up his side of the argument best: "Pinter has drawn [these characters] well -- but were they worth

drawing? For a contemporary time capsule perhaps.
Certainly this is Pinter's most immediate play, but
perhaps also his most shallow" (7 Jan. 1980; in NYTCR
41 (1980): 391-92). British critics would agree with
that view. Kerr, however, answered this argument in
the Times by not questioning whether these characters
and the implied bourgeois topic were appropriate for
Pinter. Instead, he dealt with the play as a production and found theatrical value in it, not worrying
about its moral import:

> Some audiences may find its stringent,
> reserved facade too chilly for comfort.
> But the play isn't designed for comfort,
> it's designed for the excitement of the
> chase, for the fear that truth may elude us
> if we aren't quick enough to snare it, for
> the almost surgical satisfaction of seeing
> life honed to the injured bone. I found it
> fascinating (7 Jan. 1980).

As with The Birthday Party and every play in
between, Betrayal attracted its share of positive and
negative reviews. The criticism of Betrayal was a
microcosm of the types of critical response that
Pinter has received during his career. The response
ranged from that of Walter Kerr of the New York Times
and Jack Kroll of Newsweek, experienced Pinter critics
who understand the greater importance that style
commands over substance in these plays; to that of
Irving Wardle of the Times and other London critics,
reacting defensively to Pinter's experimentation,
ignoring the innovation, and judging the work strictly
on the basis of Pinter's past work and on their own
expectations of what Pinter plays should be like.
This unusually wide range of opinions on a Pinter play
-- the widest received by his work since The Birthday
Party -- may indicate that a major reevaluation of
Pinter's work is underway, during which the definition
of the Pinter norm may be updated to include the
techniques of Betrayal and subsequent works.

This brief examination of reviewers' responses to
Pinter plays in performance allows us to see how
various elements of what is not considered Pinteresque
in the theatre came to be identified and understood by
newspaper critics. Certainly the evolution of the
identification of other playwrights' dramatic techniques could be traced in the same fashion. In terms
of wider application, the study's greatest worth may
be simply to cause a red flag to be raised when the

209

tone of a review written by a previously friendly critic is disparaging or bitter. This reactionary sarcasm often seems to stem from a feeling of personal betrayal due to the playwright's exploring a direction not expected or understood by the critic. It will be most interesting to see what innovations Pinter's next full-length play will or will not employ, and how newspaper critics respond to its innovations or its sameness.

The Lacerations of Apartheid: A Lesson from Aloes

Albert Wertheim
Indiana University

In the past decade, the South African playwright Athol Fugard has emerged as a major playwright of our time.   His first play to receive international attention was The Blood Knot, which opened in Johannesburg in 1961.   Since then, Fugard has made his mark with more than a dozen important plays as well as several films.   A South African playwright whose material is generated by the experience of living in South Africa under apartheid rule, Fugard is at the same time an international playwright whose South African settings can be seen to serve mostly as a local habitation, a backdrop for exploring universal questions of race, art and existence, the three large topics on which Fugard's plays tend to center.   He seems, in short, able to turn what could be labelled South African regional material into universal significance by preparing it for non-South African, very often American, audiences.   But Fugard must be recognized as far more than simply a political playwright, for he is primarily a stunning understander and presenter of the psychodyamics of human relationships.   His plays about race are, in fact, as effective as they are because the political and social tensions they raise are by-products and outgrowths of personal and psychological interactions.

In what may be Fugard's finest play, A Lesson from Aloes (1978), the psychological tension among and within the plays's three characters dominate the play -- so much so, that they seem to overshadow the play's statements about race.   This has sometimes led reviewers to denigrate A Lesson from Aloes claiming that it does not focus squarely enough on South Africa's racist policies.[1]   The reviewers, alas, miss the point, for Fugard is not attempting to write an agitprop play that will radicalize an audience and

---

[1] This attitude seems to be shared by Dennis Walder, Athol Fugard (New York: Grove Press, 1985), 117-118 and by Russell Vandenbroucke, Truths the Hand Can Touch: The Theatre of Athol Fugard (New York: Theatre Communications Group, 1985), 175.

sent it out of the theatre clamoring for revolution
(as Fugard might be said to do in the plays he wrote
in conjunction with his actor-colleagues, John Kani
and Wintson Ntshona, Sizwe Bansi is Dead and The
Island). Rather in A Lesson from Aloes, he wishes to
depict how racism affects whites and non-whites,
Afrikaners and British; and how in South Africa
apartheid leaves its scars on all parties, whites as
well as non-whites. He wishes also to suggest that,
paradoxically, reform South Africa may finally be the
doing of Afrikaners, from among whose ranks the
greatest oppression nowadays stems.

A Lesson from Aloes is divided into two acts. In
the first, Piet and Gladys Bezuidenhout wait for
Steven Daniels and his family to come for a light
collation a few days before that family's departure
from South Africa on an exit visa to England. Steve,
it is revealed, is a middle-aged coloured man who has
been involved in anti-apartheid activities, been
consequently placed under a banning order, and then
imprisoned because an anonymous informer apprised the
Special Branch of the police that Steve had broken
his banning order. Now, out of prison, he has
decided to take leave of his homeland forever through
an irrevocable exit visa, a euphemism for exile
permit.

The first act of A Lesson from Aloes is shared
entirely by Piet and Gladys, he of Afrikaner stock
and she of British. From the moment the play begins,
the audience is subtly made aware of the differences
between husband and wife. Piet is sitting in his
garden actively absorbed in identifying aloes that he
is raising in tins. Gladys sits motionless. The
stage directions tell us that "he is wearing spectacles, short trousers, no shirt and sandals without
socks. GLADYS, behind sunglasses, sits very still on
a garden bench" (3).[2] The stage image is one that is
brilliantly indicative of their characters. Piet is
the active Afrikaner, thoroughly open and unashamed as
his lack of clothing suggests. He is indefatigable in
his project to name aloes and wears his spectacles to
help him both to identify the aloes and to bring into

---

[2]Unless otherwise noted, all references to the
play are from Athol Fugard, A Lesson from Aloes (New
York, Random House, 1981). Parentheses indicate page
numbers in this edition.

focus the world around him. Gladys, by contrast, has
no project, is disengaged, motionless, and fully
clothed. Her glasses are sunglasses meant to screen
off the outside world and its glare. Taken by itself,
this interpretation might seem an over-reading of some
simple stage directions, but Fugard is a master of
dramaturgy, and the interpretation gains validity as
the play proceeds and as the personalities of Piet and
Gladys become increasingly apparent.

Very quickly in the first act, Piet's forthright
statements in combination with his botanic zeal and
his semi-nude body clearly suggest a certain hardihood
that fits well with his surname, Bezuidenhout, the
name of a well-known rough-and-tumble pioneer South
African frontier family. Like his Boer forebears,
Piet seems to harbor a need to control and explore his
world. Clearly his desire to identify and name his
aloes suggests this. Examining his uncatalogued aloe,
he explains to Gladys:

> According to the Bible, that was the very
> first thing Adam did in Eden. He named his
> world. "And whatsoever Adam called every
> living creature, that was the name thereof."
> No. There is no rest for me until I've
> identified this. (13)

Even his frequent quotations from poetry reflect an
attempt to face and control the world by being able to
fit each moment with an appropriate phrase or thought.
Piet's interest, furthermore, is in the living world.
His hobby is horticultural, much of the poetry he
quotes--like Keats' "Ode to 'Autumn " and Roy Campbell's "The Snake"--is nature poetry, and his own
background is one of farming. He is, moreover, a
gregarious person, a lover of people whose occupation
is driving a public bus, who has worked with others in
political organizations, and who is now concerned with
making the visit by Steve Daniels and his family into
a genial occasion.

Gladys, by contrast, is fearful of nature. She
fears the sun and burns easily in it. A descendant of
British settlers, Gladys has none of the hardihood of
the Boers. With remarkable dramatic economy, Fugard
suggests the difference between husband and wife when
Piet comments on how his Boer ancestors learned to
cope with the intensity of the African sun and the
dangers of sunburn to which Gladys is prone: "The
voortrekker women had the same problem. That's where

the old white bonnet comes from. Protection" (7). Gladys' whole tone and manner, moreover, make it clear that she is emotionally as well as physiologically a woman with a sensitive skin. Unlike Afrikaners such as her husband, she is, furthermore, unable to cope efficiently with that sensitivity.

In A Lesson from Aloes, Athol Fugard bears many similarities to his British contemporary, Harold Pinter, for as in a Pinter play, the denotative meaning of what is said is far less important than the connotative meaning.[3] Subtext, in short, supersedes text. This is particularly true in the presentation of Gladys. The subtext of her recollection of childhood is one that argues for a vision of the world as a place of urban waste, savagery, and conflict:

> All I remember of the outside world was standing at a window and watching the dogs in the street go beserk when the dirt boys came to empty the bins. Heavens! What a terrible commotion that was. A big gray lorry with its mountain of rubbish, the black men banging on its side shouting, the dogs going for them savagely. (7)

Likewise the subtext of her comments on the Daniels family, who are coming for a meal, constitutes a powerful statement indicating that she rejects them and that she rejects Piet as well. Although she and Piet have known the Daniels family for several years and although they are the godparents of Steve's son, Gladys tellingly cannot remember how many members of the Daniels family there are, she cannot remember the name of little Pietertje who is named for her husband and is Piet's godson, and she makes a point of not wishing to sit next to little Pietertje at the table. Again, when Piet projects himself as a South African Adam distinguishing among his aloes and naming them, Gladys replies, "they all look alike to me. Thorns and fat, fleshy leaves" (13). The subtext pointedly implies that she declines the role of Edenic consort,

---

[3] Fugard may well have learned Harold Pinter's subtextual style while staging Pinter's The Dumbwaiter in 1961. See Vandenbroucke, 96.

that she does not wish to share Piet's interests and life, and that she rejects the country that Piet's aloes represent.

There is surely more than botany involved, when Gladys and Piet state their views of roses and aloes:

> GLADYS   Well, they're not pretty plants, you know. Is there a good word for something you can't and don't want to touch? That would describe them.
>
> PIET   A rose has also got its thorns.
>
> GLADYS   There is no comparison! They've got a lovely scent, they're pretty to look at and so many beautiful colors. But these . . . (She pushes the aloe away) No, thank you.
>
> PIET   This is not fair to them. An aloe isn't seen to its best advantage in a jam tin in a little backyard. They need space. The open veld with purple mountains in the distance. (14)

Piet's description leads him to recite the paean to the aloe in Roy Campbell's poem "The Snake"[4] and then to make clear the connection between himself and the aloes. Like the aloes he catalogs, Piet is a succulent plant able to withstand long periods of hardship and drought, and like the aloes he is seen to best advantage in his homeland veld and not in his jam tin urban flat. Piet, too, like the aloe, has a tough protective skin yet given proper conditions he will bloom as brilliantly.

The relationship between Piet and the aloes is not merely one of personality, for the political ramifications of the botanic discussion are apparent as well. The survival of the aloes has not merely something but has everything to do with Fugard's

---

[4] Roy Campbell, "The Snake," in The Collected Poems of Roy Campbell, vol. 1 (London: The Bodley Head, 1949), 55-58.

notion of the human need for survival amid the arid political and social climate in South Africa. Gladys exclaims, "Is that the price of survival in this country? Thorns and bitterness." To which Piet replies, "For the aloe it is. Maybe there's some sort of lesson for us there" (15). The foundation of Piet's idea is there in the work to which he alludes, the monumental work on South African aloes, Gilbert Westacott Reynolds' The Aloes of South Africa, complete, as Piet reminds us, with a foreword written by General Smuts. Surely a playwright who writes with the economy of Athol Fugard does not drop such an allusion for nought. When we then consult Smuts' foreword to Reynolds' tome, we quickly realize the purpose of the allusion, for Smuts, writing in praise of Reynolds' endeavor, says, "By so doing [cataloging the aloes] he is helping to preserve the country's life blood--its living mantle, the flora on which the fauna of the land depends."[5] Indeed, Piet Bezuiden-hout is the country's life blood, the flora, the aloe on which the others in the play and the others in South Africa depend if they and South Africa are to survive.

In the second act of A Lesson from Aloes, Steve Daniels arrives late and alone, and the conflicts and alliances among the three characters are carefully set in motion, sometimes through small but important touches and subtextually. Gladys, for example, keeps Steve at psychological arm's length by calling him Steven, much the way she tries to transform her Afrikaner husband, Piet into something British by always referring to him as Peter. The two men, who share similar politics, also share a love of their country. Revealingly, they drink native South African wine while Gladys sips that favorite among British light alcoholic beverages, sherry. In fact, the acting edition of the play has Piet italicizing the separation of Gladys from himself and Steve by saying to her, "Here, my dear. A glass of your sherry?" (italics mine).[6]

---

[5] Gilbert Westacott Reynolds, The Aloes of South Africa (Cape Town and Rotterdam: A.A. Balekma, rpt. 1974), ix.

[6] Athol Fugard, A Lesson from Aloes (New York: Samuel French, 1981), 55.

In Act II, Fugard gives Steve two dazzling and extended dramatic moments. In one, he recounts the savagery of the South African Group Areas Act and the ways it affected his life and thought. In the other, he poignantly recounts his political and psychological breakdown at the hands of the Special Branch of the South African police. Steve first recounts a deeply moving anecdote about catching a thirty pound fish with his father on Port Elizabeth's Maitland Strand. The moment is one of joy and achievement mixed with the pleasure of discovering that a racial acquired habit has succeeded:

> The white boys used to come past with their
> fancy rods and reels empty-handed, while we
> had Steenbras tails flapping around us on
> the sand. The old man had patience. That
> was his secret. (62)

But Steve's exultation is succeeded by a profound and angry sadness as he recalls his father's tragedy. The Group Areas Act forcibly removed the old man far from the Maitland Stand removing him inland to Salt Lake, a body of water obviously devoid of living things. "Fairview was declared white and that was the end of us. ... He hadn't just lost his house and his savings, they also took away the sea. I mean ... how the hell do you get from Salt Lake to Maitland on a bicycle?" (63). His once proud and now broken father is tragically led to assert, "Ons geslag is verkeerd," our race is a mistake. In the performance playtext, Steve, too, reacts not with revolutionary anger but with pathetic, near tragic, resignation as he tears the snapshot that has inspired the reminiscence of his father.

But Steve's impending departure from 'South Africa and his father's removal from the vitality of the Port Elizabeth Indian Ocean coast links Steve with Piet, who has also been forced to leave the natural vitality of the South African veld. In Piet's case, the drought and the death of a black child from the effects of the drought, led him to move to the city and abandon Alwynlaagte, the Bezuidenhout family farm. For any speaker of Afrikaans in Fugard's audience, Alwynlaagte means, tellingly, Valley of Aloes.

The second of Steve's dramatic moments recounts his arrest after an anonymous informer tipped off the Special Branch that he was breaking the banning order that had been placed upon him. Once again movingly,

217

Steve recalls his mental breakdown in the course of the police interrogations. He reveals, further his resultant castration, not physiological but mental, as well as his consequent desire to emigrate irrevocably to an England he has never seen. It is then that he suddenly becomes spiritually allied with Gladys.

She, too, has been broken by the Special Branch. In investigating possible subversives in Steve's political circle, the Special Branch made a thorough search of the Bezuidenhout house. Ironically, Piet's home, named Xanadu in honor of the dream-like city that housed the pleasure dome of Coleridge's Kubla Khan, became the environment of Gladys' nightmare when the police arrive in the middle of the night and in the course of their search for political secrets and banned literature confiscate the diaries in which she has written her inmost thoughts and feelings. For Gladys, the moment is one of rape, a rape of person-hood more intrusive and destructive than its sexual counterpart. Like Steve, she is broken by the even leading her not to prison but to incarceration in a hospital where, like Steve, she has been mentally violated. Furthermore, at the end of the play, she, like Steve will go to England, but in her case it is not to England the nation but to Fort England, the mental hospital in which she will play out what remains of her life.

Gladys and Steve are allied as well by their both connecting Piet with the source of their wounds and their defeat. Like his black and coloured comrades, Steve has come to suspect Piet, the white Afrikaner, as the most logical police informer. As a result, Piet has been ostracized by his former friends, Steve's wife Mavis has refused to come to the farewell meal at the Bezuidenhout home, and to some extent Steve himself has come on the evening of the play to find Piet innocent or guilty. Gladys, whose suffering has been analogous to Steve's, instinctively senses Steve's suspicions and plays with them savagely to sunder the last thread that bind Steve and Piet. In coming to terms with what she has done, Gladys reveals Fugard's brilliant insights into not merely the biographical analogies between Gladys and Steve but in the dilemma of South Africa:

> That's my business. Yes, mine! My reason
> for telling you an ugly lie, which you were
> ready to believe! . . . is my business. I
> accept, Steven, that I am just a white face

on the outskirts of your terrible life, but
I'm in the middle of mine and yours is just
a brown face on the outskirts of my own
story. I don't need yours. I've discovered
hell for myself. It might be hard for you
to accept, Steven, but you are not the only
one who has been hurt. Politics and black
skins don't make the only victims in this
country. (74)

As Gladys proceeds to recount her sufferings in shock
therapy she italicizes her alliance with Steve by
saying, "They've burned by brain as brown as yours,
Steven" (76). It is an alliance, moreover, than she
herself only seems to understand at that moment; for
it is only then, in her last line of farewell,
"Goodby, Steve" (76) that Gladys for the first time
addresses Steve familiarly and as a comrade, as Steve,
rather than as Steven. Thus with brilliant dramatic
economy and with equally brilliant use of subtext,
Fugard forges a new pattern of relationships. Whereas
Gladys had stood outside the bond of camaraderie and
political commitment that existed between Piet and
Steve, now it is Piet who is excluded from the spiritual bonding between Steve and Gladys.

Clearly Gladys, the white woman of British
descent and sensitive skin, cannot, like the roses she
adores, withstand the climate of South Africa.
Likewise the political climate blasts her and seres
her, so that like a rose exposed to South African heat
and aridity she turns brown. She is a hothouse flower
unadaptable to South Africa and the South African
soil. She can only survive in the controlled climate
and atmosphere of the sanitorium. Early in Act II,
when Gladys and Steve are momentarily left alone with
each other, the subject of botany and politics arises:

> GLADYS Peter's new hobby, now there's no
> politics left. Aloes. He takes
> it very seriously. He's got a
> little book and he knows all their
> names.
>
> STEVE   I prefer flowers myself.

```
GLADYS          That makes two of us. We tried to
                lay out a little flower bed here
                once. . . Roses! . . . But the
                soil is very poor. Come, let's
                sit down. So, Steven, you're on
                your way to England. I couldn't
                believe it when Peter told me.
                (56)
```

Likes Gladys, Steve prefers roses to aloes; and the
subject of roses here naturally seems to provide a
prelude to a discussion of Steve's imminent departure
for England. The point is made here subtextually and
developed as the act progresses is that although
Steve may not be a hothouse rose like Gladys he is
also not an admirer of the aloes, the hardy South
African succulents. In order for Steve to survive the
current spiritual and political drought conditions in
South Africa, he must escape the South African climate
and atmosphere to transplant himself and his family to
the English spring, to the more nurturing landscape
depicted in the pastoral "Sunset in Somerset" painting
at which Gladys gazes in the shock treatment waiting
room at Fort England hospital.

Steve and Gladys display their psychological
wounds, wounds suffered at the hands of the Special
Branch and the apartheid system; and each, moreover,
displays an inability to survive in the destructive
biological atmosphere of contemporary South Africa.
Further, both Steve and Gladys to some extent hold
Piet responsible for their fates. The victims of A
Lesson from Aloes, then, is Piet, who is left remain-
ing and alone at the end of the play. Bereft of his
wife and her love, bereft to Steve and his friendship,
Piet stands personally and politically isolated in the
second act and as the curtain falls. He is also the
Afrikaner devoid of the English speaking whites,
symbolized by Gladys, and of non-whites, symbolized
by Steve. Piet, like the South African aloes, remains
to face the drought that is South Africa. Like those
succulents, he must rely on his tough skin and on his
ability to do without nurture for long periods. He
is, after all, recalling General Smuts's words in the
Foreword to Reynolds' The Aloes of South Africa, "the
country's life blood".

Piet Bezuidenhout is an Afrikaner, a Boer. When
Steven derogatorally refers to the Special Branch, he
calls them "those boer-boys" (68); and Gladys clearly

connects Piet to the police, the most savage extension of the apartheid system and its enforcement, when she says:

> He looks like one of them, doesn't he? The same gross certainty in himself. He certainly sounds like them. He speaks English with a dreadful accent. (73)

What Fugard is evoking here is that Afrikaner patriotism, hardiness, self-righteousness, self-possession, and ability to survive enabled the Afrikaners to survive and tame South African wilderness, survive the onslaughts of the British and the Boer War, and to institute and vigorously maintain the full apartheid system. The boer-boys with their Afrikaans accents have created the apartheid climate that destroys Gladys and castrates Steve psychologically and politically. Yet, suggests Fugard, in the character of Piet, those very survival traits will enable Piet to survive the political climate and to continue to work toward the dismantling of apartheid. Like his Boer forebears, Piet has the patriotism, self-possession, hardiness and will to survive. It is, moreover, these very traits, which helped to build and maintain apartheid, that may also, in the hands of people like Piet, be that system's undoing: more so than perhaps the maneuvering of liberal English speakers of the tactics of revolutionary non-whites. The questions that remain, however, at the end of Fugard's play are how long an aloe can survive adverse conditions and whether, when the long South African drought is over, it will be over due to nurturing rains or blood bath?

DATE   DUE
